# Vital Connections

*Why we need more than self-managing schools*

Cathy Wylie

NZCER PRESS

2012

NZCER Press
New Zealand Council for Educational Research
PO Box 3237, Wellington

© Cathy Wylie

All rights reserved

National Library of New Zealand Cataloguing-in-Publication Data
Wylie, Cathy.
Vital connections : why we need more than self-managing schools/Cathy Wylie.
Includes bibliographical references and index.

ISBN 978-1-927151-57-0

1. New Zealand. Dept. of Education. Tomorrow's schools.
2. School management and organization—New Zealand—Evaluation. 3. Education and state—New Zealand. 4. Educational change—New Zealand—Evaluation. I. Title.
371.200993—dc 23

Designed by Lynn Peck, Central Media
Printed by Pinnacle Print, Petone

This title is also available as an e-book from
www.nzcer.org.nz/nzcerpress

Distributed by NZCER
PO Box 3237, Wellington
New Zealand
www.nzcer.org.nz

To my parents, David and Ruth Wylie,
who brought me up to care and to question.

# Contents

| | |
|---|---|
| Acknowledgements | ix |
| Introduction | 1 |

## Chapter 1 High expectations and the support they need — 11

| | |
|---|---|
| The value of education | 11 |
| Improving education: Why policy matters | 13 |
| Hallmarks of effective infrastructure for a good public education system | 15 |

## Chapter 2 A semi-ordered freedom — 19

| | |
|---|---|
| The 1980s: Interconnections and porous boundaries | 19 |
| Teacher and school latitude before *Tomorrow's Schools* | 20 |
| The interconnecting inspectorate | 22 |
| The source of inspectors' authority | 25 |
| Creative use of the "marvellous weapon" | 27 |
| Challenges to sharpening school capacity | 32 |
| Joint work to advance reading | 34 |
| The advisers | 39 |
| Limits on the sharing of new practice | 41 |
| The reality of bureaucracy before *Tomorrow's Schools* | 43 |

## Chapter 3 Strengths, weaknesses and tensions in the 1980s — 48

| | |
|---|---|
| Impressions of the OECD examiners | 49 |
| Primary learning | 53 |
| Tomorrow may be too late | 59 |
| Life and limits in secondary schools | 61 |
| Fundamental challenges in secondary education | 65 |
| Making sense of New Zealand student performance in an international context | 67 |
| Challenging Māori statistics | 69 |
| Interconnecting roads not taken | 71 |
| The 'community' road | 72 |
| The school takes centre stage | 74 |

## Contents

### Chapter 4 Shaking up and separating out — 77
- Self-management as a solution — 78
- The Picot taskforce — 79
- Responses to the Picot report — 82
- *Tomorrow's Schools* — 85
- Fleshing out the bones — 88
- The cost of haste — 89
- Fear of connections: The Lough report — 93
- Long-term shadows — 96

### Chapter 5 A fragmented freedom: Schools in the 1990s — 98
- Principals and their new role — 99
- The demanding twins — 103
- Competition between schools — 105
- Development of the governance role — 108
- Cautious reconnections across temporary bridges — 112
- Safety-net intervention — 115
- Holes in the safety nets — 117
- Schooling improvement: Attempting some reconnection — 118
- ERO: The watchdog and scold — 122
- *Tomorrow's Schools*: Still too late? — 124
- Missing connections — 126

### Chapter 6 Piecemeal changes: Teaching and learning in the 1990s — 130
- Seeds falling on shaky ground — 130
- The new curriculum development — 131
- Making sense of the new curriculum — 134
- Mixed messages on the purpose of assessment — 136
- Question marks over primary student performance — 138
- The 1999 Literacy Taskforce — 140
- Maths: The costs of an insufficient infrastructure — 142
- Science stagnates — 145
- An absence of useful focus: Schools and Māori learners — 148
- Particular challenges for secondary schools — 151
- Changes to secondary qualifications: Promises and pitfalls — 153
- Costs of fragmentation — 156
- Lessons from the 1990s — 159

## Chapter 7 Trying to 'steer at a distance' — 162

Getting inside schools' heads — 163
Can ERO improve school self-management capability? — 167
Whose responsibility? — 169
Governance becomes more focused, but no simpler — 171
Growing school leadership — 174
Growing the knowledge needed for effective school leadership — 175
Thwarted connections — 178
The new local links: Grounds for hope? — 181
Challenges for Ministry–school connections — 183
Pressure on system funding from school self-management — 186

## Chapter 8 New frameworks for teaching in primary schools — 189

Support for change — 189
Shifting numeracy teaching — 190
A way to go — 192
Shifts in writing — 195
Schools inquiring — 197
Strengthening school professional inquiry cultures — 198
Constraints on achieving shifts for all schools — 199
National Standards: Trajectory interrupted or a new pathway? — 201
The low-decile challenge — 207

## Chapter 9 A new framework for secondary achievement: Gains and challenges — 214

Are schools places where students want to be? — 215
PISA and the questions it raises for us — 218
Reframing qualifications: Secondary outcomes and NCEA — 226
Challenges beyond the low-hanging fruit — 230

## Chapter 10 What self-managing schools need to succeed — 236

1. The cost of equating school self-management with stand-alone schools — 237
2. Costs of fragmentation — 247
3. Hidden costs — 249

Making the most of self-managing schools — 251

## Glossary — 257
## References — 261
## Index — 276

# Acknowledgements

I am deeply grateful to the Stout Trust whose award of the 2011 J D Stout Fellowship allowed me the luxury to work full time on this book in the supportive atmosphere of the Stout Centre for New Zealand Studies, Victoria University of Wellington. I am also deeply grateful to Robyn Baker, NZCER's director, who encouraged me to apply for the Fellowship, and allowed me to extend my time away from NZCER to bring this book to completion.

This work has benefited greatly from discussion and reading of drafts along the way. For their belief in the value of the book, and their encouragement coupled with pertinent critique, I am most grateful to Robyn Baker, Joanna Beresford, Jacky Burgon, Geraldine McDonald, Johanne McComish, Ruth Mansell and Stephen Lungley, and to Noeline Alcorn, Adrienne Alton-Lee, Ben Levin and Lynne Whitney for their review of the draft manuscript.

The book has gained considerably too from opportune comments, material, and questions from my NZCER colleagues, particularly Sarah Boyd, David Ellis, Jane Gilbert, Rose Hipkins, and Edith Hodgen. Thanks also to Ray Prebble for his copyediting of the book, Shelley Carlyle for proofreading Diane Lowther for indexing.

My thanks too to other NZCER colleagues for their help along the way, particularly Beverley Thomson and Susan Tompkinson, Rachel Dingle, Ally Bull, Juliet Twist, Charles Darr, and Jenny Whatman, and to Marie Cameron for insightful discussions and Auckland hospitality.

I am very grateful to the educators and officials who spoke with me in 2011 about their experiences and prognoses for the future of our education system; and to the many teachers, principals, trustees, officials, policy makers, parents, and, not the least, students, who have contributed to the research that is used in this book.

During this work, I was reinvigorated by spirited excursions with Tararua Tramping Club companions, shared music, conversation, food and humour with other friends and family, and Stephen Lungley's loving and deeply-valued support.

# Introduction

The principal of an award-winning Canadian school raised his eyebrows and said in some bemusement, "You do *what*?"

"Yes," I said, "our schools are self-managing, like your school, and every school has its own board of trustees elected by parents, and they employ the principal."

"You have no district?"

"No, nothing like that. Each school gets its funding directly from the Ministry of Education, and a separate government agency reviews them every 3 years, more often if there are issues."

The principal shook his head. "We were going down that route some 20 years back, but it was too costly in terms of competition between schools. No-one was thinking of the system as a whole. We were wasting a lot of effort, spreading ourselves too thin. Our district board canvassed parents and they didn't want the responsibility. They wanted to know how their kids' school was going, and to have some input, but not to employ people."

"We have national collective agreements, there are handbooks, a national school trustees' association funded by the government to provide advice, schools employ consultants …"

He shook his head again. "So where is the career path for school leaders? How do you make sure you have enough good leaders and support them, and how do you get people working together?"

My turn to shake my head. "It varies."

"I bet," he said, and then we moved on to talk about the ways in which the Edmonton public school district operates, so that its self-managing schools make their own decisions but are also part of communities of sharing and joint responsibility. It wasn't a system in which everything worked without criticism, but it had achieved gains for its students, and it had the capacity to keep developing and meeting new challenges.

At the end of that intensive week in 2007 talking to Edmonton's school principals and district office staff I was both wistful and excited. Excited when I thought of what was possible, of where we could take our own self-managed schools. Wistful when I thought of our own situation in New Zealand, where "it varies" was a diplomatic way of saying it was too often the luck of the draw.

The school-level freedom promised in 1988 in *Tomorrow's Schools*[1]—the radical shake-up of our education system that cut many connections between schools and the government agency responsible for education—did augment an already existing latitude in terms of curriculum and programme at the school level. But all too often this freedom means reinventing the wheel. Promising new approaches may be confined to the school that developed them because there are no regular channels for knowledge to travel, to be tried in different contexts and supported systematically. It can mean that educators don't know what they don't know, so in all good faith they continue or embark on teaching practices that are not effective.

It has also not been hard for a school to get into difficulties, either without anyone else knowing until things were bad or, what is worse, knowing but being impotent to help a school that did not seek or want help. We have made school self-management into a barrier, not the channel of responsiveness envisaged in 1988. It has taken almost two generations of students before we have seen shifts in student achievement. Only recently has it been possible to start to see some real progress in Māori student engagement and achievement levels, although meeting "the particular needs of Māori education" had been a key aim of the *Tomorrow's Schools* reforms (Minister of Education, 1988, p. iv).

I come from perhaps the last New Zealand generation where the inbuilt inequity of School Certificate (with marks scaled so that half the candidates had to fail) was not widely challenged because there were jobs and interesting work with good pay that did not require a secondary-level qualification. Now the education system must ensure that school engages all students, and that all the country's students—not just those like me, with book-clad homes and unquestioned assumptions that education would continue past secondary schooling—leave school with lifelong-learning dispositions and well-exercised minds that can keep learning in a world that keeps changing.

---

[1] *Tomorrow's Schools* did away with the 10 education boards that had employed primary school staff, and where Department of Education staff advising and inspecting primary schools were based. Secondary schools already managed their own budgets; *Tomorrow's Schools* extended that responsibility to primary schools. The policy also gave parents a greater role in school governance, through each school's parents electing their own board of trustees, the body legally responsible for the financial and educational wellbeing of the school. It also emphasised parental choice of school, as a lever for school performance. At the same time, the Department of Education was split into the Ministry of Education, what became the Education Review Office, the Qualifications Authority, and several smaller government agencies. The policy was designed to improve the flexibility and responsiveness of schools to their students, and thus to improve educational opportunities. Chapter 4 describes the *Tomorrow's Schools* policy change in more detail.

This is not just a matter of fairness, which was a major concern when *Tomorrow's Schools* began. It is also a matter of national viability and wellbeing. As economists and businesspeople increasingly began to realise in the early years of the 21st century, we need much higher knowledge and skill levels across all social groups, along with the ability to work together in new ways to ensure the use of existing knowledge and the creation of new knowledge.

What we need from our public education system now, and for the even more challenging times ahead, is therefore even more demanding than it was in 1988, when the Government put its faith in schools acting for themselves. In New Zealand, self-managed schools were not positioned within webs of well-informed support and challenge, an environment of knowledge-building in which to solve shared problems and advance teaching practice, well-constructed frameworks of thinking and processing, a shared purpose and responsibility, a good infrastructure. Many of those involved in the reforms did not appreciate at the time how important these interconnections are to building and sustaining good-quality public education.

When we look at what has been achieved over the past two decades, it is in the relatively few initiatives and policies that support these kinds of interconnections that we find some progress. The value of vital connections of this kind—ones that support sustainable development in individual institutions and a sense of common purpose and responsibility—is also increasingly clear in international research. This research shows the benefits of positioning individual schools within more collective systems. Now there is a substantial body of robust analysis that we can use to rethink our self-managing schools approach, as we need to do if we are to create the dynamic learning system we need in New Zealand.

This book tells the story of our self-managing schools so far and the lessons we can learn from this, on the whole, less-than-successful turn. It looks at the frameworks, conditions and connections schools and teachers need if they are to meet our continually growing expectations of education. Chapter 1 looks at the purpose that our self-managing schools should achieve, what we expect of education and what lies behind good teaching. To understand the changes of the past 20 or so years we need to go back to how our schools were supported and challenged before *Tomorrow's Schools*, and the strengths and tensions of the previous system. Chapter 2 describes the latitude and productive connections with education officials that schools actually enjoyed before school self-management, something all too often ignored because of the diagnosis of 'over centralisation' that was central to the reforms. It also shows how this latitude may have made schools confident about taking on school self-management, but that school leadership and cultures were not as strong as they would need to be to really make the most of school self-management.

Chapter 3 depicts a system that OECD examiners in 1983 found had substantial strengths as well as tensions that needed political will to address. These OECD examiners noted that New Zealand spending on its schools was lower per student than other comparable systems—a pattern that has persisted and remains the case today. This chapter describes the progress being made before *Tomorrow's Schools* to address the tensions our schools faced, and some of the gaps in knowledge that would make it difficult to do so—gaps that were ignored when it came to expecting so much of school self-management.

In Chapter 4 I explore why it was that school self-management seemed the answer to the tensions that educators and officials had been grappling with since the 1970s, and why it took the radical form it did, largely because education administration was tackled in the same generic way as other parts of the public sector that were being reformed. We were—and still are—the only country that has built its national school system on schools operating on their own.

The costs of this separation of schools from government, of 'operations' from 'policy', coupled with the haste of the changes when they occurred and the loss of knowledge and momentum in some key areas of education, are evident in fragmentation and deepening mistrust and defensiveness through the 1990s. Chapter 5 also describes how the new school administrative roles consumed attention and energy that were needed elsewhere, and how the Ministry found it could not in fact step back from working with schools, particularly those struggling with the new responsibilities. The 1990s also saw a new national curriculum framework, with the rapid rollout of new curriculum for different areas and efforts to move to a new national qualification framework. But student engagement and achievement remained static overall. Chapter 6 explores why this was: what the new system lacked in the way of knowledge-building and connections that could change teaching and learning.

By the end of the first decade of the new system, seeds had been sown for the Ministry of Education, working with educators, to develop new frameworks that would better support changes in teaching and learning—changes that would allow schools to better meet student needs. This was the knowledge, with support and better connections, that allowed many schools to develop in ways that self-management alone could not achieve. At the same time, however, school self-management in schools without any interconnections remained the prime vehicle for change. Chapter 7 looks at the increasingly evident challenges to ensuring every school could have sound leadership and governance, and the continuing difficulty of funding growing expectations. It also traces what was done to change the ways schools worked to make the most of their resources.

Chapter 8 describes shifts in the professional culture of many primary schools, and the role of Ministry-shaped or Ministry-funded professional development and joint work between schools, researchers and professional developers, which brought and created new knowledge that schools were keen to use. It also looks at the new challenges encountered by schools that are working hard to change their practices, particularly schools in low-income areas. Chapter 9 describes how secondary schools continue to face some of the same tensions in engaging adolescents in learning that were identified well before *Tomorrow's Schools*, and the gains they have been able to make through the introduction in 2002 of a fairer qualification structure, the NCEA.[2]

Considerable progress has been made over recent years. The question now is whether we have 'plucked all the low-hanging fruit' with the way schools currently operate. Chapter 9 includes an analysis of patterns of New Zealand achievement on the international PISA[3] assessments. On the one hand, ours is a relatively efficient system: we continue to spend less per student than other countries also rated as high performers. On the other hand, the PISA comparisons show the issues we face related to social inequality, inequality which grew over the 1990s and 2000s, making the work of New Zealand schools and teachers more demanding.

In Chapter 10 I conclude with the lessons I have learnt from writing this book, especially through comparing the good intentions and bold statements of what would be achieved with what actually resulted. Putting that analysis together with the knowledge base we now have, here and internationally, I am convinced of the pressing need to rethink our self-managing schools, to locate them in more constructive connections with government. That means rethinking the nature of how government works with schools and educators at the local and national levels, and ensuring that policy is inclusive and better based on robust evidence.

---

2   National Certificates of Educational Achievement.
3   Programme for International Student Assessment.

The *Tomorrow's Schools* system is simply not strong enough to bear the weight of our expectations for schools and learning. If we continue as we are, we will not be able to make the progress we need to make. We are unnecessarily handicapping ourselves. The conclusion zeroes in on the fundamental flaws of our system and offers a new setting for self-managed schools.

In writing this book I drew on my own experience as a researcher who has tracked and written and thought about the impact of *Tomorrow's Schools* since it began. I came into educational research in 1987 with a background in wider social policy and a keen interest in how policy has a bearing on the reality that organisations and individuals make. For me, policy is not just something that happens in buildings in Wellington, something abstract and separate from everyday life.

Linked to this interest in policy and its effects is an appreciation derived from my doctoral study in social anthropology of just how important concepts of freedom and equality are in New Zealand society, to the point where different interpretations lead to sometimes fierce clashes (Wylie, 1980). Both of these concepts played a role in the development of self-managing schools, and the expectations of them, with the same words promising different things to different people.

My own expectations of *Tomorrow's Schools* were cautiously open. With other colleagues at the New Zealand Council for Educational Research (NZCER), I had reviewed the existing educational research on educational opportunities and outcomes for a range of different social groups. Our conclusion was that there were concerning inequities in the system (Benton, 1988; Wylie, 1988a). I was asked to provide an overview of education policy and public views on education for the Royal Commission on Social Policy—a crash course for someone new to education in the issues identified by various inquiries and reports, and the existing research on effective teaching, the role of assessment and qualifications, and the importance of what would later be called 'student engagement'.

This work for the Royal Commission also brought me within the orbit of the Picot taskforce and a discussion with its chief executive on its intentions to make schools self-managing. I knew from the existing overseas examples of self-managing schools that it was important to design funding and staffing systems that did not disadvantage schools serving students in low-income and rural areas; that treating schools equally in the sense of treating all alike would no more remedy disadvantage than treating all students as if they were identical. It seemed important, too, that goals of improving educational opportunities for groups who were not as well served as others, such as Māori and those from low-income homes, were shared across the system and were used to hold schools accountable (Wylie, 1988a). But, like others at the time, I took for granted that there would be a supportive infrastructure for schools' work.

As the detail of *Tomorrow's Schools* became clear, I saw how important it was to have ongoing evaluation of what this radical change was producing. Fortunately, my institution, the NZCER, had the independence to pursue in 1989 what became a regular series of national surveys of primary schools, and from 2003 secondary schools, gaining the perspectives of principals, teachers, trustees and parents. These surveys have served as the backbone for a range of connected studies I have undertaken over the years, including principal and governance roles, how schools manage their finances, how they review and plan their work, how schools change their teaching practices and the way teachers work together, and how schools improve student engagement and achievement.

I have also thought about the way our system works by taking part in evaluations of particular programmes, initiatives and policies, and in inquiries into whether bulk funding (where schools receive funding for staffing within their operational grant, instead of having staffing paid for centrally) improved Māori learning opportunities, the role of school competition in our system and in other countries, and a review of the Special Education 2000 policy for the Government. All through this work I have sought evidence that would test whether what was intended in policy actually occurred: that the assumptions behind the policy, about how it would work to achieve its purpose, were well grounded. I continue to be optimistic that we will learn from such work and that well-researched evidence and analysis can feed better policy, though this optimism has been sorely tested at times over the past two decades or so.

This book draws, then, on more than 20 years of seeking to know how our schools were working and why, and how well positioned they were for what we needed them to provide all our students. It also draws on official publications, a wide range of reports and studies, and personal accounts. During 2011, when I was fortunate to be able to focus on this book full time as the J D Stout Fellow at the Stout Research Centre for New Zealand Studies, Victoria University of Wellington, the material I considered was substantial. I read and thought about far more than I could directly use in this book. Within the braided river of *Tomorrow's Schools* there are two important developments in particular that are beyond the focus of this book, but whose stories need to be written by those with in-depth understanding.

First, kura kaupapa Māori have become an established part of the educational landscape: it is once more possible for Māori to use their own language in educational settings that nurture Māori identity, and with evidence of considerable success in secondary qualifications. Yet the demands of school self-management and the absence of a strong infrastructure mean that these gains have been hard won and are not present in every kura.

Second, students with special needs are now better integrated into classrooms, though their needs throw into often uncomfortable relief the need for better integration of knowledge into school practice, better integration of services working with schools and parents, and the difficulties in our current system of ensuring that all self-managing schools can give these students the acceptance and learning they need.

This book also draws on interviews undertaken in 2011 with some 30 educators, officials, researchers and school advisers, people who I knew would provide me with a range of perspectives on the gains from school self-management and the possibilities for New Zealand education to make further progress. Most are known to me through contact over the years in research projects and policy discussions. They are thoughtful people who are not just mouthing a cliché when they talk about trying to make a difference to children's learning. They are people who have lived through the changes of the past 20 or so years, and who have worked hard in various roles over that time to make the most of the *Tomorrow's Schools* reforms. My understanding deepened through our discussions, and their reflections provide vivid illustrations of the reforms in practice. These are by nature optimistic, energetic people—as so many educators are. But they were largely unsure whether the gains they had seen could be sustained within the current structures and frameworks, let alone spread further so that every school can provide the quality of learning we want for all our students.

Despite many people's efforts, and some changes in the frameworks and support for schools, the issues self-managing schools set out to address remain with us. Promising developments that would have addressed some of these issues were halted in 1989 as all the attention went onto making the new structures work. There has been a price to pay for taking school self-management so literally and making it the kernel of our schooling system. Failing to learn from what self-managing schools can and can't achieve, and why, is wasteful. As a country, we cannot afford to pursue ineffective policy that does not make the most of our public funds and our human potential. Continuing as we are will not successfully address the continuing gaps in student learning. It is high time to change our education system, to make it more dynamic. I hope this book and the recommendations with which it concludes contribute to a much more productive phase in the story of New Zealand's self-managed schools.

Vital connections

# Chapter 1

# High expectations and the support they need

## The value of education

We value education so much that we make schooling one of the very few compulsory experiences of all New Zealanders. Less than 1 percent of students between the ages of 6 and 16, when schooling is compulsory, are home-schooled (Ministry of Education, 2010).[1] The vast majority of us gain skills, knowledge, interests, understanding and friendships, and encounter difference and uncertainty, in classrooms, school halls, playing fields and school trips. We rely on our teachers, and we learn to give and take with our peers.

But we don't start school as blank slates or empty vessels. Our schooling experience is filtered through our previous experiences, particularly the opportunities we have had to engage with words, symbols, patterns and movement, and to experience the interest and support of adults who encourage us. Most of us can also augment the learning opportunities we get at school with other learning experiences if our homes and neighbourhoods offer us opportunities to try different things, to pursue goals that require growing skill and knowledge, and encounters that deepen our understanding of the world's subtleties and complexities. Yet compulsory schooling still often provides the core of our growth, and it is the core we rely on as a society to ensure the next generation will be well equipped to make the most of life.

Over time we have asked more and more of schools as our society and economy have changed, and with them the kinds of livelihoods and

---

[1] The total number of home-schooled students in July 2010 was 6,782. Over half of those who completed home-schooling in the previous 12 months had 4 years or fewer of home-schooling, suggesting that many home-schooled students also have some regular school experience in their educational journey.

contributions individuals can make. Without some qualification, work opportunities are now scarce. Fewer opportunities are available to learn on the job for those who find nothing in school to motivate them and who leave without a qualification. The success of 'second-chance' post-school learning in attractive-looking vocational certificate courses is often patchy, especially if the second-chance learners have not acquired sound learning habits at school, have no clear idea of what interests them, or have received no sound advice about choosing a course that will progress them (Patterson, 2011; Wylie & Hodgen, 2011).

We are more aware of the costs to both individuals and society when students leave school without a secure platform of skills, knowledge and good communication habits, and without the will to keep learning, to try new things and to persist. We are also more aware of the long-term corrosive effects of failure in schoolwork, of being labelled 'dumb', 'lazy' or 'cabbage', and of student experiences of teachers who show no interest in or respect for them as individuals. Most of us come through school with both good and not-so-good experiences of learning and teachers. We can recall classes where everything seemed to come together to absorb us: often what we recall is the passion of a teacher, the way something was lit up. But we also know people who have been scarred by bad school experiences, who in later life regret the learning they lost by being steered into courses that bored or did not challenge them, or that caused them to walk away in defiance, and who as adults scorn those who teach or pursue knowledge and understanding.

Not so long ago we did not expect every student to find school worthwhile. Now we are asking schools to succeed with *all* their students. We want schools to engage each individual student's interest and effort daily through experiences that both nurture and challenge them, that enlarge their knowledge of things that matter, and that give them the confidence, initiative and resilience they need in an increasingly complex and uncertain world. This world is also calling for more 'higher-order thinking skills':

> We need to learn to generate, process and sort complex information; to think systematically and critically; to take decisions weighing different forms of evidence; to ask meaningful questions about different subjects; to be adaptable and flexible to new information; to be creative; and to be able to identify and solve real-world problems. (Dumont & Istance, 2010, p. 23)

This is an essential, and tremendous, task that requires considerable sophistication and coherence for teachers and schools to achieve.

No matter what knowledge and skills students bring to school when they enter at the age of 5, or how they have spent their time out of school, we ask schools to ensure that all school-leavers are equipped with a meaningful qualification that will both provide them with a platform for ongoing learning and participation and signal this to others. Qualifications now carry greater weight, and marked progress in qualification success has been achieved. Sixty-nine percent of the school-leavers of 2010 stood on the platform of at least NCEA Level 2 or its equivalent, up from 52 percent in 2005. The Ministry of Education describes NCEA Level 2 as "a benchmark, which young adults need to complete to have a basic prerequisite for higher education and training, and for many entry-level jobs" (Ministry of Education, 2011c, p. 41).

Around twice as many Māori students, so long underserved by schools (Benton, 1988; Penetito, 2010), achieved NCEA Level 2 or its equivalent in 2010 compared with 2003. But we are far from being able to rest on our laurels—not that such a thing is ever possible in education! We still need to improve the education of those 52 percent of Māori school-leavers, 40 percent of Pasifika students and 31 percent of school-leavers overall who in 2010 entered the adult world without this level of qualification.

## Improving education: Why policy matters

Improving education is no simple task. We often think of education as we remember it from our own experiences, fastening on individual teacher traits. Enthusiasm usually inspires. ("If you're not passionate, just fake it!" was the advice of one student to the 2009 international conference on school effectiveness and improvement; he brought the house down.) But enthusiasm without real knowledge—knowledge of a subject area, of one's students, of the strengths and difficulties these students have—is not enough for good learning. And knowledge of the subject and the students is not enough without an understanding of how the two can come together in ways that are helpful for learning. A teacher needs strategies they can use and make explicit so that learners can value, initiate and pursue their own understanding and competency. Finally, knowledge and strategies are not enough without the relevant materials or resources to work with. Every teacher who succeeds with their students must bring all these together in a synergistic rather than a mechanical way. To improve education we have to ask whether our education policy sufficiently supports teachers to undertake this intensive and complex work.

What we remember when we remember individual teaching that inspired us is just the tip of the iceberg. It takes a good system to produce and keep good teachers. It takes well-grounded, deliberate policy to ensure that we have sufficient good teachers in every school, to match our expectations of what education now needs to provide. It needs attention paid to ensuring that the knowledge and strategies that go into good teaching are circulating, and continually building to match an ever-changing and increasingly complex environment. Policy needs to be framed to ensure that teachers are part of a vibrant, inquiring, professional school culture, and that they are linked with others who are also sharing and building knowledge of good teaching and learning, beyond their own school.

Policy and regulatory frameworks are not what come to mind when we think of good teachers we have experienced, and yet it is difficult to achieve good teaching and learning unless these frameworks are designed to foster good teaching and learning, and to build on the evidence already available about how best to do this. It is also difficult to improve teaching and learning if there is a lack of coherence in education policy, if various policies pull in opposing directions, distracting energy and attention from what should be the core focus of teaching and learning.

New Zealand's experience since *Tomorrow's Schools* gives a sobering example of the significance of policy frameworks in what teachers and schools can achieve, and the cost of incoherence in policy. Qualification rates did not change over the first decade (and longer) of school self-management. There was no improvement until 2002, when the introduction of NCEA fostered new approaches to teaching and learning. It was too difficult for secondary schools and teachers to increase qualification success until they and their students no longer had to work within a long-criticised and outdated qualification framework that set artificial limits on the proportion of students who could succeed. This framework had been clearly identified as one of the major barriers to improving educational outcomes for Māori, whose educational opportunities were of particular concern to the Picot taskforce and to the *Tomorrow's Schools* policy.

Changes to the qualifications framework that had been gearing up at the time were sideswiped by the shift to school self-management. That shift took up too much of the policy space and too much energy throughout the system. Changes to administrative structures also had first call on government funds— funds that reduced rather than increased, just as more was being expected of schools. The nature of the shift to school self-management fragmented curriculum-based networks and the porous connections between schools. Schools found it harder to share, to collaborate, in a more competitive environment. Strong interconnections between schools and government no longer existed to keep building a shared and trusted platform.

Ironically, secondary schools had already exercised much self-management before *Tomorrow's Schools*. A real brake on secondary schools improving their students' performance was not their connections with government, but the structure of the qualifications framework of the 1980s. Arguably, putting the shift to self-management ahead of frameworks that supported change to secondary teaching and learning came at an unnecessary cost for secondary students in the 1990s, and resulted in a decade's delay in our making progress towards doing better by students who had been consistently underserved.

It would have been difficult to increase qualification success even with the change to the more relevant standards-based qualification that NCEA has provided since 2002 had there not been nationally funded opportunities for teachers to connect with others and make sense of the new standards. The introduction of NCEA was flawed, and like any qualification or assessment system it needs regular review and development to ensure it supports new understanding of how students learn best and our expectations of what they should be and do (e.g., Bolstad & Gilbert, 2012), as discussed in Chapter 9. Nonetheless, it has made possible some new approaches to teaching and learning that have had positive effects.

# Hallmarks of effective infrastructure for a good public education system

The quality of our schools reflects the quality of our educational policy. What they are able to achieve is not just a matter of desire and effort on the part of teachers and principals. Good policy needs to ensure that our educators have frameworks that allow them to use knowledge well, and connections that ensure they have the capability that is needed.

In 1989, when I drafted the first of NZCER's national surveys of the impact of *Tomorrow's Schools*, I looked for indicators of effective schools that we could include to chart changes over time in the capability and capacity of self-managing schools. Only a handful of strong studies existed. Now there is a wealth of studies, not only on effective schools but also on how schools become effective, how they improve, and particularly how we improve learning for those who come to school without the advantages of well-stocked early childhoods and well-founded expectations that school is for them. There is also much research on how the systems in which schools are located can either support them to do their best by their students or make it difficult for them. We are much better placed now than we were in 1988/89 to design policy to make the most of self-managing schools, and to think carefully about the quality of the infrastructure on which *their* quality depends.

There are six principles from this existing research-based knowledge that have informed my thinking as I examined the changes in our schooling system. These are principles that can be used to examine the soundness of the infrastructure built by our educational policy. I have therefore framed them here as questions.

1. *Interconnections*
    - Are there inbuilt, ongoing relationships of both support and challenge, and purposeful work between schools and different parts of the system, that foster the sharing and development of knowledge and a shared idea of the issues and action needed to continually improve teaching and learning?

2. *Coherence*
    - Is there alignment between policies and processes at the national and school levels, and with the roles of teacher education and development?
    - Are there common values and goals that allow attention to be paid to the deep issues of education, and that provide a common purpose that enables teachers and policy makers to work respectfully together?

3. *Knowledge development and use (including capability)*
    - Is sound existing knowledge the kernel of national and local frameworks for teachers' and schools' work in terms of teacher education and development?
    - Is new knowledge actively generated by building on existing knowledge using interconnections?
    - Is policy evaluated in ways that allow ongoing learning, and refreshing or reframing?
    - Are students and their learning sufficiently at the heart of our endeavour?

4. *Capacity*
    - Is time for teachers to evaluate and develop their own work, to find out and think about new knowledge related to their work, and to work and learn together, included in everyday school processes?
    - Is the availability of good teachers and principals independent of the location of the school?

5. *Initiative*
    - Is there scope to exercise initiative in the classroom, the school and the roles that work with educators? (Only in the informed action taken in response to a particular situation—in the 'teachable moment' and its equivalent—are student, teacher or school needs well served or new possibilities explored, and new knowledge able to be created.)

6. *Shared responsibility*
    - Is the improvement of educational experiences and outcomes, particularly for the underserved—Māori, Pasifika, students from low-income homes, those whose parents' own education was limited and those with special education needs—really shared across the system's layers and roles?
    - Is the system a learning system, able to use its knowledge and interconnections to keep developing in more productive ways?

All these principles matter. For example, we are unlikely to see better teaching and learning if initiative is exercised without good knowledge or a sense of shared responsibility. Good interconnections that ignore sound knowledge do not benefit students. Good interconnections that exist only for some schools and are used by them to make the most of their own situation will only benefit some students, without contributing to improvements for all.

The knowledge I am talking about is not of isolated facts or of guaranteed recipes. It is research-based or supported by solid practice evidence. All knowledge needs to be interpreted in the light of other knowledge, such as of the out-of-school lives of one's students or the traditions people bring to a situation. It also needs imaginative thought and real discussion, since in our current era we do not have the luxury of being able to support systemic change through increasing the public expenditure on education. We need to be able to make more of what we have. We need to look for policies and frameworks that can serve several purposes, that give us dual value by interweaving the use and growth of knowledge with connections across the system. Indeed, I cannot see how we can come closer to meeting the high expectations we now have of education unless we ensure we frame educational policy and provision through such informed and inclusive discussion.

It is also clear that for any education system to stay in good health and keep developing it takes concerted understanding and commitment, including from outside the education system. Political whim and ideology can all too easily derail long-term progress, particularly if they replace well-founded or well-developing infrastructure and frameworks with ones that are not supported by existing evidence and that ignore the lessons of the past.

The era before *Tomorrow's Schools* had some considerable challenges. It also had some strengths that may not have been as clear to people until they were gone. The next chapter takes us back to that time to show how the system worked before *Tomorrow's Schools*. We need to understand its strengths and shortcomings if we are to understand how well positioned schools and teachers were to take on the responsibilities asked of them in the reforms, and whether we could have expected *Tomorrow's Schools* to improve educational opportunities.

# Chapter 2

# A semi-ordered freedom

## The 1980s: Interconnections and porous boundaries

In the 1980s interconnections between New Zealand schools and Department of Education officials were such that despite much greater latitude over curriculum and day-to-day teaching decisions than in many other countries, there was a marked consistency of approach. New knowledge was generated and travelled through these interconnections more organically than bureaucratically. The Department of Education initiated projects to draw on practice knowledge, alongside research and specialist curriculum knowledge, linking people in different roles.

Such joint work over time led to new frameworks and new resources for teaching, and helped make the boundaries between educators and officials porous. So, too, did the relatively close relationship between inspectors and schools. Inspectors were part of the Department of Education, but they worked as teams within the 10 education boards that were responsible for primary schools, or out of regional Department offices if they worked with secondary schools.

In this chapter I outline the latitude that schools already enjoyed before they were given self-management, and the role played by interconnections to support and develop the quality of teaching, with particular attention to the role of the inspectorate and advisers. Several illustrations are given of the kind of joint work that brought teaching expertise and officials together to create frameworks and resources that would be used in many schools without having to be imposed.

I also look at some of the innovative work being done in the 1980s to change the nature of school cultures, and how evident it now is that while New Zealand schools did have considerable latitude—far more than one would think from reading the Picot taskforce report—they were not well prepared to work as professional collective cultures, as they would need to in order to make the most of school self-management.

There were certainly layers of approval needed for schools and those who worked with them to make certain decisions. These approval processes did not sit easily with the latitude around curriculum and what happened inside classrooms. I also look at the areas where decisions affecting school life were made by those beyond the school gate, and the real barriers to changing how those decisions were made: generic public service and Treasury rules and political focus.

# Teacher and school latitude before *Tomorrow's Schools*

The Picot taskforce's essential criticism of the New Zealand education system as over-centralised and bureaucratic lay behind the frequent bemusement of overseas visitors when they came to ask me about the implementation of *Tomorrow's Schools* in the 1990s. How was it possible that New Zealand schools had made the transition to self-management so rapidly given such over-centralisation? How was it possible that our system actually worked? It was certainly difficult for most visitors to imagine that their own country's schools could work well if they were disconnected from the district they belonged to. Indeed, none of the countries that came to suss out our reforms adopted them.

The latitude that New Zealand schools already enjoyed on a day-to-day basis is a key reason why it was possible for them to take on the wider responsibilities of self-management without the difficulties envisaged by people from more hierarchical education systems. On paper, things could look centralised: we had national secondary qualifications, for example, and the national office of the Department had to approve certain allocations of funding and staff. But the reality was more complex.

Prior to *Tomorrow's Schools,* teachers and schools were already accustomed to working within national frameworks that provided guidelines rather than tight prescription (other than for some senior secondary subject examinations). There were syllabuses for different subject and skill areas, but the materials used in teaching and the pace of teaching were left to individual teachers. Their choice of materials (such as textbooks at the secondary level) was constrained by what the school already had or could afford, but it was not regulated. At the primary level there were no regulations about the hours each subject should take. At the secondary level there were regulations for the number of hours the three core subject groups (English and social studies, mathematics, and science) should take, but this left around half the class hours for allocation across other subjects. It also allowed schools, if they wished, to integrate core subjects by designing a course of lessons that included aspects of these different subject syllabuses. At the primary and junior secondary levels there were no mandatory assessments. The constraints on secondary schools programmes were most acutely felt in the three-tier examination structure, which dominated the senior secondary school (then Forms 5 to 7, now Years 11 to 13).

Individual principals could vary considerably in how they enacted their role. Many seemed to see their role as the *principal-teacher*, first among peers, providing advice and support, securing resources for their fellows, and taking on the administration tasks on behalf of the school as a whole. A 1976 study found that around a fifth of 'non-teaching' primary principals' time was in fact spent in classes. Most of this time seems to have been spent teaching in order to release senior staff or to use their own expertise to teach a specific curriculum area, though some time was spent assisting new teachers (Coleman, 1976). Just over half the primary school principals in the mid-1980s had their own classes as well, which made the principal–teacher role an easier fit conceptually. Also making this a more appealing role was the autonomy of each teacher, which came with primary teachers having their own class and with secondary teachers having their own subject classes. The primary teachers in the 1976 survey certainly felt they had the freedom to teach and plan as individuals, with the back-up of the principal.

Secondary principals had more authority than primary principals by virtue of the school rather than the education board making staff appointments, and secondary schools had more control of their own budgets. However, Noel Scott's 1977 cross-country visits to secondary schools to provide a report to the Department of Education on what was needed in the way of new support for schools found principals too often working alone, heroically shouldering administration and all the interactions with the world outside the school gate. They provided both the outward face of the school as well as the initiative and discussions to secure resources. This could mean the staff experienced the principal as working 'behind closed doors'.

So within schools there was considerable latitude experienced by class teachers and by principals in how they carried out their roles. This would contribute to confidence in becoming fully self-managed with the *Tomorrow's Schools* reforms. But the schools were not left alone. They had ongoing connections with the inspectorate, the advisers and curriculum subject experts in the Department of Education. The inspectorate played a particularly interesting role in supporting schools and the development of new knowledge, and in maintaining connections across schools, especially for primary schools.

## The interconnecting inspectorate

The inspectorate had once spent most of its time grading and making decisions on individual teachers, a role that had begun in order to bring national consistency and fairness. They had ceased inspecting individual secondary teachers in the 1970s. Primary inspectors in the 1980s spent about a third of their time inspecting (passing judgement on) individual teachers, deciding whether new teachers should be certified and whether those who were interested in promotion (some 15 percent of the primary teaching workforce) should be regraded to enable them to apply for higher positions. They also played a pivotal role in the (rare) process by which incompetent teachers were removed from their school.

There was ambivalence all round about the continuation of individual inspections, though they also served to connect schools and to develop networks that could change practice. But the framework for the grading of individual teachers suffered from the same artificial allocations as the secondary qualifications. How fair and objective was the grading for promotion purposes when it rested on a normal curve of allocation, meaning that the top grades were limited to a certain number, no matter how many might be performing at a similar standard? Ex-inspectors tell stories of colleagues making trade-offs for 'their' candidates, or gradings decided by the strongest voice rather than the strongest case.

Teachers did not always trust those who inspected them. The criteria for grading were transparent but, like any criteria, required interpretation. Some teachers encountered inspectors with set views on teaching methods (though teaching methods were not prescribed), discouraging innovation. Others encountered inspectors who discouraged them by appearing to be bored or simply going through the motions, adding little other than tension throughout a day of having one's planning scrutinised and one's teaching observed. And the observation of one's teaching was not a frequent experience for teachers once they were certified. Their work was with 'my class', behind a closed door. Principals and those who headed syndicates (such as the junior classes in primary schools) or subject departments in secondary schools did not assume that their position gave them authority to open that classroom door as they pleased.

Yet these individual inspections could also connect individual teachers with expertise. As one highly experienced teacher told me, "I was having trouble with reading groups and the inspector put me in touch with a really good teacher in a nearby school." It was much easier in the pre-*Tomorrow's Schools* era for such cross-school connections that improve teaching to occur. Inspectors went in and out of schools in a geographical patch. They knew where good practice was occurring. Schools saw themselves as part of a wider system, and were usually pleased to have a teacher from another school come to observe and discuss what they saw. Inspectors could also provide teacher relief time to support the connections they made for the teachers.

Grading also helped the inspectorate to identify talent, and led to invitations to join working groups, often in the form of invitational 'in-service' courses, which again the inspectors had the discretion to resource. Their requests to principals to have their staff seconded were rarely refused.

Schools were inspected by teams of inspectors every 3 or so years. These inspections would yield advice for the principal, and inspection teams would also meet with the school committee (primary) or board of governors (secondary). The inspection reports went to the education board (primary) or the regional office of the Department (secondary). They were not made public.

Each school also had a liaison inspector, who would visit the school several times a year and discuss things with the principal. The liaison inspector was, as one secondary principal told his staff, to be "welcomed as a friend and adviser" (Day, 1984, p. 134). For the principal it was an opportunity to get another (usually, but not always) well-informed view and advice about options and possibilities, and to gain access to resources decided by the inspectorate or in which they had a say. Some liaison inspectors followed up on the advice and observations in the 3-yearly or so team inspection; others did not.

Secondary inspectors also had the responsibility for finding other schools for suspended students. This part of their role increased in the 1980s. Suspensions increased because more students were staying longer in school without necessarily being more engaged in learning. At the same time, the secondary-age population had decreased. Secondary schools became more concerned about their reputation, more ready to suspend students who were not conforming to school rules. Competition between secondary schools for reputation grew in the 1980s in some areas, even before *Tomorrow's Schools* placed greater emphasis on parental choice of schools (OECD, 1983, p. 44).

Inspectors approved school schemes—an approval rarely withheld. One ex-principal, who also spent a few months as an acting inspector (temporary positions allowed both the principal and the inspectorate to try out each other's roles), expressed his frustration when, as the new principal of a school that turned out to have major long-standing problems, he was visited by a team of seven inspectors "who turned up to tell me how to turn the school around". Not that this confident principal thought he had to take any notice of them! He asked them why, if they had known about these problems at the school, they had not done anything. He received the answer, "We're not the principal." However, others have stories of liaison inspectors picking up that a principal was struggling and going in to work with them—or move them out—before things got too bad.

Inspectors drew on their interactions with teachers and schools, and others, to form overviews of local capacity, and they shared their knowledge of issues, gaps in knowledge or difficulties that seemed beyond individual school resolution. They also often used their connections with advisers and Department officials to devise responses. Their overview could lead to in-service courses, new developments in syllabus or resources, and sometimes to innovative networks. They had latitude themselves in making these responses. Some acted as stirrers in the system. Because their role took them between schools, the Department and groups of specialists and researchers, they could often informally develop and circulate knowledge. On the whole they probably enlivened education, and they often kept it moving.

They also contributed to the perhaps otherwise remarkable consistency of approach that was evident in the schools, through their reactions, advice on and contributions to the resources and frameworks teachers wanted to use. It was consistency, but not uniformity.

Inspectors were all experienced teachers themselves, usually expert practitioners who had come to the notice of existing inspectors or advisers and had been given the opportunity to contribute to in-service groups working on developing a syllabus or teaching resources (materials), or tackling wider issues. Primary inspectors had taught in primary schools; secondary inspectors had taught in secondary schools. Much of their training for the role was on-the-job, and hence dependent on their peers and district or regional senior inspector. Their judgements were based on their own experience of what they had seen working in their own teaching and in others' classrooms, their discussions with colleagues, their participation in in-service courses with teachers, advisers and officials and researchers, their reading, and their participation with colleagues in school inspections.

# The source of inspectors' authority

One of the key criteria in grading primary teachers emphasised

> Success in achieving an ordered freedom, i.e., a lively and happy atmosphere, together with firmly established but unobtrusive class routines, and a good working tone.[1]

This "ordered freedom" which inspectors looked for in primary teaching seems to me to also characterise the manner of their relationships with schools, though perhaps that should be "semi-ordered freedom".

Inspectors' authority over schools did not lie in any direct command relationship. Nor were they in a position to hover too closely. The liaison inspector role was only one of their tasks. In 1986 there were 102 primary inspectors over the 10 education board districts, and 57 secondary inspectors, with a further 24 seconded secondary teachers usually working on particular curriculum areas (Clark, 1988). Secondary inspectors were responsible for around nine schools in the liaison role (Day, 1984, p. 127) and primary inspectors for around 20 schools.

Their authority lay in their own knowledge and the way they conveyed it, and in the resources they could allocate, particularly teacher release days and inclusion in a professional development course (then often called 'in-service'). Inspectors made decisions about priority areas and priority schools: they did not leave this up to chance, or to 'first in, first served'. The strength of this district-wide discretion of allocation was that if the judgement was sound, decisions on scarce resources meant a fair prioritisation for schools with higher student need, or prioritisation for schools that would make the most of the professional development, which could then be used as a resource by other schools.

This overall strategic decision making also had other benefits:

> If the DSI [District Senior Inspector, who headed the team of inspectors in each education board] called a meeting, said, 'I would like you all present', all the principals went. Not just because of their authority, but there was a sense of the collective.[2]

---

1 These criteria are given in Ewing (1963, pp. 52-53). Ewing was then the Chief Inspector of Primary Schools.
2 Interview, July 2011, with former principal.

The inspectorate could also connect the dots. For example, to enable principals and teachers in rural areas to be part of in-service courses, the Wellington inspectorate tackled the shortage of relieving teachers and put some of its discretionary resources into training for teachers returning to the workforce. It tackled the high turnover of young teachers in the Porirua area, which was due to the particular demands of teaching in a low-income area coupled with what the inspectors saw as a loss of hope or agency among school staff that they could in fact raise achievement levels.[3]

Inspectors also had authority in relation to opportunities for individuals. Some saw this positively, some with wariness:

> It was about people with a combination of moral and educational authority. When you put those things together you thought, hmm, this person can help create an opportunity for me, but this person's opinion is actually also worth something.[4]

> The inspector's power came largely through knowledge is power. You know, they were the people who knew when the curriculum was going to change or when the exam syllabus would alter. They were the people who actually controlled probably 90 percent of all the in-service development that you were ever going to have. So if you upset them too much it didn't matter that your principal or HOD [Head of Department] thought you should go off on a particular professionally improving activity, they could veto it, and they did.[5]

Yet inspectors had also been a (too) rare source of feedback for this critic of the miswielding of their authority. His further comment shows how schools were accustomed to operating more as bands of individuals than as professional collective cultures:

> But the only person who gave me adult feedback was an inspector. Once every few years somebody might have come round and said, 'That wasn't too bad.' You were pretty much on your own. And so it was quite nice to have somebody, particularly if you held them in some regard, who would come in and say they thought you'd been on the right track, or a lesson had gone well. Yeah, but it was sort of a long time between meals.

---

3   These examples come from reports and notes from inspectors included in the National Archives files for the Wellington primary inspectorate.
4   Interview, July 2011, with former principal, former Ministry of Education official, and current consultant.
5   Interview, July 2011, with former secondary teacher, inspector, ERO and Ministry of Education official.

In the Wellington primary inspectorate archive files the tone of letters to principals in the mid- to late 1980s is respectful, and the advice is couched as suggestions and questions. I don't know how typical this is: the material saved is patchy rather than comprehensive, and this was only one of the 10 inspectorate teams in the country, and probably one of the more progressive ones. Inspectors may have used a different tone when speaking face to face. The use made of the advice would also depend on whether a principal was looking to change schools or roles,[6] or seeking their own or their staff's inclusion in professional development, and therefore the impression they wanted an inspector to have of them. And a great deal would depend on the inspector's own expertise and credibility in the eyes of the principal and teachers.

In other words, although inspectors were above principals in the educational hierarchy, their actual authority and influence on what happened in schools depended on the nature of the relationship they had with principals and teachers, their knowledge, and their ability to make connections and facilitate useful knowledge building or sharing across schools and with others. Teacher release days, said one ex-inspector, were a "marvellous weapon" in the inspector's kit.[7]

# Creative use of the "marvellous weapon"

Teacher release days could be used to satisfy individual or school interest and need. They could also be grouped to create frameworks, resources and networks that would be likely to change practice and create a common language that teachers could use to discuss what they were doing and how it was working. They included the development of resources for teachers in Mangere and Otara to work in multicultural settings with Māori and Pasifika students.

The Wellington primary inspectorate used release days to develop the Wellington maths units and the Schools Without Failure kitsets. The Wellington maths units were developed by the district's maths adviser,

---

6 Inspectors were part of the committees that made decisions on appointments, including appointments of principals. But they did not necessarily decide these appointments. One ex-primary principal recalled that while he had inspectors' support for taking on the principal role, his path was blocked by an elected board member without educational expertise who had taken against him. It was only when this person was absent that he was able to be appointed to his first principalship. Interview, July 2011.

7 John Ennis, personal communication, 5 December 2011.

working with teachers, and with advice from curriculum experts in the head office of the Department of Education. The units were trialled before they were published. They were available on request, as befits the latitude schools enjoyed, and were well used in the Wellington area, backed by in-service courses and advice. They provided some "specific direction on balanced programmes … a strong emphasis is placed on teachers having pupils work at different levels within each class".[8] Such specificity was not unwelcome when it came from credible sources, using a process of development that respected teachers' practice knowledge while taking it further.

The Schools Without Failure project dealt with the much more knotty issue of the development of school cultures and values. It is worth looking at in closer detail, both for how it was developed and for what it tells us about the views of people who were concerned about the patterns of unequal educational outcomes in the years before *Tomorrow's Schools*. We get an insight into their ideas about what might improve things, and about the channels available to them to influence principals and teachers.

## Schools Without Failure

The inspectorate was the catalyst for the Schools Without Failure work, spurred by the challenges of areas such as Porirua. It was work that relied on interconnections for its success. This ambitious project acknowledged that social inequalities played a role in educational performance, but "the project team saw no reason to apologise for their commonsense belief that teachers can make a difference and that schools without failure is a goal worth striving for" (Mansell, 1985, p. 3). The team of seven primary and secondary teachers, identified through their previous participation and good use of in-service training in curriculum areas, produced five kitsets that focused on the relationships between students and teachers and on how best to continually motivate children through everyday school practices.

There is material in these kitsets that would not go amiss today, though it would be phrased differently—particularly the title of the first kitset: *Self-esteem and School Learning* (including the affirming of a child's cultural identity). The other four kitsets were as follows:

- *The Evaluation Process: How Does It Affect the Child?* encouraged assessments that involved clearly understood objectives for learning that were set by

---

8  Archives R20472 921.

the teacher and learner together, and that were privately communicated. It also showed the shortcomings of pacing work for students based on classifying them too much in terms of a normal distribution.[9]

- *Changing School Climate for Children's Success* emphasised warmth and openness, and teachers working together and with their school community.
- *Using Groups for Success: Co-Operative Learning* included cautions about rigid ability grouping that limited teacher and child expectations and effort.
- *He Tumanako mo te Ao Hou: Success at School for Māori Children*.

Included in the kitsets were booklets with cartoons; course leader notes; taped interviews with children, parents and others in the community; case studies and scenarios; reprints of a range of articles with different viewpoints; references for further reading; and suggestions for small-scale action research.

The authors were aware that "teachers are likely to change what they do only when they themselves have been closely involved in deciding what was needed" (Mansell, 1985, p. 5). The kitsets aimed to steer a deliberate middle course to encourage change, which is never simple when it involves giving up something one had taken for granted or thought was working. Elements of strategies "jolting people into changing by exposing the damaging effects on children of their present practices" sit alongside strategies

> gently leading towards changed attitudes by first giving reinforcement for whatever they were presently doing well, and suggesting ways to build on those strengths, remembering the need to maintain the self-esteem of the adult learner throughout the insecurities of change. (Mansell, 1985, p. 6)

---

9 Along with notes on the normal curve used in norm-referencing and its shortcomings as a diagnostic tool, and questions for teachers about how useful such ranking actually was in planning to meet children's needs, the evaluation booklet (p. 11) gave a cartoon with this limerick:

Said the sad reading teacher, Miss Raill:
"Young Jack and his friends always fail.
While I won't say they're dumb,
there will always be some
who fall at the end of the scale."

Said Jack who was quick to concede:
"There are others far out in the lead.
While I am willing to serve
as a tail of a curve,
I'd rather be able to read."

There was a focus, too, on "small steps and attainable goals" as well as "a long-term vision" (p. 7).

Connections across the system were used by the project team. Over the several years of the kitsets' development (the teachers worked in bursts of activity covered by the inspectorate's "marvellous weapon" of teacher release days between their usual teaching responsibilities), they discussed the work with over 100 people: in schools and the Department of Education, with educational researchers, academics, teachers college staff, and Māori and Pasifika groups. Sixty schools volunteered to trial the kitsets in 1981 and 1982. Designed as stand-alone resources, they were found to be most effective long term in schools that already had good experiences of staff working together for a common purpose—far from a universal experience. Time for teachers to work together was also an issue.

These findings about some of the conditions that are needed to change school and teacher practice—involving using and fostering the collective strength of teachers working together to support change in individual classrooms—are all too similar to findings in evaluations of professional development and school improvement initiatives funded by the Ministry of Education after *Tomorrow's Schools*. Simply shifting to school self-management was not enough to spur people to gain the knowledge and capacity to develop the kinds of productive school cultures that are one of the essential ingredients to keep improving the quality of education and the outcomes for students. Interconnections that produce useful resources are necessary too. Schools cannot do everything on their own.

There was a heartening interest in these kitsets; heartening because it indicates there was interest both in the school-wide approach and in improving teaching. Other districts heard of the resource and sought it out. The Department funded the further production of 90 kitsets nationwide, which could be lent to schools by inspectorates. The Wellington inspectorate supported members of the project team to work with schools using the kitset for several days; a national in-service course was held for a week, with each of the 10 districts sending one person. Course participants' ability to influence things—to interconnect—varied. Some were principals whose influence might be limited to their own school. Networks of schools using the kitset were set up in some areas but not in others. A key person would change position and connectivity would drop. Feedback was only informal, but positive.

Mansell (1985) noted that the new curriculum developments of the 1980s—the health education syllabus, a draft starter resource (developed by the Department's Māori and Island Education Division with the New Zealand Educational Institute's[10] Māori Advisory Council) and the major new curriculum review—rested on schools undertaking collective work, often involving parents and the community. These new curriculum developments spanned subject areas that were the usual means for allocating advisory support and providing curriculum anchorage in the national office of the Department of Education. They were about the importance of coherence in the practice of teachers in a school, and the interactions with students and parents that would be most likely to enlist their positive participation in learning. They were about ways of teaching (pedagogy) that are most likely to engage student effort and persistence with learning—for all students, in their diversity of talent, knowledge and confidence. They were about the vitality that comes from schools that work cohesively and systematically, evaluating their effectiveness with students, and using student performance and feedback as useful information to decide what could be developed further in a culture of support for continual learning. They were about the kinds of capability schools would be expected to have as the self-managing units of *Tomorrow's Schools*. The experience from the Schools Without Failure project shows both that this capability was not well developed and that its development generally needs support.

Here we come to a real shortcoming of the system prior to *Tomorrow's Schools*. It could foster innovation, it could foster new thinking and practice, but there was no national, systemic way to support schools in the work of development and real change; no way to keep building networks or share experiences of what schools were doing and develop the work further. Curriculum areas tended to have stronger networks. But this essential work on pedagogy—on *how* one knits together learning in ways that motivate and really engage students, and on how one develops schools as collective adult learning places—had no national anchorage. We have a much stronger platform now for knowing how important it is that schools work in this way. But it is hard not to look back on the Schools Without Failure project and wonder how much better equipped schools might have been to make the most of the self-management they were given in 1989 if there had been some way to build nationally and systematically on this work, both before and after *Tomorrow's Schools*.

---

10 NZEI, the primary teachers' union.

## Challenges to sharpening school capacity

By the early 1980s quite a few inspectors and other Department of Education officials were seeing the need for schools to change their way of working as organisations. They were also seeing the need for more attention to be given to the principal's role in working in a more cohesive way at the school level and making the most of new knowledge brought into the schools. The inspectorate had been frustrated by all too often seeing no change in schools after a teacher had gone on an in-service programme of some length, indicating to them that principals had not ensured this new knowledge for the school had been used to develop the school's teaching capacity. Such professional development was not cheap, and it was one of the resources that needed rationing.

Principals won appointment on the basis of their strength as teachers. Most had had some additional responsibility beyond the classroom when they applied for a principal's job, but there was little training for the role of principal. Support came from the school's liaison inspector and a principal's own personal networks. Principals' associations and the two teacher unions also provided opportunities for discussion of shared issues. Colleges of education had started to offer courses for principals and school managers.

Appointed to her first principalship just before *Tomorrow's Schools*, a now highly experienced principal recalled her first day in the role:

> I didn't know what to do when I went into that office. I did not know what a principal did. There was a book. It told me every single thing to do. It was all stuff like what to do if there's a broken window—ring the Education Board. That was it. No focus on raising student achievement, on teaching, on appraisals. It was about accommodation and furniture.[11]

In the mid-1980s some district inspectorates began to provide professional development to principals that would enable them to focus on building a more collective and deliberate school culture, one that went beyond camaraderie and sharing of teaching materials. This principal was able to take part in workshops funded by the Wellington district inspectorate to start to address this crucial gap in the system. These workshops focused on school development and ran over 2 years. Principals taking part undertook change projects in their schools, and discussed their projects and their learning from them in the workshops. Sharing of their endeavours, gains and failures, linked the participating principals together. This linking was to prove particularly

---

11 Interview, June 2011, with highly experienced principal and principals' adviser.

useful for those fortunate enough to have taken part in the workshops in the immediate post-*Tomorrow's Schools* era, when principals were left to make their own way in uncharted waters. The Wellington inspectorate also set up a principals' consultancy group of current and respected principals that people could use, providing "support without condemnation".[12] This group of principals came to the fore in the Wellington region in the days immediately following the introduction of *Tomorrow's Schools*, pressing for more systemic support for principals while continuing to provide informal support themselves.

Teacher release days were not plentiful: fewer than one per year per teacher if you tallied them across the country. The OECD examiners whose observations about New Zealand education in 1983 are a valuable reflection of what well-informed outsiders found distinctive about our system (which I look at more closely in Chapter 3) thought this quantity compared poorly with overseas systems.

Harvey McQueen, a former secondary inspector and Department official, who later worked in Prime Minister and Minister of Education David Lange's office during the final development of *Tomorrow's Schools*, wrote a series of columns in 1986 for the *National Business Review* under the heading 'Education: Pointers to a crisis' (McQueen, 1986). The crisis was mainly around a sense that pressure was mounting for changes that could not be provided within the current system. In his third column he focused on in-service training:

> During the cuts of the Muldoon years, inservice training was regarded as the soft underbelly of the system. It was here that the knife went in. For a short-run, diminishing end, a needed infrastructure was slashed.
>
> Thousands of dollars are spent on curriculum development, a new syllabus is promulgated and then very little money is allocated for its implementation. When the syllabus does not work it is criticised, often the process is repeated, extra money is allocated for further development.
>
> Principles underlying a new syllabus need face-to-face explanation. Teachers receive little assistance to learn the required skills, or support to develop suitable programmes and change their strategies. There are usually few resources to support implementation.
>
> If a coherent, consistent programme is to be implemented nationally it needs planning and support. (McQueen, 1986, column 3, p. 1)

---

12  John Ennis, personal communication, December 2011.

But even before these cuts in the early 1980s left a gap in in-service training and development, support for teachers was not plentiful, nor were opportunities to develop new frameworks and resources that teachers would want to use. One can see why it was important that the inspectorate could connect people across schools and use their various roles to identify particularly good practitioners for temporary working groups that would develop knowledge collectively. One can also see why it was important that their roles allowed them to energise teachers and principals and spread knowledge. It was a relatively efficient way to make the most of limited resources—albeit a slower mode of working than government is now used to. Porous boundaries between classroom practitioners and 'experts', and joint work to create frameworks and resources, made the results acceptable to teachers, and this is crucial to any development and widespread use of educational practice. On the whole, the approach probably provided considerable value for money.

# Joint work to advance reading

The joint work approach was most fruitfully used by the Department of Education to develop primary teachers' capacity to teach reading through the creation of practical and interesting frameworks. The Ready to Read series has been used in New Zealand schools since 1964, replacing the British-based Janet and John series. It gave junior schoolteachers a sequence of progressively more demanding stories, with New Zealand content so that New Zealand students could see their world in what they were reading. They were published by the Department of Education, with every school receiving some copies of each story. The stories were graded in terms of their difficulty. Teachers thus gained a dual resource: more appealing stories, plus a framework to assess and meet individual student needs, which became the common backbone to the teaching of reading across the country.

In 1975 the series was revised through

> intensive consultation with teachers, reading advisers, curriculum developers, inspectors and college of education lecturers. This process may explain why the series is so widely accepted and used in our primary schools today. (Wagemaker, 1993, p. 18)

The revision included better coverage of Māori and less stereotyped gender roles.

The way the original series was devised, using New Zealand teachers' practice as a fulcrum for inquiry, also contributed to its near universality in a system that did not prescribe. Here is Bill Renwick, then the Director-General of Education, talking about its genesis:

> It began with an assessment of what was best in the practice of New Zealand infant teachers and of what seemed to be of most enduring value in what had been researched and written about the beginnings of reading. The project was firmly rooted in the practice of the teachers and the day-to-day reality of New Zealand infant classrooms. The development set out to tap the knowledge and experience of everyone in the teaching profession with a contribution to make to the learning of reading in the early stages. There was much trialling of materials, counting of heads, sifting of opinions, and testing of hunches about how best to introduce new entrants to reading, what materials to use, how they should be used by teachers, how teachers could best be trained to teach the beginnings of reading, and how they should be supported in their work. The end result was not only a new set of reading materials and the validation of an approach to the teaching of reading but, no less important, the creation of a national network of teachers of the beginning of reading. Ready to Read grew out of the experience of the teachers, advisers, inspectors, lecturers and others who participated in its development.
>
> ... [the work was] carried out in the spirit of critical inquiry, and it made use, where appropriate, of research tools and techniques ... One of the central ideas of the series, the use of the children's own experience and the language of that experience as a vehicle for the teaching of reading, was an idea born of experience rather than research. At the time ... most of the published overseas research and other writings on the beginnings of reading were preoccupied with basic word lists, it was an idea ahead of its time. Its justification was that it seemed to work in the hands of New Zealand teachers in New Zealand junior schools. (Renwick, 1981, p. 19)

Here we touch on another distinctive aspect of the New Zealand approach to education: the idea that learning, at least in the primary school, had to be couched in terms that made sense to individual learners. Educators—inspectors, advisers, officials, along with teachers—did not always immediately grasp just how different individual learners could be, or how much their own perceptions were filtering what they thought would cater for individuals. Thus it is not until 1975 that there is better provision for Māori and girls, so that these individuals could see themselves more directly in the reading material. Nonetheless, this emphasis on the individual learner had the power to prod ongoing review, such as the 1975 revisions, and lead to improvement to meet a wider range of student need.

The Ready to Read framework was not sufficient in itself. It needed to be used by teachers who had a sound introduction to the teaching of reading, to working with students as individuals. In 1972 Doake was noting that most teachers who had their training before the introduction of the 3-year teaching diploma would have spent no more than 8 to 10 hours on reading courses, most of these focused on the new entrant stage. The 3-year course meant that students were now getting anywhere between 30 and 70 lecture hours on teaching reading. However, Doake concluded after examining more than 3,000 student-teacher reports of diagnostic reading conferences with children that too many were failing in reading because teachers did not know enough about how to adapt their teaching to different students and give them strategies to use when they encountered new words. In his experience from 6 years of teaching at the Christchurch Teachers' College, 60 lecture hours was "the absolute minimum to provide student teachers with merely a basis from which to begin to learn the complex task of teaching children to read effectively" (Doake, 1972, p. 27).

Having sufficient time to learn how to teach reading well, to discern what individual students need and what strategies to emphasise with each individual, remains an area of concern in the design of initial teacher education even now.

Reading Recovery was developed and trialled in different parts of the country between 1976 and 1983. Marie Clay, its originator, noted that it was designed to allow children to catch up with their classmates if they had fallen behind those classmates at the end of their first year of school. It was customised to individuals because:

> The aspects of the complex learning [of reading] that are most troublesome will vary from child to child. This is one reason why no classroom programme in the first year of instruction will be adequate for all children: those who fail have problem diagnoses which differ one from another. (Clay, 1990, p. 62)

Two things are striking in this passage. First, there is the New Zealand emphasis on the distinctness of each individual student. But accompanying this is an acceptance that one could not expect a class programme—a single teacher—to cater for every individual. Official messages have increasingly conveyed the expectation over the last 5 to 7 years that teachers will cater for every individual in their class, creating a new tension but also an impetus for more collective school cultures to share expertise and responsibilities.

Reading Recovery has been such a hallmark of New Zealand primary education, adding much to our already existing international reputation for good reading programmes, that it may come as a surprise to realise that fewer than half the primary schools were using it by the time of *Tomorrow's Schools*. As with other major initiatives, its expansion had to be rationed, partly to build up capacity through establishing a national network of tutors who could train experienced junior school teachers. This national network built consistency and the opportunity for ongoing learning within it.

What also came out of this programme of research and development on early reading difficulty that led to Reading Recovery were assessment tools that could easily be integrated into teaching, particularly the use of running records (structured observations of a child's oral reading). These could be included in two highly influential in-service courses.

ERIC, the first of these courses, is still spoken about some 30 years later by people who were teachers at this time as a watershed in professional development. ERIC was not a magician, but the (inexpensive) Early Reading In-service Course. This provided a set of linked units, using film, which could be watched by teachers when it best suited them. It was first available in the early 1970s, but resources were not available to take it to all districts until 1978. It reached 20,000 teachers, and markedly influenced teacher thinking and reading programmes in the early years of primary.

A follow-on programme, LARIC, focused on reading from Standard 2 (now Year 4) to Form 2 (now Year 8) and was introduced in the early 1980s. It was developed by a Department of Education team after wide consultation among reading advisers, college of education lecturers, inspectors and teachers. Of particular interest were the changes made in light of the ERIC experience, successful though many thought it had been. It sought to boost schools as professional collective cultures and to provide some interconnection. It focused on group discussions of what teachers saw or heard and their experiences from what they had tried in the previous unit. The groups were linked beyond the school: one teacher would have had some external training as a tutor, or an adviser would attend.

Feeding into LARIC's development were interviews with 138 teachers from 34 schools and observation in 24 classrooms. Only 40 percent of these teachers had attended any in-service course on reading, and many had little or no help in planning their reading programmes. These reading programmes mainly focused on written comprehension. LARIC put more emphasis on guided silent reading, giving children reading practice to counter the growing time given to television viewing in their leisure lives. It grouped children in terms of their interests in reading material rather than ability, and used more thoughtful questioning, running records and miscue analysis to diagnose reading difficulties.

The programme was effective in changing the practice of many who took part. Particularly stimulating was the opportunity to observe others' teaching and its effect on students: "Most teachers rarely observe continuously other practitioners in action with a group of children" (Elley, 1985, p. 43). Other LARIC participants were pleased to find that what they were doing was in line with "the official philosophy of the Department", an interesting pointer to the uncertainty teachers could feel with the latitude they had, both within and outside their school.

In the mid-1970s Doake had also made some pertinent observations on secondary reading, which—rather soberingly—could have been made even today. He thought it important to include courses in teaching reading in secondary teachers' training, particularly if secondary education were to move from the teacher as imparter of information that students copied, to students playing an active role in learning, well framed by teachers.[13] Teachers have tackled these issues individually over the years, but it was not until 2006/07 that we had a specific national secondary literacy professional development approach that emphasised the importance of a collective approach within secondary schools. The issues Doake describes affect all learners, but particularly those who have fewer home resources and who come with less knowledge of the subjects school can make available. What might have

---

13 I include his summation here in full because it points so well to some continuing tensions in secondary education that concerted effort has only really started to address with the greater freedom of NCEA.

"If a basic course in reading were studied by our prospective teachers for our secondary schools, what might be some of the possible effects of the knowledge and understanding that should develop from this study? How, for example, would the full understanding and acceptance of the concepts of independent and instructional levels in reading alter the use made and the selection of the textbooks for study in the secondary school? What is the effect of having pupils constantly read at their frustration level?

And if our secondary teachers learned and applied the principles of the directed silent reading type lesson to any reading they required their students to do, how would this affect current classroom practice? If, for example, they developed their students' readiness for their required reading by ensuring that they each possessed an adequate background of knowledge and experience to deal with any new concepts met during their reading, that their interest in the subject matter to be read had been stimulated to such a stage that they actually wanted to read the material; that relevant and realistic purposes had been established so that each student understood clearly why he was reading the material and what he was expected to find out from his reading and retain—if all these things happened, how would the applications of these simple but basic principles as to the use made of books in our secondary schools? Boyd's (1965, p. 15) investigation with Dunedin sixth form students disclosed that for these pupils reading for set purposes was a new idea.

The complaint that subject-teachers usually make in response to the suggestion that they should be 'teachers of reading' is that they do not have sufficient time to 'teach everything'. They seem unaware … that a dichotomy need not exist between content and process. They seem to be unaware of the principle that 'the teaching of a particular subject is the teaching of the study of that subject; and that makes inescapable the fact that every teacher is a teacher of reading and study.' (Artley, 1969, p. 433)."

happened to the progress of these learners if we had had the infrastructure to approach this systematically? We did not have it before *Tomorrow's Schools*, and we did not get it with *Tomorrow's Schools*. Our reforms focused on structure, to the detriment of knowledge-building and sharing to improve learning opportunities.

## The advisers

Advisers were another interconnector, working closely with the inspectorate, which was responsible for their use. They were recruited from the classroom or principalship to provide sound practice knowledge to teachers and principals, responding to requests from schools to run courses, workshops and demonstrations, and to work with teachers, principals and others on the development of new syllabuses, resources and teaching methods. More than 80 percent of the 940 primary teachers surveyed by Bayly in 1983 (Department of Education, 1983) said they would request an advisory visit at least twice a year. They particularly valued 'hands-on' modelling from someone with credible experience. Most had positive experiences:

> I'd dropped science at the fifth form, and when I had to be the resource teacher for science at our school—the confidence to do that was really because the science advisor spent the whole day with me and a group of the students, working with these lovely resources that had been developed by teachers working with advisors, resources they had written as a result of practical work with kids, that touched on science, social studies, art, writing. I needed his advice on how to offer the scientific knowledge to kids. It was hard work, but so good—the kids did not want to go home, they found it so exciting.[14]

Advisers were sought most when there were new curriculum developments, or new resources: they were the interpretive links teachers needed. They were also sought out when teachers gained new responsibilities, such as leadership in a curriculum area, and when classes contained students with special needs. (Mainstreaming or inclusion in regular classes of students with special needs was introduced in the early 1980s, and teachers were not confident about doing this well.) Some also sought them out after an inspector's visit.

There were not enough advisers to go around: 165 nationwide in 1986, reduced from 180 in 1982 as part of the cutbacks in public spending. They were also used less in secondary schools after this cutback. Most education boards had just one or two advisers in each curriculum area. The weight

---

14 Ruth Mansell, personal communication, 7 September 2011.

given to reading in New Zealand education showed in more positions (21 nationwide) than in maths (17), though there were also generalist advisers; for example, for Māori and Pacific Island education (26), junior classes (22) and rural schools (21).

Advisers came from schools. If they returned to schools it was usually as a principal. The advisory services also provided a route into the inspectorate, thus circulating the accumulated knowledge both ways. Like the inspectors, they had variable specific training for their role working with adults rather than children. A 1986 review called their development inadequate, though it included induction training of 1 to 2 weeks working with an experienced adviser in another district, participation in regular national courses, and some regional meetings and working groups (Nelson, 1986). The physical education, science, and arts advisers had originally been developed as separate national cadres, anchored in the Department of Education, and they mourned the loss of their national identity and leadership when *Tomorrow's Schools* localised the advisory service in colleges of education. Those in curriculum areas that had not had such national anchorage did not miss it, perhaps because for some, such as those who worked on English, there had been strong recent developments in reading and writing that provided an alternative anchorage and stimulus.

The 1986 review of advisory services noted tensions between the advisers' interconnecting roles and their direct work with schools, raising questions about whether the first was occurring at the expense of the second. What this indicates is that there was simply not enough time to do both. Indeed, the review suggested more use of secondment of teachers to support new curriculum developments, and that more advisers were probably needed. It also suggested more clarity around purpose and objectives, coupled with feedback on the quality of performance. The inspector who carried out this review (on a 12-week secondment) noted that:

> The processes of goal setting and evaluation are central in school development. Support and advisory services must be able to model them as a function of their own services if they are to exercise optimal influence in their work. (Nelson, 1986, para 6.1.5)

So while the advisers were playing a vital role in building the knowledge and capability of individual teachers and schools, the very open-endedness of this role increasingly raised questions. It was a role that was open at both ends. Demand outran supply, but the demand was also voluntary. Teachers and schools that were open to learning sought it, while those who saw new learning as an admission of failure, or something that was not an ongoing part of being a professional, did not seek it and could fly under the radar. This problem of uneven use of new knowledge to develop learning and school quality existed before *Tomorrow's Schools*, and the even greater latitude that school self-management brought simply made the problem deeper.

# Limits on the sharing of new practice

Schools used their latitude to try things out for themselves. Jack Shallcrass, one of the doyens of New Zealand education, made two compilations of teacher and principal descriptions of changes they had instituted in their schools. Over 40 percent of secondary schools responded to his request for descriptions of "experiments and innovations" for the 1973 compilation published by the Post Primary Teachers' Association (PPTA), the secondary teachers' union; 68 schools (around a quarter of secondary schools) were represented in the book (Shallcrass, 1973). He used around 75 descriptions of changes in primary and intermediate schools in his compilation published by the primary teachers' union, NZEI, in 1978 (Shallcrass, 1978). The unions' support for this work indicated their interest in the ongoing development of schools and the teaching profession.

Changes described in these two collections ranged widely. Some would have school-wide implications and had a number of dimensions, indicating profound thought. Others are more in the way of modifications of existing approaches, which might be confined to a single class. Their effectiveness was often described in terms of improved student engagement in learning, or a deeper quality of student work.

Several national compilations were also made by officials at the head office of the Department of Education from the descriptions of school innovations sent in by inspectorate teams in the mid- and late 1970s. These innovations were fed back to schools that showed interest, but the national compilations do not seem to have become a regular feature. Few schools made wholesale changes.

Thus while schools had the latitude to try out different things, the sharing of their approaches tended to be sporadic, up to individual connections and district impetus. There would be some informal national networks, particularly in secondary subject areas, supported by national in-service courses and subject associations. There were some local networks in Mangere–Otara and Porirua, the two areas where urban concentrations of new housing and poverty were most acute. These were co-ordinated and supported through the district inspectorate. But on the whole there were no systemic ways to build national knowledge on particular issues through connecting schools that faced similar challenges. To carve out distinctly new networks of support needed either a reallocation of the "marvellous weapon" or new funding from the national office of the Department of Education. This is where ideas for change did indeed encounter bureaucracy: the need for someone else to approve, the need for someone else to release resources.

Individual inspectors and advisers could chafe against the need to get support and approval for initiatives to improve teaching and learning that needed access to the inspectorate's discretionary resourcing. Some DSIs were more receptive and confident than others; some were more likely to activate the chain of authority above them to seek approval. Some inspectorate teams appear to have worked well as teams; others could make it hard for newcomers. From the tone of letters from the Department head office staff to district inspectorates, one again has the impression of those above in the hierarchy seeking to influence rather than command. The limits on sharing new knowledge and building on it to create wider change do not seem due to a tight bureaucracy, driven from the centre.

Department of Education head office staff sought to influence district practice by sharing what seemed to be good initiatives, and by putting issues on agendas for discussion and sharing of local strategies at regional and national conferences. For example, in the mid-1980s the regional senior education officer, covering most of the lower and eastern North Island, sent round a paper outlining concerns about the quality of rural education.[15] There is an interesting analysis indicating that rural areas were having difficulty attracting good staff, country service no longer being seen as a necessary step for promotion, with many recruits coming from the "local community with their sometimes limited expectations". Teachers and principals were not keeping up with their professional learning, partly because of the additional expenses involved. Parents might have low expectations for children's academic growth. These are all themes that would surface again in the era of *Tomorrow's Schools*, which, ironically, would see these same communities being given greater responsibilities with reduced support. Uneven quality of rural education has been an ongoing issue in New Zealand, unresolved by school self-management.

---

15 Archives R20472 921-0, letter from Ken Rae, Regional Senior Ed Officer, to the DSISS; DSISps Wellington, Wanganui, Taranaki, Hawke's Bay; the SEdOic Gisborne, and RSEdoECE, with an attached paper from George Bowers based on work by Don Burney.

The paper also set out the Wanganui inspectorate's plan to deal with these problems. This plan centred round knowledge building and interconnections: the inspectorate would build support teams of advisers and inspectors, who would go into a given area to work with all its schools on school development, with follow-up visits. Implicit in this plan is the hope that neighbouring schools would then share a common language and interest and be able to provide support for each other. The district inspectorate could not address on its own the more systemic issues of attracting teachers to rural communities. What it could do was focus (some) resources on those who were already there.

# The reality of bureaucracy before *Tomorrow's Schools*

So where was the bureaucracy, the over-centralisation that would be seen as the major impediment to the flexibility required to meet particular student needs and that was so key to the Picot taskforce? It was in the regulations to do with staffing, with property, and with resources for teaching. Primary teachers and principals had to wait for an education board's monthly meeting to have such things as leave applications or secondments, or expenditure on resources, approved within set limits. Approvals that seemed straightforward could therefore take weeks or months to come through. Primary appointments were decided by district appointment committees, with representatives from the education board, the inspectorate and NZEI. Principals could state their preference in terms of a long-term reliever but not for new appointments. Part of the reason for this was to ensure fairness in appointments, giving fresh faces as much opportunity as those who were known. Dismissals or moving on of staff also involved the inspectorate, and principals sometimes felt they had been "passed the parcel" of a teacher of questionable quality or who struggled to make good connections with their particular students.

*Tomorrow's Schools* certainly had its attractions when it came to property, staffing and equipment. When submissions were made on the draft policy:

> The first letter we opened was from a primary principal, elated at the prospect of having a say in the selection of the staff of the school and the chance to get the electrician of his choice to fix the staffroom Zip. It was the first of many supportive letters from principals. (McQueen, 1991, p. 90)

When principals talked about their new freedom after *Tomorrow's Schools*, they talked about being able to repair a broken window straight away instead of going through the education board to have it fixed. Secondary teachers talked of having money to buy resources for learning, such as science equipment, that they knew how to use and that suited their curriculum emphasis, rather than getting resources from the standard list of equipment that they did not need or did not know how to use. One primary principal told of three pianos being delivered when no-one on the staff could play them; others could show you materials in storage that they would take years to use, or would not use, when they had lists of other materials they kept running short of.

These materials spoke to them of waste, as well as 'bureaucratic' formulas. The intention behind the standard issue—to provide equality of educational provision—was lost on teachers as they focused on what they could do for their particular students. Indeed, without additional infrastructure to link equipment with pedagogy, without the training that would make equipment useful and pertinent, this intention behind standard issues could not be realised, as the Committee on Secondary Education had pointed out in 1976 (Committee on Secondary Education, 1976, p. 84).

There were also the regulations about how much time should be allocated to core subjects in the first 3 years of secondary school, which McQueen thought had made schools more uniform than they needed to be (1986, p. 2). As we have seen, schools actually enjoyed considerable latitude over their courses: the hours were not specified per subject but in groups of subjects, and took up just over half of the school week. It was the qualifications that really dominated the scope of the senior secondary curriculum. These were the most formidable obstacle to making changes, as renowned educator Charmaine Pountney makes clear in her recounting of the seminal changes she made as principal of Auckland Girls' Grammar School in the 1980s (Pountney, 2000).

The barrier to any changes here stood at the political level. In 1979 the School Certificate Examinations Board, backed by the Employers' Federation, made the case for a wider standards-based system to replace the inherently unfair system of the scaled norm-referenced School Certificate. As Charmaine Pountney recalled:

> The minister said, 'No, as long as I am minister we will have percentage marks and a pass-fail system and 50 will be a pass and 49 will be a fail.' I was at the School Certificate Examinations Board meeting where this profound utterance determined the continuing inadequacies of our national puberty ritual. (2000, p. 241)

The following Minister was also not disposed to major change (McQueen, 1991, p. 47), despite the heft of the 1970s sector work showing clear reasons why it was needed.

The DSI of secondary schools had to approve time allowances for staff to act in roles other than for class teaching and school management, such as guidance teachers or work experience classes. The DSI could also grant additional staffing to provide education for students with special needs. Education board staff interacted with schools, particularly the board's property supervisor, and most secondary principals discussed their planning for the year with departmental officers at least once a year, half more often (Day, 1984, pp. 106, 107, 126). Most secondary schools sought some advice from the Department of Education, with an increase in those doing so between 1975 and 1985 (Department of Education, 1986, p. 47).

Secondary boards, which could already appoint staff, attend to their own maintenance and run their own budgets, focused on finance and property. And they could ignore the regional superintendent of education if they wished. A rare occurrence, to be sure, but as David Lange found out when he tried to resolve Nga Tapuwae College board's "lengthy and costly litigation against a staff member", "the Minister could not interfere, and had no power to dismiss or discipline the board" (McQueen, 1991, p. 59).

Indeed, while there were many regulations and local board rules about what to do (the 'green' book that was the only guidance for the new principal quoted earlier), there were known ways around these regulations, and there was scope for interpretation that could well differ from the original policy intention.

Bureaucracy was also experienced by schools in the degree to which funding for school activities was allocated through tagged funding, which meant limited budgets for specific activities, and by approval systems that applied across the public sector. These generic approval systems meant that education boards were unable to make all the decisions themselves and had to refer some decisions to the Department of Education. It is interesting to find Bill Renwick, then Director-General of Education, hinting at why it was that the Department was in the position of having to continue to approve a range of school expenditure in 1983:

> It is a fair criticism of the system that, except for the universities, educational controlling authorities in this country are placed under undue restriction by the requirements of ear-marked grants. Some of us in the department have long been persuaded of the desirability of a change of policy that would give controlling

authorities more financial authority without reducing accountability. I still hope for the day when it will be possible to recommend to a minister that he take up the recommendation of the Educational Development Conference for greater devolution of financial responsibility to controlling authorities. (Renwick, 1983, pp. 11–12)

Some political support appeared to be forthcoming: the 1986/87 annual report of the Department of Education reports discussion with "education authorities" on amalgamating grants so that resource allocation could be local and more flexible. It noted that this meant increased accountability, and that some standardisation of account codes and annual accounts formats would be needed to track expenditure so that the adequacy of grants could be periodically reviewed—a concern raised by some educational authorities. It thought that the greater responsibility (to manage the funds within budget) would require advice from the Department and "perhaps, training" (Department of Education, 1987b, p. 50).

Operating grants covered "basic teaching programmes and essential administration services". A 1986 review recommended greater targeting to reflect special educational needs (a term that then included Māori and Pacific students). The 1986/87 Department's annual report casts careful doubt on the adequacy of the operating grants to cover the basics, let alone additional targeting: "Increasing levels of parental support for day to day school operating costs are prima facie evidence that basic funding levels are losing ground in real terms" (Department of Education, 1987b, p. 51).

Lyall Perris, Acting Secretary of Education in 1995/96, looking back on the run up to the *Tomorrow's Schools* reforms noted that:

> The Department was a soft target to criticise. Much of its life was spent saying 'no' to people who wanted more money spent on something, and who did not realise that the Department could allocate only the money which it was given by the government, and then only in the ways that the government approved. Along with other departments it suffered through the growth over the years of volumes of rules for everything. Decisions seemed to take an interminable time (frequently because they had to be referred to the Minister). (Perris, 1998, p. 8)

Most of these approvals that took longer than seemed necessary, that seemed to need too many others involved before an individual could act, were about identifiable matters needing a decision about money, time, property or appointments. They were not about what happens in classrooms or how school staff work together; the everyday practices of teaching that create the learning opportunities that *Tomorrow's Schools* was intended to improve (Minister of Education, 1988, p. iv).

*Tomorrow's Schools* would tackle bureaucracy in the schooling system by whittling down these layers of involvement in decision making. But this removal of layers came at a price. Key roles in the former schooling system's interconnections—that vital part of any schooling system that initiates the creation of knowledge and brings knowledge into schools in ways that can improve teaching and learning—were played by people who were also part of the decision-making chain. In chopping out the decision-making links, most of this knowledge connectivity was removed from the New Zealand schooling system. It is no wonder that what many senior educators missed most after *Tomorrow's Schools* were the interconnections, the external challenge and support and opportunities to gain a wider perspective and contribute to the profession's development that had been provided by and through the inspectorate.

# Chapter 3

# Strengths, weaknesses and tensions in the 1980s

*Tomorrow's Schools* was intended to improve learning opportunities. What did teaching look like before *Tomorrow's Schools*? What were the tensions the schooling system found difficult to surmount? This chapter gives us some benchmarks to return to in later chapters, to see what differences *Tomorrow's Schools* has made and, just as importantly, what differences one could expect it to make given the nature of the schooling system in the 1980s.

The OECD examiners' 1983 report on the New Zealand system is the starting point for this chapter. Then I turn to what primary school teaching looked like. The challenge of providing good-quality education in low-income areas, and the challenges for secondary education, follow. Several roads beckoned as ways to improve education and student performance, and I outline these.

Some of the pressure that built towards *Tomorrow's Schools* was created by the following:

- Secondary school programmes and the qualifications regime that framed these programmes had serious shortcomings. These had been described and discussed by a number of national committees and reviews, and recommendations had been made to politicians since the mid-1970s (Openshaw, 2009).[1]

- Interconnections between schools and their communities had also been recommended since the mid-1970s, sometimes in the sense that each had something to offer the other which would strengthen it; sometimes in the sense that the community, however (un)defined, should contribute more to deciding what a particular school might emphasise (Barrington, 1990).

---

[1] Openshaw gives a very useful and lively history of issues, attempts at change and the roles of different players and interest groups in the changes that did result.

- Māori were clear that the education system was failing them, falling far short of providing the learning their children needed in order to succeed in school, maintain and develop their identity as Māori, and have real options for adult life. Alarm bells had also been rung about the likely loss of te reo Māori if it was not more widely used and better taught in schools (Penetito, 2010).[2]

All of these needed more fundamental action than the existing system could provide.

## Impressions of the OECD examiners

In the early 1980s the OECD undertook a series of reports on member countries' educational systems. The report on New Zealand gives a very useful picture of our strengths and weaknesses, and the tensions we were grappling with in the run-up to *Tomorrow's Schools*, from knowledgeable people who were looking from the outside. The three OECD examiners who visited New Zealand in 1982 brought with them comprehensive experience of educational policy and infrastructure.[3] They were struck by the degree of basic trust in, and agreement with, the existing educational provision. This trust was not universal, but the educational policy-making style was "consensual and incremental, guided by a combination of individualism and tolerant conformity within what has been, at least until recently, a society characterised by common values to an unusual degree" (OECD, 1983, p. 10).

The OECD examiners were also struck by the lack of a division between teachers and educational administrators, noting that not only were most of the latter ex-teachers, but they were strongly committed to improving teaching and learning. "We found very little cynicism or time-serving" (p. 11). New Zealand education administrators struck them as giving less prominence to "instrumental, economic, job-oriented values" than they saw in other

---

2 Wally Penetito provides a compelling history of the cumulative frustrations Māori have experienced within the New Zealand education system, and the hard questions that accompany these, in his 2010 book, *What's Māori about Māori Education?* The knowledge at the time about Māori experiences with education and the structural barriers that contributed to so many gaining too little, and indeed losing from the experience, is summarised and discussed in Benton (1988).

3 Peter Karmel, the chairman of the examiners, was then Vice Chancellor of the Australian National University; the Karmel report for the Australian Government in 1973 on the quality of Australian schools and their resourcing led to some substantial changes in Australian education. William Taylor was the Director of the Institute of Education at the University of London, one of the key English institutions for teacher training and research in education. Ingrid Eide had been the Under-Secretary of State in the Norwegian Ministry of Education.

countries, perhaps reflecting their origins as teachers and the "person-centred values of New Zealand education" (p. 18).[4]

They saw better equipment and resources in schools in "better-off" communities, noting this as an inevitability "in a system that depends on the willingness of parents and the community to find resources to supplement those provided by government". But they were also impressed by the efforts to provide rural areas with resources and curriculum opportunities, and thought it important that New Zealand take care with its policies on secondary school zoning to avoid the kind of differentiation between schools that marred other countries' provision.

They thought the system was economically run,[5] noting higher pupil:teacher ratios than in other OECD countries and, as noted in the previous chapter, lower spending on professional development for teachers. They summed up the New Zealand system like this:

> Within a context of much consultation and the local management of schools, policy-making and administration are highly centralised in the Department of Education in Wellington, for which the Minister of Education is responsible. The result is a combination of local initiative within guidelines firmly laid down by the centre. (OECD, 1983, p. 13)

Firmly laid-down guidelines they might be, but they were often not in black and white. And these were guidelines that usually arose from careful consultation, from the effort to bring together those who had an interest and would be affected. The OECD examiners noted criticism that sometimes more time and money were spent than was warranted for a given topic, and wondered if this participatory approach was feasible in an era of cuts to government departments (OECD, 1983, p. 23). Departmental curriculum officers were spending only 8 percent of their time directly developing new syllabuses; the rest was spent working with teachers, inspectors or advisers, or providing information and briefings. The examiners were not impressed with syllabuses that were more than 20 years old, though they were told schools could and did seek approval for their own revisions. (One wonders whether these revisions were collated, or circulated so that others could think

---

4   Noeline Alcorn's biography of Beeby, the Director-General of the Department of Education who played such a seminal role in the spread of this focus, provides an illuminating and highly readable story of how these characteristics of New Zealand education came together and grew (Alcorn, 1999).
5   McQueen (1986, column 4, p. 3) cites UNESCO comparisons of per student spending for 1981: Australia, $3,071; Japan, $2,985; New Zealand, $1,686 (US dollars).

about them and build on them.) But they could also see value in having wide participation in syllabus change, allowing such change to provide useful in-service professional development.

Interestingly, although they described the system as highly centralised, the OECD examiners did not find more people chafing at the bit than in other countries they had encountered. Their comment here is wry:

> There are few countries where those responsible for particular levels of administration—heads of individual institutions, local officers—do not feel that their own efficiency would be enhanced, and savings would accrue, from their possessing greater autonomy and referring fewer matters 'up the line'. We found no more and no less of this type of feeling in New Zealand than we have encountered elsewhere. (OECD, 1983, p. 23)

The examiners were struck by a longer primary school experience than in other countries, often running till children were 13,[6] and they thought that, coupled with the compulsory school-leaving age of 15, this resulted in "a somewhat truncated secondary education" for a sizeable minority (p. 35).

They were also struck by our schools being comprehensive (open to any student, rather than some schools being competitive in entry through tests) and by what they found to be low levels of streaming (assigning students to streams of classes using ability testing). The examiners applauded this, on educational and social grounds, but they also noted that teaching a homogeneous class was much easier:

> Unstreaming ... makes demands on teachers that must be met by improved levels of initial and in-service training, and where possible an improvement in pupil/teacher ratios in order to provide time for diagnosis, preparation and assessment. (OECD, 1983, p. 35)

They went on to recommend selective improvement in pupil:teacher ratios ("as distinct from class size") and recruitment of primary teachers from university graduates, because it was often too late to "remediate" any problems at secondary school. They noted that teacher turnover was high by international standards. Like others, they thought that in-service training was inadequate, finding the single mandated teacher-only day for school-initiated professional development much less generous than in other countries.

The OECD examiners also thought that in-service programmes to improve the knowledge and skills of teachers in order to improve the educational

---

6   To some extent this shows how structures can outlive their origins and take on new life. Intermediates were originally intended to be 3-year junior secondary schools; they were cut back to 2 years during the late 1920s–1930s Depression as a cost-saving measure.

opportunities and achievement of Māori students were particularly important, especially given the new caps on teacher recruitment. There had been more than a doubling of Māori teachers, from 3 percent in 1971 to 8 percent in 1982, but this was still much less than half the proportion of Māori students in the school population:

> It is clear that if teachers are to be successful in incorporating what has been called 'active Māoritanga' into the work of schools, in helping to raise the academic accomplishments of their minority pupils, and in incorporating such contents and styles of language teaching into the curriculum as are best calculated to maintain and enhance culture and identity, without detriment to scholastic progress, they will need much more systematic and thorough knowledge of the research evidence bearing on these issues ... and a first hand awareness of the practice and procedures most likely to achieve their objectives. (OECD, 1983, p. 87)

The examiners reported Benton's 1979 survey results showing that only 15 percent of Māori aged under 15 could speak Māori, and they shared the concern that this did not augur well for the continuation of the language unless there was a major effort to develop a bilingual policy and adequately resource it. This was not something that could be "resolved quickly by administrative decision. Any consistent or effective course of action in this area will require a major political initiative and commitment" (OECD, 1983, p. 88).

Changes occurring to secondary programmes to provide "more scope for the boy or girl whose interests are not primarily intellectual and who is not likely to pursue a post-secondary course requiring university entrance standards" (OECD, 1983, p. 39) were viewed positively by the OECD examiners. But they also saw such changes as liable to being undercut by traditional approaches to secondary school ethos and organisation, such as the almost universal school uniforms and the use of corporal punishment in the majority of schools. They also wondered if "the apparent unresponsiveness of many school regimes to the values of the youth culture" was contributing to the alienation of some young people, including those who were members of minority groups (which would include Māori) (p. 40).

Principals and teachers they met noted the constraints imposed by the University Entrance examination: "At present, too much attention is given and status attached to an examination relevant for only a small minority of the total secondary population" (OECD, 1983, p. 42). This excessive focus on academic curriculum was evident in all six examinations that occurred in the course of senior secondary school. It struck the OECD examiners as overly narrow. The contradiction between the comprehensive ideal of the secondary school and what shaped what students were offered and could achieve is the subject of their strongest recommendation: the secondary curriculum needed to be broader. They found that most of those they spoke to agreed with them, but there was no consensus on what should change, and no sense of urgency. Change would mean tackling the range of separate agencies involved; for example, the School Certificate Examination Board had no links with the Universities Examination Board, and the development of syllabuses was done separately for the senior secondary school and Forms 1 to 4.

The overall impression is of a system that was ambitious in some respects, such as wanting to provide comprehensive education and tackling this at the classroom rather than school level, but dogged by legacies that structured secondary schooling and that would make it hard to meet Māori needs and keep te reo Māori a fully live language. The inclusionary approach to the development of the frameworks teachers and schools used attracted these knowledgeable outsiders, but they also saw some shortcomings, some treading of water, and the need for political action. The need for political action these OECD examiners identified was not due to the need to break up a hierarchical, bureaucratic system, but because the issues that limited teaching and learning most were issues of resourcing, and structures of qualification and schooling that had outlived their original purpose.

# Primary learning

The OECD examiners' suggestion that primary teachers should have a university education points to the knowledge they needed for what is a sophisticated role, particularly in a system that has what Ramsay (1993) called

> a distinctive pedagogic style ... built up over many generations of teachers ... Fundamentally it is child centred with an emphasis on grouping of children for a range and variety of activities, coupled with an individualised approach with a considerable amount of non-directive teaching leading towards independent learners who own their knowledge. (p. 26)

New Zealand primary classes were not (and still are not) dominated by workbooks or textbooks and a standard pace. Mandated tests were, and at this stage remain, absent. Guidance to teachers, then and now, emphasises knowledge of the child as well as knowledge about, say, what learning to read entails, to bring the two together in engaging and active learning that keeps children motivated to learn. This gives primary teachers a strong sense of a two-fold purpose to their work. In a study of children's progress over the first 3 years of school, I found junior school teachers aiming not just for the acquisition of specific reading or mathematics skills, but to instil confidence in the school environment, confidence that one could learn through one's own efforts and that learning was worthwhile (Wylie & Smith, 1995). Reading was better framed for teachers (they had the Ready to Read series with its progressions) than mathematics, and they were generally more confident themselves with the written word than with numbers and fractions.

This emphasis on children experiencing themselves as making progress, and succeeding, also lay behind a desire not to 'rush' children, or to focus on quick attainment if it was at the expense of solid understanding. It lay behind the care with which most of the teachers in this study approached judgements of children, and their emphasis on personal growth rather than ranked public comparisons with others. The New Zealand classroom walls had nothing like the ladders of children's names ordered by their grades that I read about in the American research. The groups children worked in were usually operating at different levels, but children were 'giraffes' or 'tigers', not 'the top group' and 'the bottom group'.

This did not stop children knowing that some groups had 'harder' work than others, or wanting to be in the group that had 'better' work (children did move between groups). But they were not constantly being told where they belonged, as if performance was a given rather than something that changed with action and time. Most of the children we followed in this 3-year-study thought of learning in terms of something gained by making an effort rather than something coming from innate ability, an important association to make because it allows ongoing learning, whereas a label of low ability taken to heart early does not (Dweck, 2000). So there were considerable strengths in this general approach.

## Drawbacks in primary teachers' knowledge and support

But teachers were not always accurate in their knowledge of where to pitch work for students so that they could be both confident and challenged to keep developing, and of how to check student knowledge. Studies around the mid-1980s found that many students had been given material to read that was too far ahead of their reading competence (Wagemaker, 1993, pp. 19–20). Teachers could also pitch reading too low for students, so that they kept going over the same ground. Glynn, Crooks, Bethune, Ballard, and Smith (1989) found that some students who had made progress during their Reading

Recovery course with individual lessons slipped back once they returned to the classroom, often because the class teacher and Reading Recovery teacher did not connect, and the class teacher had given them reading work at a lower level than they could now tackle. Another possible disconnection between class practice and Reading Recovery gains was the practice of 'holding back' students a year in the junior school: around 22 percent were not in the year level most appropriate to their age. This was most likely to occur for Māori boys (McDonald, 1989).[7]

Teachers were also working with the frameworks they were used to and that were available to them. Running records (the structured observations assessing a child's oral reading as part of everyday classroom work) were not in widespread use until the mid-1980s. The legacy of earlier general classifications was also still evident in shaping teachers' perceptions of their students and the progress they could make, as noted by the Wellington inspectorate in 1983:

> Although teachers continue to identify slow learners and generally provide for them at their level, the bulk of children in the average group have little which will identify those who could do better or have work which will extend them. Teachers' expectations generally still coincide with the traditional so-called normal distribution curve. Consequently inspectors have a general concern for under achievement across the board.[8]

Their note goes on to say that diagnosis of learning difficulties and how to respond to them had been included in all the inspectorate's in-service courses, but a smaller range of these courses was able to be offered in 1983 (part of the political cut-backs to professional development that McQueen had seen as hobbling the progress of the system, as noted in the previous chapter).

Teachers might draw on common resources in a school to devise units in social studies or science, but without a clear and agreed school sequence

---

7 Because of the desire to match learning material with children's working levels, in the junior classes we studied there was quite a variation in the individual learning opportunities within a given class. It was possible for a student in a Year 2 class to be working on Year 1 or Year 3 material. New Zealand students who were kept back did not seem to be simply repeating the same ground, as they often did in the US, where there is a consistent finding that 'holding back' disadvantages students. However, keeping students back a class could affect their secondary career and chances of gaining a qualification if these students reached the legal school-leaving age without having also reached the year level when they could be assessed for qualifications. The data are no longer available to know if keeping students back a year is still occurring.

8 This is from the Wellington inspectorate's 1983 contribution to the Department of Education's national compilation, monitoring of progress on the recommendations in 'Educational standards in state schools' (Archives R20472 921-0).

this could mean repetition of topic content for students rather than a deeper understanding over time. So the latitude given to individual teachers, if it was not supported through joint work and knowledge building with their colleagues, could undermine the effectiveness of their teaching.

Reading Recovery provided the basis for sharing responsibility for a student between classroom teachers and a specialist teacher. In many schools, however, this specialist role seems to have led class teachers to think that there were students whose needs could *only* be met by temporary specialist teaching. This led to class teachers and Reading Recovery teachers operating separately, as teachers were used to doing. It meant that the Reading Recovery teacher did not operate as a school resource, working with class teachers so that they could use the knowledge and strategies within classes before children reached the age of 6, so reducing numbers who might need one-to-one teaching (McDowall, Cameron, & Dingle, 2007).

Indeed, many primary schools could be thought of as a set of separate classes, with each teacher responsible for her or his class, focused on the individuals who constituted that class. The criteria for teacher certification were focused on the teacher in their classroom, not as a member of a collective, sharing and developing knowledge across the school.

This sense that the class was the paramount form of school organisation was very clear in my first research topic in educational policy, the development of the 1:20 teacher:pupil ratio in the junior school. This policy added more teachers to schools to support the shift from 'whole-class' uniform teaching to more differentiated approaches for different children's needs. While the guidelines were clear that these additional teachers were not to be used to create new classes, that is exactly what two-thirds of the schools receiving them did in 1985, the first year of the policy. That is how their staffing was organised and how they were used to working: in single cells, separately. In response, inspectors and advisers used their normal channels of advice and influence, and the proportion of schools receiving new staffing that created a new class did halve in 1986 (Wylie, 1989).

Looking back, this is also a good illustration both of the latitude that schools were used to and of the cost of insufficient coherence in introducing a new policy that is intended to lead to change in practice, to increase the effectiveness of practice—as all new educational policy should. As with too many new policies in New Zealand education, the 1:20 ratio came into place too rapidly after its announcement, in this case less for political reasons (the usual cause) than because schools were keen to have the additional staffing in place. There was insufficient attention paid to explaining the aims of the policy so that teachers understood and accepted it, to preparing them to work in teams, or to enhancing their knowledge of how to diagnose the needs of individual children (Renwick, Vize, & Smith, 1989, p. 61).

## Strains in the system

As the OECD examiners noted, the New Zealand approach called on considerable teaching skills. Improvements to teachers' ability to gauge performance levels (particularly to recognise underachievement, to move children further) through improved pre- and in-service training were among the recommendations of the inspectorate's 1978 report on national standards, which at this time meant the levels and quality of student achievement and teaching (Department of Education, 1978, pp. 88–90). This comprehensive review, based on information from school inspections (including classroom observations, documents such as school reports, and assessments) was spurred by one of the periodic surges in public critiques of student performance in the 3Rs (reading, writing and 'rithmetic).[9] It provided some reassurance that levels of reading performance had been maintained, but reported a slight decline in listening skills and a somewhat greater decline in arithmetic skills. The inspectorate noted, however, that where there had been some improvements, they had occurred for "better than average" students, and that "in some subjects, the performance of the poorest students is not as good now as it was in earlier years" (Department of Education, 1978, p. 18).

This report on the quality of education in New Zealand schools in 1977 provides a fascinating read. It covered most of the curriculum: music and physical education, as well as reading, writing, maths, science, art and craft, health, and outdoor education, and made some general comments on primary and secondary schools. In each of these curriculum areas the inspectorate described the range and quality of the lessons it had seen, the resources used, student interest, time allocation, teacher competence, and recent developments, among them some gains in student engagement and teaching. So its judgements of the levels of student performance were made in the context of teaching quality, and the frameworks and support teachers operated with.

---

9 A lively account of three of these periodic surges of concern is given in Openshaw and Walshaw (2010).

Recommendations were also made in the inspectorate's report. These recommendations are not soft. They go across the board: for teachers, schools, the Department, teachers colleges, provision of in-service development, and the inspectorate's own responsibilities. The unit of analysis was not, as it has been since *Tomorrow's Schools,* schools; it was the system. The inspectors were part of the Department of Education, but they were not defending it or putting it in the best light. Nor were they singling out it, or any element of the system, for criticism or blame. Their recommendations offer a developmental evaluation.

The report concluded that student performance levels were "mixed", with achievement levels in the middle years of primary schools a particular concern. The inspectorate saw the need for principals and senior staff to be helped to work more with teachers, "to be better managers of the total resources of their schools, and to promote effective school and class organisation" (Department of Education, 1978, p. 99). Teachers also needed more support and advice as their classes became more diverse, with a particular challenge relating to "the difficulties often faced by students whose cultural background is not Pakeha" (p. 102). More attention on pedagogy was needed. The system as a whole needed research and development and understanding to help it work better for students at risk of failure, particularly in their early school years.[10]

There is no comparable overview of what was happening in schools in the 1980s. A periodic national review of levels of student performance and quality of teaching that was followed up by joint action to work on specific aspects of concern could have been a real spur to the system, and indeed was suggested by the inspectorate (Scott, 1980).

Warwick Elley, a prominent assessment specialist, concluded that our reading performance was stable in the 1970s and 1980s, resulting in the

---

10 The report ends with a spirited if somewhat exasperated defence against critics of the failure of the education system to ensure that no child failed:

> If there were any simple way by which standards could be improved and failure removed, it would have been discovered and applied by now. The stubborn fact, however, is that the conditions of successful learning are still far from being understood; learning theory is still far from being an exact science ... More research will be needed into the causes of failure. More development work will be needed to try out methods that are successful. More will need to be done to help teachers become better equipped to deal with failing students. And if it is to be done, it can't be done for nothing—if the community really wants higher standards from children, teenagers and adults with low levels of attainment, it will have to pay more to get them. (pp. 105–106)

Some 30 years later there is much better knowledge available about successful learning, and about the conditions that support it, in and out of school. The challenge lies in aligning the knowledge and the conditions, in using the knowledge in policy.

patterns evident in the 1990 IEA (International Association for the Evaluation of Educational Achievement) reading assessments, which have also been "remarkably stable" in subsequent decades (Elley, 2004). As a country we were among the high performers. But the 1990 IEA survey made clear what had not been so evident in previous descriptions of differences between low and high performers. Our high average country score masked a wide spread of scores. Our average was pulled up by a substantial proportion of highly performing readers. We had a considerable proportion of poor readers, mainly made up of children from low-income homes with few books, Māori and Pasifika boys, and children whose English was a second language. The challenges noted in the 1978 report had not been addressed by a growth in knowledge and capacity to address these students' needs.

# Tomorrow may be too late

Some of the changes that would be needed to give useful knowledge more footing in schools to successfully meet these students' needs were described in *Tomorrow May Be Too Late* (Ramsay, Sneddon, Grenfell, & Ford, 1981). This was a thorough, year-long study, funded by the Department of Education, of the use of the additional staffing and funding supplied to Mangere and Otara. These low-income areas faced substantial social and educational challenges resulting from rapid growth during the 1960s and 70s with the waves of Māori migration from rural hapū and iwi homelands and Pacific migration from their island homelands. They had the unenviable reputation of being Auckland's ghetto. Principals and teachers who wanted "to make a difference" were recruited, but there were not enough of these, and not all stayed. *Tomorrow May Be Too Late* was the first report to document the area's high teacher turnover and the difficulties this caused. As we shall see, such turnover remained an issue that *Tomorrow's Schools* could not resolve.

In 1981, on average, half the staff of a school in Mangere–Otara would be different each year (Ramsay & Sneddon, 1983, pp. 79–84), making it very difficult for the schools to keep developing. Although the area benefited from young enthusiasts, it also gained some who found it hard to grapple with its additional demands. It was easier to gain promotion by taking a senior job in the area's schools, but it was harder for the area's senior staff to win promotion elsewhere. So not everyone who stayed was there by commitment, or as energetic as the area needed.

Some collective knowledge-building and support occurred. Enthusiastic teachers worked together with advisers and the support of the district inspectorate. For example, the Otara Language Group met weekly between 1974 and 1977 to share ideas and support each other's work. Out of this came two booklets of locally developed and tested language units (which the Department printed for every Otara teacher). The whānau concept of organising secondary students in vertical groups rather than separate form classes came out of Hillary College. Workshops and courses were ongoing, with the inspectorate and advisers playing key roles. But these were insufficient to build the knowledge needed. The high teacher turnover meant that a critical mass of well-informed expertise and knowledge about the school community, fostering enduring relationships that developed important trust and respect, could not be sustained.

Peter Ramsay (who would later serve on the Picot taskforce) and his colleagues in the *Tomorrow May Be Too Late* study found some of the Mangere–Otara schools to be much more effective than others in engaging students in learning. To sustain these schools, which tended to have more experienced staff, and improve other schools, they recommended government action to ensure that schools could recruit, retain and keep developing good teachers. This should include the development of several "resource, experimental and development" centres that could support schools with in-service training, induction of new teachers and development of appropriate resources, so that teachers and schools were not always having to reinvent the wheel and were able to share and further develop effective practice through deliberate experimentation.

These recommendations would have provided useful interconnections, capacity building and knowledge development to tackle the shortcomings in a system that left students in these areas so underserved educationally. The Department did part-fund some resource centres in the poorer parts of Auckland, but with more modest scope than this. The resource centres, which would have provided the hubs essential for joint work, did not make it through into the *Tomorrow's Schools* policy. The only recommendations from this study that did make it into *Tomorrow's Schools* were those related to school resourcing, allowing schools their own choice of materials and providing more funding to schools serving high proportions of Māori and Pasifika students in low socioeconomic areas.

That both this report and the policy share the word *tomorrow* appears to be accidental, though in some lights ironic, given the long time it has taken—is taking—to grapple with the issues the report highlighted. The policy title was one of several options given to David Lange from his office team, and he chose it because it "has the right futuristic ring" (McQueen, 1991, p. 92).

# Life and limits in secondary schools

The open approach that so struck the OECD examiners is evident in the Department of Education funding and publishing two studies that gave an unvarnished look at how teachers and students experienced secondary schools in the mid-1970s. They show how strong the subject and examination framework was, and how school cultures were often not well organised to allow teachers to work together, to learn from each other and to create school-wide responses to the needs of their particular student body—as *Tomorrow's Schools* would later assume they could.

Elizabeth Campbell from the University of Queensland was commissioned by the Department of Education to explore what was actually happening in secondary schools, in relation to the "authoritative intentions" of the three major reviews of education and their sets of recommendations that had occurred since 1969. She surveyed randomly selected teachers and students at 76 secondary schools, around a quarter of the national total. She obtained survey responses from 635 teachers and 1,883 students (Campbell, 1978, p. 82).

Campbell found that national curriculum guidelines were widely used, but with little of the recommended local adaptation. If local adaptation occurred, it involved teachers and left out students, parents and the community. Schools remained strongly "subject" oriented, and were more "discipline" than "person" oriented. Despite the desire in the authoritative intentions of the national recommendations to have a balance of "product" (content coverage, with students "receiving" knowledge, with an emphasis on memorising facts for assessments) and "process" (more development of cognitive and learning skills through active student participation), product was more prominent and most teaching was whole-class.

Comparison with identical survey items asked of secondary teachers in a 1966 survey found little change over the decade (Campbell, 1978, p. 86). There was moderate integration of assessment and learning experience through project work, but tests and examinations dominated assessment. Teacher satisfaction with teaching as a career was generally at a moderate (50 percent) or high (37 percent) level, but teachers also thought their practice was not able to match their professional ideals, partly because of their workloads. Students' satisfaction with school was more likely to be moderate (68 percent) than high (8 percent), with interest expressed in changes to subject range, depth and relevance (particularly in Forms 6 and 7), uniform regulations, and physical facilities for recreation.

Campbell thought that the gap between the intentions of the reviews and what was actually happening in schools could be attributed to heavy teacher workloads, large class sizes, big schools and school design. She thought, too, that not enough was known about how to change educational practice. Teachers were often left to their own devices:

> It has been claimed that typically the teacher is isolated in his classroom, with few opportunities to see what else is happening in his school, or how other teachers are meeting their problems. In this unhappy context, he is being exhorted to innovate, be imaginative, try out new ideas, and experiment with new materials. (Campbell, 1978, p. 88)

This theme of the need for more collective school cultures and the importance of a more systemic approach to developing and building practical knowledge for teachers if practice were to change is also present in Noel Scott's more trenchant report. Scott, then the principal of Makora College in Masterton, went on to chair the select committee on education within the Fourth Labour Government, which took a pivotal role in the *Tomorrow's Schools* changes.[11] In 1976 he was seconded by the Department to spend a year visiting secondary schools and provide a report "to identify important areas in which the Department could consider developing new approaches" (Boag, 1977). Scott talked with principals, teachers and students. His 21-chapter report, each chapter covering a different aspect of secondary schooling and its support, was wide ranging. It expressed frustrations, but also noted some improvements in student and teacher experiences of schools. For example, after speaking with "dozens of groups of seniors" he noted that they were mainly positive about their teachers and were experiencing less authoritarian attitudes from them. Students did not like the way exams dominated their schooling but saw exams as a fact of life.

Some of the frustrations expressed in Scott's report related to the lack of action on the issues already identified through the Education Development Conference (in which some 60,000 took part, with 8,000 written submissions) and the review of secondary education. This review started with a national

---

11 Scott had contributed several accounts of innovations at Makora College to Jack Shallcrass's 1973 collection; he went on to join the inspectorate and then went into politics; and he was Associate Minister for Education during the Labour Government of 1984–90, chairing the 1986 select committee into the Quality of Teaching and working on the *Tomorrow's Schools* policy.

conference in 1971, providing a booklet that could be used in school and community discussions of the nature and purpose of secondary education. A second national conference brought together a wide range of people in 1972, resulting in more specific suggestions. In 1974 there was a co-ordinated approach for secondary schools to undertake self-review. Twenty seconded teachers and principals worked with four inspectors and a curriculum officer from the national office of the Department to hold local meetings attended by several representatives of each school in the area, followed by 2-day meetings at each school. This fed through into the 1976 McCombs report.[12]

When Scott went into secondary schools, the Education Development Conference and review of secondary education process meant people in the schools had thought about the issues affecting what they could do in secondary schools, and many were ready for change. The following points are of particular interest in Scott's report:

- There was a need for more clearly defined national goals and guidelines on the purpose of secondary schools to guide local interpretation and development. Scott found a wide range of views, but at their core he could identify agreement on the need for schools to provide sound academic development for all students, in ways that developed individuals as a whole (while acknowledging their differences) and provided a range of experiences in warm, supportive and tolerant environments.

- There were tensions between this purpose and the traditional nature of community expectations of schools, along with the growing expectation that schools should change, resulting in uncertainty for schools.

- Principals were key, but they too often worked alone. They received little training for their role, and the same was true of the senior and middle school managers. Scott also saw an "immense pressure of time and workload under which top and middle management exist", resulting in sometimes slow responses to urgent matters, as well as too little time to reflect. There was little administrative assistance, not just for school managers but also for the inspectorate and head office staff.

---

12 Named after the chair of the New Zealand Committee on Secondary Education responsible for the report, Sir Terence Henderson McCombs, who had been a Minister for Education 1945–47, and the founding principal of Cashmere High School. It was serviced by Harvey McQueen and Ormond Tate, both then working for the Department of Education. McQueen gives an interesting account of the background to the sector and community-including committee, its workings and his own role on it http://stoatspring.blogspot.co.nz/2009/08/secondary-education-review.html. The report itself is: New Zealand Committee on Secondary Education. (1976). *Towards partnership*. Wellington: Government Printer.

Scott saw conflict between different sections of the Department: between the 'policy forming' and the 'policy implementing'. Schools were critical of the Department; sometimes, he thought, making situations worse because their own administrative operations were inefficient. The issues he singled out as causing friction between the Department and schools were: buildings and equipment; inadequate funding and restrictions on the use of funds; teacher salaries; syllabus and examination requirements; too many forms to be filled; too many circulars that were hard to understand; and slowness to respond to urgent requests.

He saw much innovation occurring around trying to better meet a wider range of student needs, including greater variation in teaching methods, but

> Documentation is unfortunately fragmentary and flimsy. A great need exists to evaluate developments and disseminate information. The role of the Curriculum Development Unit and inspectorial teams in this field could be greatly extended. The results would be greatly appreciated within schools and would encourage co-operation between the sections of the Department and schools. (Scott, 1977, p. 10)

Teachers were interested in moving away from the 'chalk and talk' teacher-centred lessons, yet most lessons seemed to be of this kind. He saw some broadening of senior programmes, but on the whole examinations dominated the timetabling, along with "subject syllabuses which are so broad and demanding as to require large amounts of teaching time to cover" (p. 5). He noted that there was nothing in the departmental regulations that prevented schools from integrating subjects: it was tradition that was holding back such change. He also found that although School Certificate was often criticised, teachers were hesitant about change: they wanted national comparability, and they doubted their own ability to internally assess and develop their own syllabuses without considerable training.

Scott noted teacher criticism of follow-up of in-service courses. He thought they could take some initiative themselves within their schools to ensure that in-service courses did contribute to school development as well as individual teacher development. But he also saw a need for more national co-ordination. He noted the positive development of local in-service programme planning committees made up of teachers working with an inspector. There was also far too little in-school in-service training, which he put down partly to schools' reluctance to make time for teachers to work together.

Finally, he noted that with the abolition of grading, and secondary schools making their own appointments, there were more internal appointments within large schools and less mobility of teachers from small and isolated schools, making these schools increasingly less attractive. He thought there needed to be more movement possible across schools in different areas.

What strikes me particularly in Scott's comprehensive consideration of what could improve secondary schools is the need for interconnection, and for national frameworks that are coherent. Secondary schools already enjoyed much self-management, but on its own that was not enough to develop and circulate the knowledge and confidence needed to change practice. School appointment powers were also increasing the unevenness of capability across schools in different areas. What is also sobering in the light of *Tomorrow's Schools'* assumptions about the gains to be made from shifting decision making to the school level is the difficulty secondary school leaders already had in managing their workload, probably exacerbated by the lack of training they had had for the role.

# Fundamental challenges in secondary education

Another prime source of observations about secondary education in New Zealand in the pre-*Tomorrow's Schools* era is the collection *Directions in New Zealand Secondary Education* (Codd & Hermansson, 1976). One arresting aspect of this volume of 24 papers is that six of them were written by current officials of the Department of Education, and the rest by academics and college of education lecturers, with one from a serving teacher. The officials' papers read as their own, reflecting the scope and knowledge of the work they have done, acknowledging the issues that have no straightforward solutions and the complexity within which educational policy and practice occur and change. I cannot conceive of such an inclusion of government officials in a comparable volume now, or their being able to write such reflective papers. Few government officials in the high-level jobs held by these writers now have similar in-depth educational knowledge. They cannot be as frank these days, nor so invitational of debate. They operate within a less open system, where their prime accountability is to their Minister and that Minister's public reputation.

The other arresting aspect of this collection is that key points made in this volume apply as much today as then, almost 40 years on. In other words, increasing school self-management, without also substantially improving the infrastructure for teachers and schools and the ways teachers can work together, has not been the answer needed to change the nature of secondary education.

School-based curriculum planning is a complex task. The cycle of "setting of objectives, selection of content, devising and implementing learning situations and setting up evaluation procedures to find out if the objectives are being met", as Ross (1976), formerly the Superintendent of Curriculum Development, put it, needs time, training and resources. Renner's analysis of the implementation of the new social studies curriculum (Renner, 1976) showed that teachers' positive views of it, and their confidence about being ready to implement it, were not matched by their knowledge of it. There was a strong desire to work co-operatively with their colleagues and heads of department to develop their programme, but very little of this work was occurring. Little expertise outside their schools was identified. So teachers were working on their own, following their own interpretations, which often differed from the curriculum's intentions. Renner therefore thought it likely that they would interpret the new curriculum in terms of their existing understanding rather than realise that it was asking them to approach students differently.

Munro (1976) praised the science syllabus's "splendid statement of intention". This syllabus included knowledge of basic facts, principles and theories, the ability to apply fundamental concepts to new situations, and the application of scientific method. It also went further, with a focus on the development of scientific attitudes, such as open-mindedness, intellectual honesty, a willingness to suspend judgement and a recognition of the tentative nature of theories, and on the development of a continuing interest in science. All of these have been re-emphasised in recent times as important goals that we have still to properly provide in our schools. Writing then, Munro felt the science syllabus's intention was undermined by the absence of examination items that matched many of these objectives—there was insufficient alignment between curriculum and assessment—and by syllabuses over-packed with content to be covered, something that would continue to dog curriculum changes. What was a good national framework for science provision was also undermined by teachers' and parents' own experience that equated science with facts rather than problematics, by class size, and by laboratory conditions. Barely one in 10 of 600 Auckland students tested at the end of Form 3 could cite appropriate evidence to test a hypothesis, or draw careful conclusions from evidence in relation to simple problems from their own experience.

A further useful source of information is a 1975 baseline survey (Department of Education, 1981) of secondary schools, involving comprehensive questionnaires filled out by every principal with their liaison inspector. A 1985 follow-up survey was sent to a sample of schools and was filled out by principals. In 1975, principals were most likely to identify finance, buildings, staffing schedules, incompetent staff and examination requirements, followed by community standards, as major impediments to their school's ideal objectives. Note that the bureaucracy itself was not a major impediment. Nor was it identified as such in 1985, when the set of impediments remained much the same.

Interestingly, schools' ideal objectives gave somewhat more attention to the development of personal values systems, positive attitudes to others and a desire to enquire, followed by learning skills, than to academic achievement. Schools' *actual* objectives were somewhat different, with academic achievement close to the development of personal values and a desire to enquire behind learning skills development. Again, this difference between what secondary principals would like to provide for their students and what they thought their school actually aimed to provide remained much the same between 1975 and 1985. Thus local latitude for the professionals was constrained not just by the resources available to them, but also by the academically framed curriculum and qualification structure, and the way these continued to frame many beliefs in the community about what secondary education should look like.

Quality of teachers was also something secondary principals identified as a constraint on change, and one wonders whether this related to the difficulties Campbell, Scott and Renner had found as they saw teachers working too much on their own.

# Making sense of New Zealand student performance in an international context

New Zealand was one of the early entrants into the sequences of international student assessments that began in the 1970s. The results were often comforting, as the early analysis focused on average achievement rather than ranges of scores, and we had high average scores for 14-year-olds (Form 4, now Year 10) and 17-year-olds (Form 7, now Year 13) in the first round of international assessments, for reading comprehension, literature and science.

Our reading levels in the early 1970s were supported by high average levels of parental education and the highest average number of books per home and frequency of newspaper reading of the countries in these early international comparisons. Reading in schools was described by an American researcher, Alan Purves, delving into what lay behind New Zealand's high average achievement, as using "a variety of material and opportunities" to provide "an enjoyable and a serious experience, which seems to persist through the intermediate school and into the secondary school English classroom" (Purves, 1979, p. 16).[13]

Students' own use of time also mattered, with higher scores for those whose leisure time included reading and less television watching than those with low scores, a pattern that has persisted over 40 years. Higher-scoring students were also more likely to have English teachers who were specialist teachers of the subject. Low-scoring students were in non-academic streams and had lower aspirations, but the majority said they liked their subjects (less so for mathematics).

It is interesting to read Purves's two interpretations of this pattern, particularly since the second now belongs to a different era, an era that started to lose its security in the late 1970s and came to an abrupt end in the economic and social reforms that began in the mid-1980s. Both of these interpretations would probably have struck chords with many New Zealand teachers and policy makers at the time:

> [first] It is plausible that although school may be pleasant enough, it has successfully dampened their [low scorers'] ardour for learning and, by placing them in general and vocational programmes, removed their aspiration … [second] On the other hand, these students might well represent a different kind of pupil: the child of parents who, although not well educated and not of the 'middle-class' are nonetheless affluent. The man in a freezing works earns good wages and can afford many 'luxury' items; his children see his affluence and therefore see no need to aspire beyond that state. Education and the values of literacy do not hold promises of more 'jam today', so the incentive to use school as a means to middle-class security has disappeared. (Purves, 1979, pp. 24–25)

Reading the second interpretation—that educational success did not seem important to those who could see good jobs that did not need it—brings home how much more weight is now given to education as the path to the future, how much more it matters that we can provide quality education for every child and pathways that motivate rather than "dampen ardour".

Our maths performance on the international assessments was less encouraging, with not particularly high average scores in the Second International Maths Study (SIMS) in 1981, in which 20 countries participated. Our strongest area was geometry (perhaps the emphasis on art in primary

---

13  Purves was on a Fulbright Scholarship to New Zealand.

schools contributed), and our weakest areas were arithmetic and measurement (Robitaille, 1989). Gains over the course of a year were also among the lowest of the seven countries that took part in this aspect of the study (Burstein, 1993, p. xxxvii). There were shortages of mathematics teachers in 1981, still evident in 1987 (Department of Education, 1987a, p. 62). Perhaps secondary principals' views in the 1985 survey, on the quality of some of their teachers, were also coloured by such shortages; maths was not the only subject where this was occurring.

The SIMS study was probably the first of the international studies to show an enduring New Zealand pattern. Differences between individual students contributed over half the difference in individual scores. Differences between classes in a school contributed more to the differences in New Zealand student scores than differences between New Zealand schools, a pattern that is typical of the comprehensive nature of our schools. As the OECD examiners noted, unlike many other education systems, we cater for the full range of students within each school rather than, say, having separate schools for 'vocational' and 'academic' students. We have not sorted students so much by school as by streams or different programmes within schools, and by the 1980s by the mix of courses students could choose or have made available to them. There are therefore different opportunities for learning within the same subject and the same school. The SIMS study found that classes that covered more mathematics were the ones with higher student scores. They also tended to have higher proportions of students with higher parental education levels.

New Zealand used the results of the SIMS study constructively: to revise the secondary maths curriculum and in developing tests for different maths topics so that teachers could find out what students already knew when they entered their Form 3 class, and so avoid repeating material (Kifer & Burstein, 1993, p. 341).

# Challenging Māori statistics

Missing in the reports of New Zealand's performance in these initial international comparisons and in Campbell's survey is any analysis by ethnicity. Now we take such analysis for granted, but it is one of the sources of knowledge we have that was not readily available in the 1970s and 1980s. It can not only tell us how well students are faring but also whether any differences are related to differences in educational opportunities and experiences, things we can tackle in educational policy and practice.

The system did have analysis by ethnicity in relation to the retention of secondary students in school. It also had an accumulated body of analysis showing how the underperformance at secondary qualification level of Māori students and, overlapping this, the underperformance of students from low-income homes, was related to the subjects they took and how these subjects were (unfairly) scaled for the senior secondary qualifications (Benton, 1988).[14]

Some definite progress was evident, however. In 1973, 40 percent of Māori students left secondary school after 2 years. By 1983 that was down to 23 percent. In 1966, 15 percent of Māori students left school with at least one School Certificate subject and 2 percent with University Entrance. By 1982 that had risen to 35 percent and 8 percent. But in 1986, 53 percent of Māori students still left school without any qualification, more than twice the proportion of non-Māori who left school without any qualification (22 percent). The Department of Education noted in its briefing papers to David Lange that

> on indicators of benefit from the education system such as School Certificate success rates and retention rates there has been no narrowing of the gaps between Maori and Pakeha over a long period of time. (Department of Education, 1987a, p. 129)

The Department went on to say that it thought the work currently indicated in the curriculum review and changes to the assessment framework would likely improve things in the long term.

The Department went further in its "appraisal" of secondary education for UNESCO in 1988, starting its outline of "major issues and problems" with a frank admission that secondary education was under strain: "Up to possibly thirty percent of the student body is alienated from the present system because it is not responding adequately to their perceived needs" (Department of Education, 1988a, p. 28). This included many Māori, who were "demanding answers" and wanting a system that included and respected Māori values and decision making. But those who felt well served by the current system were resistant to change.

Framing the New Zealand education system as something that had always aimed to provide equal opportunity,[15] this appraisal indicated that

---

14 See particularly pp. 346–359; pp. 364–365.

15 Renwick and Beeby both saw the New Zealand emphasis on equality of educational opportunity (equal access) beginning only after the Depression. Renwick saw that equality of equal access was no longer sufficient: in the 1980s, equality was sought in terms of outcomes, raising substantial questions about the quality of learning opportunities and the need for them to better cater for a wider range of needs (Beeby, 1986a; Renwick, 1986).

resources need to be targeted more effectively to break the "strengthening inter-relationship between economic deprivation and failure in the education system" (Department of Education, 1988a, p. 28), though it did not say how. The three major issues identified by the Department are fundamental:

- Because more was expected of education, for more students, the narrow framing of the senior secondary curriculum and qualifications was ever more apparent. The foremost issue was the academic nature of the curriculum, set for the minority heading for university.

- Next came the senior secondary qualifications (the dominance of University Entrance), the use of scaling (adjustment) of raw marks in School Certificate, which "has adversely affected the final marks of candidates in subjects regularly chosen by the less able" (p. 41) and the arbitrary 50 percent pass rate. This led to a high rate of 'failure': students leaving school without qualifications, something that mattered much more than it had a decade before, when jobs were plentiful. Because the qualification's technical structure was largely hidden from public view, the reasons for this could be (unfairly) placed at the door of schools.

- The third issue this report singled out was public concern about the quality of teaching because of the difficulty in reducing 'failure'. The Department thought this concern was adding to teachers feeling alienated from society.

# Interconnecting roads not taken

Action was under way to address these fundamental issues, as the Department had noted in its briefing to David Lange. But the two main roads offering the coherence and interconnection that secondary education needed were only to be partially mapped before they were abandoned for *Tomorrow's Schools*.

The first road would have reshaped curriculum and qualifications together. This road was mapped out in the 1986 report of the Committee of Inquiry into Curriculum, Assessment, and Qualifications, a joint work project which brought together the Department, the education sector and the business community. The first step was to replace the arbitrary School Certificate pass rate with grading, and University Entrance with a Sixth Form Certificate that offered a wider range of subjects. More fundamentally, this Committee, with its broad range of stakeholders, also recommended what would take another 16 years to bring to even partial fruition: achievement-based assessment for Forms 5 to 7 (now Years 11 to 13). To achieve this fundamental change, the

Committee recommended a board of studies, to make possible a greater coherence between secondary curriculum, assessment, pedagogy and qualifications. This board of studies would also have continued to bring into one forum educators and employers, unions and representatives of Māori. But the resulting Board of Studies, formed in 1988, lasted only until 1990, an early casualty of the *Tomorrow's Schools* reforms.

The second road not taken was that outlined by the curriculum review (Department of Education, 1987c), which attracted 21,500 submissions and a further 10,000 on its draft. This review placed great emphasis on the importance of schools developing local curricula within national guidelines,[16] using ongoing review and evaluation of their programmes and their effectiveness, along with serious community consultation. Schools would have time allocated for this work. They would not work alone, but would be supported by advisers and departmental officials, who would themselves receive training in how best to do this. A national infrastructure was sketched out, with the potential for the knowledge-building and sharing interconnections the inspectorate had used to cross-pollinate practice.

*Tomorrow's Schools* would pick up the idea of schools taking a coherent look at themselves and framing their actions in terms of desired purpose, through the school charters. But it was to leave such work to schools to work out on their own, relying on written guidance and one-off training. As we shall see, schools needed much more than this.

# The 'community' road

Of the three tensions identified at the start of this chapter:

- the need for changes in secondary programmes and qualifications, and, not unrelated,
- Māori concerns that progress was not occurring fast enough, and was not

---

16 Interestingly, this emphasis on local decision making on curriculum was linked by Renwick (1976) to the difficulty of gaining any national agreement on what was important. He wrote: "Most of the issues of any importance in current discussions of the studies and activities that teenagers should undertake arise from views of educational priorities and value pre-suppositions that are by no means universally agreed upon in the national community. They are unsuited to national prescription in the name of the State for uniform adoption in all schools. The national interest may well be adequately served if there is full, informed discussion of a proposed type of study or activity and if, following that discussion, national guidelines are set for the information of local schools and their communities. The decisive consideration then becomes what the local traffic will bear" (pp. 26–27). This suggests that some of the lack of sharp controversy the OECD examiners noted came from deciding not to force issues.

sufficiently supporting Māori identity, including te reo Māori, and

- community–school interconnections,

only the latter was included in the substance of the *Tomorrow's Schools* reforms. Centrality was given to school governance by the school board elected by the school community, working in partnership with school management and required to consult with its wider community.

The calls for more community involvement in the administration of education came from the Education Development Conference in the mid-1970s,[17] and from the 1976 McCombs report on secondary education. In 1979 Renwick identified three major reasons for the "pressure" to enlarge the role of school committees. The first presages Picot by almost a decade:

> The first is a general belief that power and responsibility should, where possible, be devolved so that decisions can, as far as possible, be made at the point where the results of those decisions are to be carried into effect. (Renwick, 1979, p. 9)

Renwick next noted a desire among parents and local communities to have more influence in their children's schools.[18]

The third reason has more to do with other government agencies' interest in schools as "a public local institution that can be used by them in the interests of various programmes that they may wish to initiate locally" (Renwick, 1979, p. 9), such as sport. Thus the school committee,

> as the statutory body with the responsibility for the care and upkeep of the local primary school, is accordingly finding itself more and more called upon to make decisions that bear not only on the use of the school buildings and equipment, but also on the working relationship that should be established between the school and other community agencies. (Renwick, 1979, p. 9)

At this stage there were distinct roles for the school committee and the parent–teacher association, with some competition between them for any enhanced local role. Renwick hoped their roles would coalesce; he also hoped the school committee would play a role in principal appointment and the school programme.

In 1981 the educational historian John Barrington attributed the lack of change in this direction to professional disquiet about lay involvement in

---

17 Around 4,000 seminar groups were organised by the "extension departments" in the then six universities, over 60,000 people took part, and 800 submissions were received (Barrington, 1981, p. 70).

18 Barrington (1981, p. 77) also traversed these reasons, and noted that the rise in parents' educational levels over time may have contributed to their greater confidence in engaging with schools.

decisions on staffing and programmes, coupled with 'back to basics' parent organisations arising in tandem with the economic downturn and the return of the National Government in 1976, with its caution about devolution in general (Barrington, 1981). Primary school committees did elect the district education board and decide with the principal whether the school would have 30 minutes of religious instruction each week, and they could comment on teacher appointments and recommend a teacher's dismissal to the education board. One Wellington study found that school committee members often felt they had no independent power, but were 'rubber stamps' for the education board and Department, "a cheap way for the board to administer the school" (Barrington, 1981, pp. 73–74). This administration was largely related to school property and administering money raised by the school's parent–teacher association. Secondary boards, despite their much wider brief and inclusion of representatives from local government and tertiary education institutions, also focused on property and finance. Neither the secondary boards nor the primary school committees had any training for their role.

The open and inclusionary approach to educational policy at the national level noted by the OECD examiners, which largely worked well in relation to the development and dissemination of syllabus, curriculum, resources and shared understanding (the professional matters of education), did not seem to work quite so well when it came to the administration of education and the role of non-educators. The 1976 Educational Development Conference recommendation that primary school committees take part in the appointment of principals to their school troubled NZEI, and Renwick was frank that within his own Department there was no consensus that this was a good idea. Meetings to discuss it involving NZEI, national bodies of the education boards, and school committee and departmental officials could not reach agreement, so "I referred the issue to the Minister for his guidance" (Renwick, 1983, pp. 10–11). The Minister thought school committees should have a role and "asked the parties to devise a scheme that would achieve this." But this was still not achieved by the time of the 1986 Inquiry into the Quality of Teaching (the Scott report), one of whose recommendations was that school committee chairs should have voting (as well as speaking) rights on the board appointment committee appointing their school's principal.

# The school takes centre stage

The Inquiry into the Quality of Teaching also called for schools to be more communicative with parents, more open and welcoming, approaching the relationship as "equal partners to achieve quality education" (Education and Science Select Committee, 1986, p. 24). It endorsed the partnership role of parents contributing collectively to curriculum and school review, as outlined by the draft *Curriculum Review*. There is a sense in both these documents that individual schools needed to be actively constructing their own community through the professionals and parents finding more common ground, focusing on what they thought was important to emphasise locally, and charting and ensuring children's progress.

While stressing the importance of schools-as-communities, the Inquiry into the Quality of Teaching outlined a much stronger role for the Department and inspectors in evaluating the quality of schools. Indeed, its recommendations included carving the inspectorate in two, separating an advisory role from a 'professional audit' role. These twin principles—the school as a distinctive 'community', coupled with a greater weight on evaluating its performance through audit—would help to shape *Tomorrow's Schools*.

Returning to the many other recommendations of this Inquiry, what strikes me now is how at the same time as it emphasises the school-as-community, it takes for granted that teachers work on their own. More in-service training for principals and senior staff is recommended, but for "their professional support roles". A new "lead teacher" role is mentioned, to provide promotion without having to leave the classroom, rather than taking on a role of working with other teachers to collectively improve the quality of their work.

There is also little sense of connectivity across the system, other than through making senior school, inspectorate and advisory roles "reviewable" or time-limited, and putting such roles on similar pay scales. This suggests that circulating individuals through these roles, or returning them to the classroom, was seen as a prime way to aerate the system. But while such circulation can bring new ideas and perspectives into a setting, it doesn't amount to the collective creation of new knowledge through joint work that shapes shared understanding so that the system as a whole can keep moving. How, for example, were individual schools to learn how to work as joint partnerships with parents? How were they to know what was possible if they did not know what they did not know? How would new knowledge and theoretical understanding relevant to effective teaching, along with new subject knowledge, changing so rapidly now in so many spheres, enter schools?

What New Zealand education would find itself relying on in order for schools to become their own communities was the latitude with which schools already worked. Teachers and principals were accustomed to taking the initiative, to responding to their particular students' needs. This was a real strength. But it is also apparent through the issues discussed in this and the previous chapter that school-level latitude and initiative were not enough. To provide effective learning—to meet needs that had been poorly met before and the new needs arising with a more uncertain society and economy—latitude and initiative needed to occur within a coherent local and national infrastructure that:

- connected teachers with the kind of knowledge, resources and tools they could use in their work and build on
- could expose teachers to evidence of levels of student engagement and achievement they may not have thought possible
- incorporated new national frameworks that were focused on ensuring real opportunities for students to achieve (rather than hobbling them in rationed qualifications, which then narrowed curriculum and pedagogy)
- connected different expertise across the system to build knowledge, understanding and purpose, things that are not well built or sufficiently owned by all those who need to make a system work well if undertaken by one party on its own.

But when the political willingness to make profound changes in New Zealand education finally came, the existing infrastructure for the development and improvement of teaching was eclipsed. No new coherent infrastructure to keep building the capability and knowledge of educators replaced it. The next chapter charts what happened, and why.

# Chapter 4

# Shaking up and separating out

An overseas observer described the New Zealand approach as "the 'earthquake method' of education reform (shake up everything) ... with virtually all the major new structures being implemented within the space of one year" (Holdaway, 1989, cited in Barrington, 1991, p. 5). Changes that gave schools self-management certainly came swiftly. These changes owed less to the pent-up tensions within education than to the determination of the Labour Government elected in 1984 to resolve the major fiscal deficit they inherited by restructuring the economy and the role of the state (Boston, Martin, Pallot, & Walsh, 1991; James, 1992).

Restructuring of government services proceeded along generic lines, based largely on analysis provided by Treasury in its 1984 and 1987 briefing papers.[1] Fundamental to this analysis was the premise that human behaviour is primarily self-interested. Government institutions and the relations between them therefore had to be designed to appeal to self-interest, offering decision-making freedom, but also to guard against it, through the separation of roles and the casting of relations as contracts with specified measures of performance. 'Provider capture' was the term used to suggest that officials' and professionals' knowledge about the development of policy and delivery of services was warped by such self-interest.

This chapter looks at why it was that self-managing schools came to the fore, and then why it was that so little attention was paid to the developmental infrastructure needed to make the most of them in the reforms that altered the education landscape between 1988 and 1991. The haste of this initial period, together with the emphasis on the separation of roles—of policy from operations, and of schools from the government agencies that replaced the Department of Education—cast a long shadow.

---

1   Economic management (1984); Government management: Vol I (1987); Government management: Vol II: Education (1987).

## Self-management as a solution

The earthquake that altered the education landscape was not the only social earthquake of the era. Some of its rationale came from the steep increases in unemployment that resulted from the government economic and public sector restructuring and the 1987 stock market crash. As always, youth were particularly hard hit. This brought new urgency to the continuing issue of the high proportion of young people leaving school without a qualification, of whom too many were Māori. The number of jobs available to them had shrunk. Improving education and training for these young people was identified as a prime means of reducing unemployment and its related public costs.

Out of the work done for the Cabinet Committee on Employment and Training, which focused on post-school options, came the diagnosis that post-school institutions were insufficiently responsive to the needs of these young people and to the needs of the wider economy (Butterworth & Butterworth, 1998, pp. 56–65). Lack of ability to respond effectively at the institutional level was seen to stem from the institutions' lack of flexibility, largely due to the way they were funded through centrally defined courses and eligibility criteria. In the prevailing logic of this policy era, the solution appeared to be more self-management of institutions. Self-management was seen as providing more local freedom and incentive to respond to local needs. Institutional freedom for post-school education and training would mean each institution making decisions on the courses and qualifications it offered, and on how to allocate the resources that would come from the number of students attracted by these courses. Because these decisions would be made directly by individual institutions, there would be a single body to hold accountable.

Institutional self-management appealed on a number of fronts. It appeared to provide solutions to the widening tensions of inequality in education, in terms of access to both opportunities and outcomes. Institutions would need to make what they offered accessible and attractive. National productivity would improve: consideration of employment pathways would foster courses that would lead to the improved skill levels needed as the economy shifted from its previous axis of manual labour and primary production. The association of self-management with more accountability also promised a means to keep institutions focused on their performance, and thus to improve the effective use of public funding.

## The Picot taskforce

"Flexibility" and "responsiveness", together with the delegation of responsibilities "as far as is practicable", framed the terms of reference for the Picot taskforce to review educational administration, covering schools and the post-school institutions other than universities. This taskforce was announced just before the August 1987 election, which re-elected the Labour Government. David Lange, the Prime Minister, now took on the Education portfolio, signalling that educational change had priority. It was also an internal signal to his Cabinet that education policy would not be dominated by the market frame favoured by the 'Rogernomics' team headed by the Finance Minister, Roger Douglas: there would be no privatisation of schools and vouchers, as the 1987 Treasury briefing paper on education had recommended. However, the Picot taskforce would pick up the Treasury report's emphasis on consumer choice as the most reliable means of steering providers, whether in relation to schools or the support for schools.[2]

The taskforce came to be known as the Picot taskforce after its chair, Brian Picot, an able businessman who had built up one of the country's largest supermarket chains. The small taskforce of five combined educational expertise and experience of management and organisation beyond education. It brought together insiders who knew the education system's tensions very well and outsiders who would not take things for granted. Joining their discussions were three officials from the Department of Education, Treasury and the State Services Commission.

The four other taskforce members were Peter Ramsay, from the University of Waikato, who had led the *Tomorrow May Be Too Late* study and had written about effective schools and the value of schools working with their local community; Margaret Rosemergy, from Wellington Teachers' College, who had also chaired a secondary school board; Whetu Wereta, a statistician working with the Department of Māori Affairs and a member of the Royal Commission on the Electoral System; and Colin Wise, head of a large firm,

---

2   For more about this period of reform, and the Treasury analysis, its genesis and its role in education reform, see Butterworth and Butterworth (1998), who also provide a chronology of the changes up until 1996; McQueen (1991); Openshaw (2009, 2012); and Wylie (1995a). Whitcombe (2008) provides a succinct description of what came to be called 'New Public Management', its appeal to the Labour Government and the National Government that followed, and the problems this approach has bequeathed. She also notes that senior Treasury officials did not anticipate the wholesale separation of policy and operations that occurred, and thought there were circumstances when it would be less effective to keep them separate (p. 8). However, such a separation is an essential part of the 1987 Treasury briefing paper on education.

who had been a member of a secondary board and of the University of Otago Council. Maurice Gianotti, who was the chief executive of the taskforce, was the acting Wellington regional superintendent in the Department of Education and had headed the Wellington district primary inspectorate. The Treasury official was Simon Smelt, who had co-written the 1987 Treasury briefing paper on education, calling for radical change, and the State Services Commission official was Marijke Robinson. There were also periodic contacts with David Lange and his office.

The Picot taskforce report, titled *Administering for Excellence*, was made public in early May 1988.[3] Its main recommendation was to make schools self-managing. Professionals and parents would come together to share this responsibility, working in "partnership". Parents would govern the school through the board they elected from parents of the school's existing students who put themselves forward to take on the responsibility. Boards and schools would operate within national guidelines and objectives but would not need to seek approval for particular decisions. The 10 education boards would cease to exist. The Department of Education would also no longer exist; government education functions would be dispersed among a policy-focused Ministry and a set of smaller government agencies. The fulcrum of the relationship between each school and its community, and with the Government, would lie in a charter that set out the school's objectives. Schools would be held accountable for meeting their objectives.

This institutional accountability sounded promising to me at the time. Perhaps this would be the lever to shift the public as well as professional complacency I had seen around the unequal provision of education and its outcomes when I was writing the overview of education for the Royal Commission on Social Policy. I thought that reporting to a national organisation might focus attention at the school level, but only if it was accompanied by real action by the national organisation. If individual institutions had to examine what they did in the light of what it resulted in and what it meant for students from different ethnic backgrounds, different socioeconomic circumstances and both genders; if as a result they had to collect and use relevant data and to (what would now be called) 'listen to student voice'; if the school-as-community (including students) discussed the picture that resulted: would this not trigger some long-overdue changes?

---

3   Taskforce to Review Education Administration. (1988). *Administering for excellence: effective administration in education.* Wellington: Government Printer. April is given as the publication month on the report itself; the copy I was given at the time has an embargo sticker indicating its public release on 10 May.

If the central government organisation collated school data into a national picture that was similarly both monitored and discussed, and used to assess how well policy was working, and if fairness of educational opportunity was made the core principle to judge progress against, would that not also trigger the changes needed? These links between policy and operations, and giving centrality to fairness of educational opportunity, were included in the recommendations of my education overview for the Royal Commission on Social Policy (Wylie, 1988a).

Consideration of the need to improve educational opportunity also focused my thinking on the safeguards that would be needed with self-managing schools to ensure that schools whose communities had better resources did not gain at the expense of those in poor communities. Such safeguards were clear in the existing research on self-managed schools, and included weighted funding for schools in poor areas and schools not being able to set their own salary scales. Looking back, it seems that it was easier for me to think about safeguards for new mechanisms in order to avoid unwanted effects than it was to think about the infrastructure of challenge and support that schools would need to really undertake the kind of work that the emphasis on institutional accountability in the Picot report assumed they could do on their own. Unfortunately, I was not alone in this.

The Picot taskforce recommended that schools be responsible for allocating the government funding they received. Thus they would choose and pay for the services and equipment they felt they needed. To make the existing government services supporting schools (such as the advisers, and the psychologists and specialists working with students with special needs) responsive and flexible, they too would need to become self-managing, and largely self-funded by making their services sufficiently attractive to schools. There would be some additional costs associated with the change-over, but the Picot report estimated "efficiency and effectiveness" gains of around $111 million.

Some checks and balances to this centrality of self-managing schools were also included in the Picot report. Some of these held a promise of connections that could support and build new knowledge and provide some coherence. Accountability would come through regular reviews of schools, based on their charter, to be carried out by a new review and audit agency. Seconded principals would be part of the review teams, offering a channel for cross-fertilisation.

Community education forums would discuss local provision and issues, provide a channel from the "flaxroots" to government, widen community understanding of education, and provide support for useful innovation. However, in keeping with the new freedom of schools, participation would be voluntary.

The Parent Advocacy Council could provide advice to parents whose needs were not being met, to the point of advising those who wished to set up a new school if a school was not being sufficiently responsive.

Policy advice to the Minister from the Ministry would be guided by an Education Policy Council that would bring together the four most senior officials in the Ministry and four outside appointments (two made by the Minister and two by an electoral college of educational groups), so that a range of expertise would be brought together within an overall policy framework (Taskforce to Review Education Administration, 1988). Policy advice to the Minister would be the core part of the new Ministry of Education, but it appeared that it would be policy informed by community education forums and interaction with education's representative groups, including the teacher unions.

# Responses to the Picot report

More than 20,000 responses to the Picot report were received, 40 percent as form letters. Most responses were from teachers and others who worked in education. Parents who wanted to comment were mainly those whose children had special needs or received specialist support, including music lessons and Reading Recovery. These parents' concerns were much the same as those of the teachers and others who responded. Opposition was strongest to the changes to the specialist and advisory services that would cut them from the national infrastructure and make them self-funding, dependent on individual school choices and budgets (Department of Education, 1988b). The other main issue raised by teachers and parents was the nature of the board of trustees, particularly the responsibility asked of parents.

Several common themes are also evident in the other issues raised by teachers and parents, including:

- how to reconcile local autonomy with national guidelines, particularly if that gave power to strong individuals without the existing safeguards of universally applicable processes
- how to ensure equal opportunities and standards, given this local autonomy, which would give power to people who might not see the need

to change the status quo, and might result in uneven distributions—a particular concern for rural respondents and Māori
- the support that would be needed for the new self-managing schools, particularly for the enlarged principal role and the new role for parents.

Māori inspectors, advisers and Department of Education officials held 222 hui across the country with iwi. While largely positive, Māori thought the recommendations fell short of ensuring that Māori student needs would be recognised and met. With boards of trustees making the decisions, it was important that Māori were adequately represented on them. Māori doubted that there was adequate understanding at this local level to really change things for the better for Māori students. Their doubt fed into strong interest in Māori managing Māori education, with a range of ideas as to how this should occur, including a separate Māori education authority. The hui were clear that Māori-medium schools would need particular support to ensure the continuation of te reo Māori and the strengthening of Māori culture (Openshaw, 2009, pp. 132–133).

Public opinion polling carried out for the Prime Minister's office in July 1988 showed divided views as well as much uncertainty about the Picot recommendations. Here, too, there was some wariness about local latitude and what it might mean for increased differences between schools. The majority opposed local choice for which subjects to teach on top of a compulsory core and also opposed boards of trustees taking responsibility for deciding their teachers' salaries (Openshaw, 2009, pp. 134–235).

Parents with students currently in state schools, when they were polled, also showed some concerns about shifting decision making to the school level. More than two-thirds thought that schools in different areas would not be equal and that boards of trustees could be taken over by parents with extreme views. Around half thought that the Government was avoiding its responsibility by shifting administration to schools, and that too many changes were taking place too quickly. Views were divided as to whether the new approach would improve educational standards (Heylen Research Centre, 1989a).

Principals' and teachers' views on how effective the reforms would be were also mixed. They shared the concerns of parents noted above. In addition, they had concerns about different schools using different measures to judge teachers' performance and reward it, given the Picot taskforce's recommendation that school operational funding should include funding for teaching staff. Linked to this was a concern that principal–teacher relations could deteriorate. Principals also saw the need for new skills for their new role (Heylen Research Centre, 1989b).

The Picot taskforce had heard from those who actively sought change in the system, but this was not the majority. Most parents tend to be conservative about large changes in education. Interestingly, in a public opinion poll run in late 1987, less than a third of parents thought there was not enough opportunity for parents to have a say in how their child's school was run. The same poll found that more than half the parents of children in primary and intermediate schools and half the parents of secondary students thought their local state school provided their idea of an ideal education very or extremely well. Those who thought it did not were very much the minority: 14 percent of primary parents and 22 percent of secondary parents (Heylen Research Centre, 1987a). So at one level—though an 'ideal' education seems a rather abstract notion—there was *not* widespread dissatisfaction. However, around a third of the parents polled did think the information parents got about what was happening in their child's school and what was taught in class were inadequate.

When this poll on education took place in 1987 it was election year, and education was to the fore. The National Party spokesperson on education, Ruth Richardson, used inequalities of educational outcomes, including the high proportion of school-leavers without qualifications, in strong criticisms of the education system. Several national media articles also took up these themes. Charmaine Pountney estimated that 80 percent of parents who participated in discussion groups on the secondary examination system in early 1987 "believed that their own school was doing a reasonable or good job; but the same people were deeply worried about the state of New Zealand education" (Pountney, 2000, p. 112). A May 1987 opinion poll showed that public views on how well 'education' was working were divided: 43 percent thought it was working well or quite well; 42 percent thought it was working poorly or quite poorly (Openshaw, 2009, p. 82). Another public opinion poll later that same year sheds some light on this level of public concern. Lack of funding, rather than quality of teaching, was identified as the main problem facing education (Heylen Research Centre, 1987b, p. 101).[4]

---

4  Funding, too few teachers, inadequate buildings and lack of resources amounted to 37 percent of the responses. Around 3 percent identified poor quality of teaching or principals. Half had no idea what problems the education system faced.

## *Tomorrow's Schools*

Just 4 months after the release of the Picot report came the Government's response, the policy document giving the structure for the new era: *Tomorrow's Schools* (Minister of Education, 1988). Most of the Picot taskforce recommendations were included, with the exception of the Education Policy Council. An overall steering and evaluative advisory group on the big picture of educational policy, which included the sector, had no place in the new era of the public sector, with its emphasis on chief executive accountability through performance-based contracts.

What evidence is there of any thought given to the infrastructure needed to support the self-management of schools and the sharing and development of useful knowledge across the education system in *Tomorrow's Schools*? Not much. A 'liaison group' would help schools develop their first charter—but only if they requested such help. The Implementation Unit would consider "ways in which principals and other teachers taking on new responsibilities can be given training, information and support" (pp. 4 and 11). However, the advisers were not immediately cut out of the system as a whole. 'General' advisers would be funded at the teachers colleges to serve schools in each college's catchment area. Two years on, the funding for these positions would be included in school operational funds, so that schools could make their own decisions about advice. Similarly, special education roles were subsumed into a new national body that would initially be contracted to the Ministry of Education, but these roles were also expected to be self-funding after 2 years, with the national body's funding redistributed to schools. Resources produced by School Publications and film and audio units within the Department were also separated off into a separate business, funded for its first 18 months and then expected to start to recover its costs. Curriculum objectives would be set by the Ministry of Education, but the Curriculum Division would cease to exist. Instead of the ongoing national anchoring, connections and knowledge-building and development it had provided, curriculum "activities" would be contracted out as required.

The general tenor of the *Tomorrow's Schools* document is that schools be left to make their own decisions, since this freedom of decision making was assumed to be the key to unlocking the flexibility and responsiveness that would improve educational provision. The companion assumption, of course, is that the services the schools would need, whether for accounting, curriculum, specialist advice, support for a child or the appointment of a new principal, would be readily available, affordable and of good quality because their viability was dependent on the schools' choice. No national approach was thought to be needed to supply such services, ensure they were available in all localities, or connect them so that there could be ongoing learning for both the services and the schools—so that the wheel did not have to be re-invented. Consumer choice would suffice.

There was also reduced linkage between the development of curriculum and resources through the loss of the Curriculum Division, the hiving off of resource production to a stand-alone agency, and the loss of the inspectorate and its interconnective role. Joint work undertaken by people with different expertise and roles in the system was no longer to be the main vehicle through which curriculum and teaching and learning resources would be developed in ways that spread them through schools. Such separation of roles and loss of nationally led joint work would make it hard to develop powerful new tools for teaching. This would not be an environment in which the Ready to Read resources could emerge, resources that had provided new knowledge that teachers welcomed, coupled with a national achievement progression framework that most teachers used without its having to be mandated.

Choice (schools choosing providers of advice; parents and students choosing schools) was one of the Picot taskforce's four pillars in its approach to improving educational administration in order to improve educational outcomes. Consumer decisions were assumed to be the best impetus for schools and providers alike to be responsive, to offer quality.

"Individual competence" was another of the four pillars. It was outlined in a positive statement of faith that makes much of good intentions and implies that to question the existence of competence (in teachers, principals and boards of trustees) is arrogant:

> Individual competence assumes that most people are competent to carry out the tasks given to them and that nearly everyone will have a genuine commitment to doing the best job possible for all learners. The presumption of individual competence encourages the development of initiative, independence, personal responsibility and entrepreneurial abilities. To assume the opposite is to cut off the education system from the benefits of commitment and enthusiasm that develop when people feel confidence and trust has been placed in them. (Taskforce to Review Education Administration, 1988, p. 4)

What is missing here is any sense that competence needs both initial and ongoing development, especially in a rapidly changing and complex world. This may have been because the Picot taskforce's abiding assumption was that it was a lack of institutional freedom that lay at the heart of education's difficulties. Yet as we have seen in the previous chapters, considerable freedom around curriculum and ways of teaching in the schools already existed, with mixed results. It was largely the senior secondary qualifications that so narrowed the curriculum for adolescents. Secondary boards and principals already had most of the freedoms included in *Tomorrow's Schools.*

In both secondary and primary schools, what was really lacking was any systematic way to build and circulate new ways of doing things; for example, improving Māori student learning and achievements. Local pockets of initiative—often linking people across schools, working with the inspectorate and advisers, and curriculum and other officials within the Department— were already occurring, but then, as now, such initiatives did not happen in *every* locality. The result, then and now, is national unevenness, both of taking initiative and of taking it effectively. It is also difficult to sustain change, especially if it is dependent on individual enthusiasm and the changes are not embedded in the system.

Only in the Review and Audit Agency (later to be refashioned as the Education Review Office, or ERO) was there a potentially knowledge-building connection that all schools had to have. As originally set out, the Review and Audit Agency would use multidisciplinary teams for its 2-yearly reviews, including members who had expertise in curriculum, administration, equal employment opportunities and equal educational opportunity, as well as a community representative and a current principal. These teams would use the school's own charter as the basis for review. Their initial report would identify strengths and weaknesses, along with recommendations for improvement. A second visit to the school would occur a term later to see what progress was being made, with a final report made at that time. Schools whose final reports included "serious deficiencies in the management of the institution or in the achievements of its students" (Minister of Education, 1988, p. 21) would be reviewed a third time 6 months later, and if significant improvement had not occurred, the board of trustees could be dismissed.

The lack of systematic linkage between school inspections and subsequent Department work with a school that was criticised in the 1986 Scott report was now being remedied. Recommendations from a review team would be a form of advice, though *how* a school was to make progress and the connections that might help it do so were to be left to the school. There were two further productive and capacity-building aspects to the Review and Audit Agency's approach: using the school's charter as the basis for review had the potential to encourage more collective work within schools, and including seconded principals in the team would encourage some cross-fertilisation between schools and educational roles.

## Fleshing out the bones

Then came the task of fleshing out the bones of this radical policy. Initially, the teacher unions and other sector groups were excluded from the working groups the Ministry formed for this task. Their exclusion brings home to me just what weight was given to the purist separation of functions in the larger public service framework in which *Tomorrow's Schools* was occurring, and just how difficult that made it for officials to understand both the contribution that hybrid roles and joint work could make to the development of shared knowledge and how important such knowledge and understanding were. In the era of separating policy from operations in government departments, schools came into the operational category.

In the past, teasing out how policy principles would actually work in practice would have involved joint work with the education sector groups: the teacher unions, the national organisations for the education boards, secondary boards, school committees, and parent–teacher associations. They were included because they had useful collective knowledge. They were also included because they were the ones who would have to make any changes work, and the new understanding developed through such joint work could be communicated by them to their members. Joint work played a number of interconnected and useful roles.

But now, in the new public sector environment, those who provided professional services were thought to be (only) self-interested. Belief in "provider capture" was what saw them initially excluded from the working groups set up to give detailed shape to the outlines of *Tomorrow's Schools*. Russ Ballard, the interim head of the Department of Education appointed to manage the change, was a scientist and change manager in large organisations who had recently returned from the United States; he had no educational background himself. The teacher unions had to meet with David Lange and convince him that the reforms would not work unless they had teachers' trust and support (something whose necessity in achieving change Beeby (1986b) had written about just recently), before they were included in the working groups.

The break from the past was signalled by including the experienced people nominated by the sector groups (including the national organisation of school committees as well as the unions), but not as their representatives. Ballard, the change manager, may well have wanted to signal that the consensus-seeking era was over. The purist framework within which he was operating appears to have made it hard for him to see that good educational policy also needed the expertise of the education sector groups and the opportunity to develop some shared understanding that could inform how people approached their responsibilities.

Indeed, the inclusion of union, education board and parent committee expertise in these initial working groups made the transition to the new era far less problematic than it might otherwise have been, as noted by the acting Secretary of Education, Lyall Perris, some years later (Perris, 1998, p. 15). Related to this lesson, he also wrote approvingly of a World Bank paper arguing "for the importance of continuous interaction between policymakers and the people affected by policy change" (Perris, 1998, p. 18). The value of such interaction underpinned much of the thinking that informed the *Tomorrow's Schools* emphasis on schools working more closely with their community, and the requirement to consult with communities was included in the regulations for schools. But, ironically, at the national level this interaction of policy makers and those affected by policy change, those whose knowledge and connections are needed to effectively design and implement policy, has often had to be fought for. It has not occurred as often as it should to achieve workable and effective policy.

# The cost of haste

There was just 14 months between the *Tomorrow's Schools* policy document and the changeover date of 1 October 1989, when the new era would begin. Publicity campaigns were mounted that successfully encouraged many parents to put themselves forward for the May 1989 elections for the first school boards of trustees. Only two out of some 2,700 schools could not find sufficient willing parents. The new boards and principals attended training sessions together, sessions that were of necessity very broad brush. A colleague who was then the treasurer on her school board recalls being told that if treasurers could manage their own household budget, they would have no difficulty managing a school budget.

The Education Act was still being drawn up. The first boards and the principals were the ones who would have to make the examples that others could follow; they had only outlines, their own thinking and experience, and their own existing networks to draw on. The Government did fund a new organisation for school trustees, as it had previously funded the national organisations for school committees and school boards. Some support came from the inspectorate before it was dismantled, but most inspectors had gone (many into the Review and Audit Agency) when boards started work on their first budgets, and a planned funding hotline was cut to save costs.

Paucity of advice, coupled with discrepancies between the indicative funding and the budgets put forward by 82 schools in a check of the new funding formulas, aroused anxiety and sometimes anger among the new boards and their principals. The Department of Education had noted funding difficulties for some years, something held against it by Treasury and the State Services Commission, who put the difficulties down to inefficiencies and unwillingness to make hard decisions. The check of the new funding formula had been intended as a high-level comparison of the indicative new budget for the school and its previous year's spending, increased by around 10 percent. But probably due to the haste of the initial implementation, something was lost in the translation of this intention to the actual work with the sample schools. Schools understood they were to compare their new budget figure with the previous year's spending, *plus* what boards thought was reasonable to allow them to catch up on more than a decade's tight funding for property maintenance and resources. This comparison showed an overall shortfall of 31 percent. Funding levels for schools were improved the following year, and involvement of "leading school principals" in the development of the formula for school funding ameliorated some of the school boards' initial anxiety (Perris, 1998, p. 20).

Somewhat ironically, property was the one area where the Picot taskforce had recommended government support for boards. It had noted that there was much work to be done to improve the quality of school environments for learning, and it put this down to the absence of specialist expertise in property management in the administrative structures of education. It recommended a separate property division within the new Ministry of Education, and this recommendation was followed (Taskforce to Review Education Administration, 1988, pp. 33–34). Property came to be the main, and often the only, point of discussion between Ministry of Education officials and individual schools. It was also the one area where there was a district approach, with district committees comprising Ministry of Education officials and sector group representatives making some allocation decisions in terms of major capital expenditure, based on individual schools' plans.

But these committees were not looking at the overall shape of schooling provision in the district and how to make the most effective use of the district's educational property, but simply measuring the strength of individual school cases against one another. The district existed only on paper. It was not a structure with ongoing processes of challenge and support, providing an infrastructure for self-managing schools.

Haste also left mistrust in its wake in the development of charters, which were to be central to creating schools-as-communities as well as framing their accountability to the Government. The *Tomorrow's Schools* document was clear that schools would be operating within national guidelines relating to the curriculum, and to equal educational opportunities, with particular reference to the Treaty of Waitangi and te reo Māori for students who wished to learn it, or learn through it. But the draft charter outline that went to schools in 1989 did not contain all that was intended to be included in the legislation. When the additions were made to the charter outline, many schools were left with the impression that an initial autonomy had been circumscribed.

Insufficient time or support also marred the development of these founding charters. They were to be given to the Ministry of Education at the end of 1989—by boards that did not start work until June. Five to six months was nothing like the time needed for people who were finding their feet in so many ways. Boards were groups of people who had not worked together before, whose chairs may never have run a meeting before. Many board members, parents and professionals alike, would never have grappled with documents like a charter, formed an organisational policy, worked with a set of financial accounts, employed someone, or worked within a set of regulations. Boards could not take this founding work lightly: they would be held accountable on the basis of the documents they produced. The original boards had just a few months to come to a common understanding of the ambitious national guidelines, the content of which some would find problematic. They had just a few months to create trusted relationships with local iwi and community groups, of the kind that would allow genuine contributions and discussion. Booklets were developed as guides to community consultation, but they were not available until after many schools had undertaken some consultation (Mitchell, 1993, pp. 56–64).

As a result, the charters that resulted were often careful documents, with nothing specified that the board and principal thought the school was not already doing or that was well within its reach. Initiative was most evident in the creation of mission statements, signalling core values as well as what people thought would signal quality (the word 'excellent' often appeared). But few charters were really the core founding document, arising out of a community-building process, that some on the Picot taskforce had envisaged. The charters were not going to be a touchstone for school planning and practice. They were going to live on the back shelf rather than be living documents in frequent use.

These initial and often vexed experiences of dealing with the new requirements for charters, and then the policies framing how the school would go about its work, did contribute to the bonding of boards and principals. The common purpose created, however, was sometimes a defensive one: the school united in frustration at the inadequacy of information or support, and sometimes united to defend what they had developed in good faith and that now seemed under threat. I do not think this threat was real in any tangible sense, but it was an environment of much uncertainty.

Another early experience that left mistrust between schools and government agencies in its wake came in mid-1990, when the Government stepped back from the status of the charter as an agreement in which a school would meet its (self-defined) charter goals in return for the Government providing the resources necessary for it to do so. Instead, the charter became what seemed a one-way undertaking of the board to the Minister of Education to meet those charter goals.[5] At the same time, the common principles such as equality of educational opportunity, which schools had used, or should have used, to frame their own undertakings, were no longer described as "paramount". Schools that had worked hard to come to terms with these and see what shape they should take in their own setting sometimes felt undermined, their effort to change given no value (Wylie, 1995b).

Training was offered to schools grouped together in geographic clusters in the hope that these clusters would continue voluntarily. Some tried, or morphed into networks dependent on personal relations. Such networks—usually between principals, sometimes between trustees—were invaluable to many. But, on the whole, the clusters that Picot taskforce member Peter Ramsay had expected schools would naturally form did not eventuate (Ramsay, 1991). The Ministry would go on to encourage schools to form clusters by using clusters as its form of funding for initiatives that required competitive applications. Schools did join others, usually for a limited time,

---

5   David Lange apparently thought the nature of the charter as a Crown–board agreement would bring educational funding difficulties to the fore (Butterworth & Butterworth, 1998, p. 162; McQueen, 1991).

and in different combinations for different initiatives. They clustered to access additional funding, staffing, professional development or equipment, particularly computer-based. They joined to take away something for their own use rather than to work together on shared issues or to advance knowledge by working collectively.

Such collective work had not been part of the birth of their new identity as self-managing schools. With the exception of the property committees, which involved just a few people, there were no longer any district structures or processes to bring people together to work to develop something. Fewer than a handful of community education forums were convened, and then in response to individual schools wanting to extend the years they catered for. These did no more than show that decisions that favoured one school at the expense of other schools could be made by the initiating school without hindrance (Mansell, 1993). By 1990, 10 percent of primary schools that catered for students up to Year 6 had applied to take students up to Year 8, a quick way to extend their roll numbers. Consultation did not mean joint work in a given geographic area to decide how best to meet student needs with existing school stock, how to make the most efficient use of government funding or what changes might best meet student needs.

Another important lesson that comes out of the birth of *Tomorrow's Schools* is that the first phase of any major policy development that changes the landscape in which people operate is not simply something that can be sloughed off, something that is just an initial messiness that goes no further. There has been an ongoing price to pay for both the way people were left to make their own way and the initial haste. Charters and policies could have been an invitation to a new way of working for schools, a closer look at what was working in their school for their students and what they needed to improve. Haste and lack of coherence and support tainted these new processes intended to support ongoing school development. For too many, they became things done largely to comply with rules that would eventually change, and therefore were not worth investing too much energy in.

# Fear of connections: The Lough report

The Department of Education, and then its successor on 1 October 1989, the Ministry of Education, was not in much shape to support the new self-management, even though its operational role was largely limited to charter approval, funding schools through the application of funding formulas and property management. Few schools' charters were not approved: most schools had no feedback at all on the substance of their charter. In her first annual report as the first Secretary for Education, Maris O'Rourke noted that "the complexity of reforming at the centre, while simultaneously restructuring all other educational institutions, was vastly underestimated" (Barrington, 1991, p. 57).

But only 6 months after the birth of the Ministry of Education, the Lough review of the implementation of *Tomorrow's Schools* was already suggesting its restructuring and downsizing. This review was chaired by Noel Lough, a former Treasury head. With him were an official from Treasury, David Greig, one from the State Services Commission, Paul Carpinter, a businessman, Donald Cowie, and Maris O'Rourke.

This review was much more rigid than the Picot taskforce in its belief that self-management of schools—with no ongoing national provision of common services, no ongoing relationships with the Ministry of Education, and no ongoing connections between policy and operations—was the key to improving educational outcomes. What school self-management needed to operate successfully, in the eyes of the Lough review, was better management frameworks and to employ administrative support. It suggested a planning and reporting framework that was akin to those used in government departments (while noting that small schools would need shorter versions of, for example, personnel plans). Operational people should develop a management framework. The Lough report recommended that principals should lead a short-term project that would devise models that schools could use, trial them, hold workshops on them, and provide advice—all within 6 months. On the one hand, schools could choose whether to use these models; on the other, the Lough report suggested that ERO could reduce its work by focusing on these school plans, with their outcomes and targets, rather than on the school charters.

The prime rationale given for this was to enable money to be redirected from ERO to the schools, to pay for the administration work that was now confronting schools and leading to inefficiency and ineffectiveness as principals undertook tasks that took them away from educational leadership. The Lough report—titled *Today's Schools*—also suggested cuts to the Ministry of Education, in part to redirect money to schools.

Shifting administration to schools had not proved cost-neutral, let alone cost-saving. A Coopers and Lybrand (1988) analysis of what it would cost to shift administration to schools in England had concluded that school self-management cost more to implement properly, not less. The Picot taskforce had this report. It also had an analysis of the future costs of school administration prepared for it by another large management consultancy, Ernst & Whinney (1987), which also pointed to the additional work self-management would mean at the school level. One wonders how, in the face of these two analyses, the optimistic Picot report identification of ongoing savings was calculated. It certainly left a damaging legacy. Such optimism that school self-management would be more efficient badly undercut the funding needed for the development of the government agencies to properly support school self-management.

There was a principals' taskforce, which produced booklets along the lines suggested by the Lough report, and all by September 1990. However, the models in these booklets did not end up as the framework for ERO reviews. ERO's initial framework emphasised joint work to support school self-review, with a hard edge focused on achievement:

> The Review Office is committed to developing a system in which reviewers work alongside governing boards, principals and teachers, helping them assess their own performance and their own systems for achieving their objectives. Reviewers will be particularly concerned with looking at the results, or effects of programmes and practices. A report will always focus on charter objectives and to what extent they are being achieved. (ERO, n.d.)

But ERO's role was fundamentally altered by the Lough report. Its staffing was substantially cut, which put an end to the thorough review process envisaged. That process would probably have provided the opportunity for some real developmental dialogue between reviewers and schools, focused on the effectiveness of school practices. Such a process would have helped to build capacity and a sense of shared responsibility in a district, counterbalancing the self-interest of schools that came with this version of school self-management.

A nationally uniform method of review which separated reviewers from school staff replaced this approach. It did pay some attention to school charters, but focused more on compliance with the new legislation, not on school development in relation to educational achievement. Lange had apparently seen ERO as a source of support for schools, but this could not happen with its now narrowed focus (Butterworth & Butterworth, 1998, p. 162).

The Lough review also pushed for the more rapid end of the advisory service so that schools could use the money to choose their own advice (Department of Education, 1990, p. 51). Fortunately, this last recommendation was not followed, allowing some continuity of individuals, and some nodes within the system for the sharing and development of knowledge, though this has not been unproblematic as advisory services (renamed 'support') competed for Ministry of Education contracts.

The Ministry of Education had established small district offices, mainly focused on the transition to *Tomorrow's Schools* and property. The Lough report was critical of this district operations role, saying that "location in the districts encourages educational institutions to continue to depend on the Ministry of Education for *operational* [emphasis in original] advice, which is counter to the intentions of the reforms" (Department of Education, 1990, p. 43). It recommended putting even more distance between the Ministry of Education and schools by reducing contact to a single national helpdesk (using phones and computers). Connections, ongoing relations and informal advice were not seen as part of an infrastructure that could support common learning and capacity development, but as a form of dependency, an undermining of school self-management. Schools were operational, the Ministry of Education was policy: they should be kept separate.

While this recommendation was not followed, it did circumscribe the role of the district offices. Ross Boyd, in his 1998 account of the changes to the Ministry of Education over the early years of the reforms, includes several graphic illustrations of what this felt like. From the Dunedin manager:

> Most of us had been helping, caring educationalists. We had to be told: National Operations provides information, we monitor compliance, we assist understanding, but we do not give them (principals) advice. We tell them: 'go back to your boards of trustees, outline the problem to them, and say let's sort this out ourselves.' Schools are self-managing. Respect this. (Boyd, 1998, pp. 160–161)

The Waikato manager showed an audience of principals graphically what this all meant by turning his back on them while explaining that in his role he now faced the Minister, not them. He put a hand back to his audience to indicate that help would continue, but the sector was no longer the main focus.

Money continued to be tight. The National Government that took office at the end of 1990 cut public spending, including to education, and this, in the context of the narrowing of the accountability of the core government service, led to further cutbacks to the Ministry's district role.

## Long-term shadows

Separation of what previously had been connected was key to the Picot report, tempered by some processes for joint work across different roles and responsibilities. Some of these processes survived the *Tomorrow's Schools* policy framework but were unravelled through a combination of the Lough review, funding difficulties and haste.

In retrospect, changing the government agencies at the same time as asking the schools to take on new roles seems a major mistake. At the very least, some continuation of support—which would of necessity involve joint work with people in schools—would have been advisable. One can understand why changing everything all at once was done from the point of view of those who had faith that school self-management would be the answer to the tensions in education, and that leaving the government department in place would preclude development. But many of those who were aware of the tensions in the education system, and who had used their positions to improve educational opportunities and achievement where they could, were in fact in the Department of Education, the inspectorate and the advisory service. Looking back from 1998, Lyall Perris thought that

> there is nothing inherent about New Zealand public service managers which makes them incapable of exercising initiative ... It is possible that Education Boards and the Department of Education could also have changed in this way, given the directions, incentives and freedoms to do so. They were not given the opportunity. (Perris, 1998, pp. 8–9)

Had ERO developed along the lines it originally heralded it may have provided the new engine for the kind of connective building of knowledge and shared responsibility that we needed and still need. But I suspect limits would have been found, since ERO itself was not connected in an ongoing way, or through any joint work, with the advisers or with the other government agencies at either the local or national levels.

So the birth of school self-management left two unfortunate and related legacies: the sense schools got that they were left on their own, and a Ministry of Education hobbled by hesitation about what guidance and advice it could give to schools. Its connections with schools were also much less systematic than formerly, so it was harder for it to bring into policy the operational knowledge necessary for policy to work well and have a chance of achieving its desired aims.

In the next chapter I explore what this meant for the first decade of a system based on school self-management, and how difficult it was for the Ministry of Education to respond to the unevenness between schools that became apparent, just as many parents and teachers had feared.

# Chapter 5

# A fragmented freedom: Schools in the 1990s

> We got distracted by the new sexy stuff: finance, property, staffing. Somewhere about 1992 or 1993, maybe even 1994, over the summer holidays, we were having a family barbeque. And my brother in law with no experience in education at all said to me, 'How is this *Tomorrow's Schools* going?' And I said, 'It's great', 'cause I loved it, I used to find the old system restrictive and I found the new one liberating. I said, 'I'm appointing staff, I'm moving budgets around, I've got property projects on the go, I'm busy as. It's the best thing that's ever happened.'
>
> 'Oh that's good,' he said. 'Are the teachers teaching any better, or, more importantly, are the kids learning any better?' I said without even thinking, 'I don't know, I haven't got a clue, I'm too busy running the place.' That answer rattled around in my head, and as I was going home I said to my wife, 'I should know, and I don't because we're doing this other stuff.' And I think we were all like that, or most of us.
>
> What gave us a systemic sort of wake-up call were the ERO reports of Mangere, Otara and the East Coast that said, there is systemic failure here.[1]

This chapter focuses on how schools learnt to think of themselves as separate enterprises in the 1990s, through their new responsibilities and the absence of interconnections. It charts how principals learnt to lead self-managing schools, and why it was that finance and property so dominated their attention in the formative years of *Tomorrow's Schools*. Competition for students to ensure school viability and reputation was a reality for schools, particularly in some areas, and contributed to schools' sense of themselves as separate enterprises. Boards of trustees also had their efforts focused on their own school.

Because the policy-oriented Ministry of Education did not have the role of active school support and challenge, it struggled when difficulties that

---

1  Interview, July 2011, with former primary principal.

schools were experiencing became public or schools sought its help. The centrality of school self-management in policy meant that any connections with schools had to be framed as indirect or temporary. New initiatives were therefore advanced by asking schools to cluster together to compete for additional funding. ERO increasingly raised concerns about uneven school quality through the 1990s, but it did not work with the Ministry to improve the support given to schools, making a virtue instead of its independences—separation—from the education sector and the other government agencies. It was a decade showing the increasing costs at a national level of the fragmentation of the schooling system that came with *Tomorrow's Schools*.

## Principals and their new role

Primary principals, whose role had expanded most, found it easiest to enjoy their new expanded role if:

- their schools were large enough to employ administrative support
- they did not have responsibility for a class (but only a third of primary principals were non-teaching principals)
- their boards had relevant expertise and also trusted their principal
- they had no difficulty finding and keeping good-quality staff (both teaching and support)
- their schools were located in areas with steady or growing student population (Wylie, 1997a).

In such fortunate circumstances, school self-management allowed decision making that could focus on improvement rather than cutting back or making do. The hours a principal worked were likely to be long—the average work week for primary principals jumped markedly over the first year of *Tomorrow's Schools* to around 56 hours. For principals whose schools had fortunate circumstances, there was reward for this additional effort.

But school self-management was sown on uneven ground. Many principals did not enjoy such a fortunate combination of circumstances, particularly those who led schools in poor or rural areas, often the schools serving Māori students, who were especially meant to benefit from *Tomorrow's Schools*.

In 1992 Peter Ramsay, who had served on the Picot taskforce, brought together some of the research on the initial years of *Tomorrow's Schools* in an article for the Principals' Federation journal. Overall, he thought that while the changes had often been accompanied by "shambles", at the cost of high principal workload, most principals and trustees were optimistic about *Tomorrow's Schools*. But he concluded with this warning:

> If research has one message to tell us, it is that the quality learning in our schools depends very much on the professional qualities of the school leaders. My greatest single fear is that as principals have moved away from their professionalism to an understanding of the mysteries of Apple Mac and of the accounting data bases, that we will lose the genuine thrust of the quality of New Zealand education. (Ramsay, 1992, p. 17)

The new management role of principals did erode the momentum that had been developing in the 1980s to make school cultures more collaborative and evaluative, and it would make it harder for principals to take a leading role in changes in teaching and learning—in other words, to what happens in classrooms. As one experienced principal put it:

> At the time *Tomorrow's Schools* came in, there had been a whole lot of young principals appointed in this area. That took quality practitioners out of the classroom, but the opportunity to help us lead pedagogical change was still there. After *Tomorrow's Schools* came in, we were reduced to systems implementation and compliance, and we lost our currency.[2]

Even for secondary principals, who had some prior familiarity with property, funding and staffing decision making, the new *Tomorrow's Schools* framework required significant learning—learning they had to largely initiate themselves. Here is one principal who was well connected before the reforms and confident, looking back on the early days:

> It was a miracle that people survived! We learnt by the seat of our pants. I had very little support from my board in the way of advice or guidance. The Ministry provided guidelines in 1990–91. They gave a bit of framework. But I also had ERO and Ministry people visiting me to help them develop manuals! I went to the Caldwell & Spinks courses,[3] and courses at the College of Education. I had pretty close relations with people in the advisory service there. The local principals' association was very important to me. I could meet colleagues and talk through issues.
>
> There was no support from the Ministry. The Ministry was policy, and schools became the operational arm. That was fine in theory compared with practice. It

---

2   Interview, June 2011, with highly experienced principal, active in principals' groups and support over the period, and some experience of working with the Ministry of Education.

3   Australians Brian Caldwell and Jim Spinks had written an enthusiastic book about self-managing schools that was influential in the early days of *Tomorrow's Schools*. They were funded by the Implementation Unit of the Department of Education to provide sessions on self-management around New Zealand.

assumed a lot in terms of people's understanding and national consistency—that did not occur. It meant there was a lot of reinvention of the wheel.[4]

There was not a complete lack of government-funded professional development and support for principals, but it was no longer systematic. Principals often needed to take the initiative, and their boards needed to be willing to fund additional costs (most professional development was not entirely free for the school or for the principal). The single systematic support was an important one. College of education advisory contracts included the provision of rural advisers to provide rural principals (who were frequently new to the role as well as more isolated) with ongoing and free support. This was often a lifeline for rural principals, and a connection to the wider world which was vital to their and their school's development. But it, too, was voluntary. Things could unravel in a school without an adviser knowing; or, if they knew, they had no authority they could use if a principal or board put up barriers.

Most professional development for principals was through contracts for which the colleges of education and other providers would tender. Evaluations of these contracts would often show variation in quality across providers. But no-one had responsibility to use this information to improve the capability of providers. There was no continuing programme of principal support (contracts for their support were not available every year, and there was no strategy for the supply of principals). The providers felt themselves to be in competition, and over time they became more reluctant to share knowledge or to work together, though evaluations and providers' own published research allowed some cross-institutional learning.

An evaluation of one of the earliest contracts for principals' professional development gives insight into the needs of principals and the shortcomings of the new approach. David Nightingale provided an account of the programmes provided by seven providers, mostly colleges of education, to 9 percent of the country's principals, within a 1992 contract "to provide professional development programmes to support principal development and curriculum leadership in primary and secondary schools". Most principals who participated were positive about their experiences. They welcomed the opportunity to focus on curriculum rather than administration. They also relished having some external expertise to look with them at their particular

---

4 Interview, June 2011, with an ex-principal, union representative and contributor to national curriculum and qualifications reviews, manager of an advisory service and provider of principal professional development.

school, something they felt they had lost when the inspectorate went and the advisory service was restructured (Nightingale, 1993). The more useful programmes had a more sound theoretical basis and development than others, which led them to emphasise this customised support to each school and to leave schools with processes they could develop further.

Nightingale was perturbed at the professional isolation of principals, and their lack of the essential support and challenge needed to keep developing. Two of the programmes had created school clusters, but these would need external assistance to continue, assistance that was not part of the *Tomorrow's Schools* infrastructure. It is telling that what he recommended to counter this isolation and its cost for ongoing school development did not try to build on any sharing between principals that had occurred in these professional development programmes. He did not try to recommend ways to keep schools connected, identifying common issues and trying out promising approaches to create common understanding and resources. This is not surprising: there was no systematic way for principals to work together. There was no longer any organisation or role that had the authority to bring principals together, to work with them on local issues, or to arrange for them to see in action a successful programme or approach in an area of student need they were struggling with.

Rather than joint work or systematic local connections, what Nightingale thought might be feasible was that principals should have one-on-one professional supervision from other principals, tertiary institutions, the Special Education Service (now separated from the Ministry) or private consultants. In the new era such support for their principal was something that was left up to an individual board to decide, to weigh its priority in the many competing calls on their school funding. Only in 1998 were professional standards for principals introduced and schools given a tagged sum of money to employ outside expertise for principal appraisal, if they chose not to do it themselves.

Few principals pursued one-on-one professional supervision. Most principals' access to some external review of their work was limited to the annual principal performance appraisal that boards were required to undertake, based on mutually agreed objectives. This appraisal has varied considerably in its quality and usefulness. It has been heavily reliant on who did the appraisal—which was often left up to the principal, if the board did not undertake the appraisal itself, and therefore dependent on who was locally available and known to the principal. Principals were also cautious about what they shared in the appraisal process, even with its two-fold purpose of identifying professional development needs as well as judging performance, because the results would or could go to the board.

Appraisals were kept within a school, so there was no opportunity to gain knowledge about area or national needs that could feed into a coherent programme for principal development. ERO could see them—it has the right to see anything within a school—but ERO's interest was in whether the appraisal process was occurring and was consistent with the school policy on appraisal, and that the school policy in turn was consistent with the National Administration Guidelines (known as the NAGs). If ERO looked at principal appraisals, it was in the context of the individual school or perhaps, later on, patterns of how appraisals were done. But ERO was not focused on the substance of those appraisals in terms of either individual school or system improvement.

Principals had to be registered teachers, but that was all. Boards usually employed external advice in their appointment of principals, but sometimes went for generic human resources advice. Advice they paid for was sometimes ignored, or not given the same weight as board views about the importance of, say, sporting interests or demonstration of a roll increase at the applicant's current school. Boards in some areas (particularly rural) often had to take who they could get, so schools with high needs would run through a series of first-time principals, many with no school management experience. Through the 1990s the complexity of the principal's role grew clearer, but so did the difficulty of finding sufficiently capable and energetic educators to fill that role.

# The demanding twins

Property and finance loomed large for principals from the early days. They were the two areas of school life that dominated board of trustees' work right through the 1990s. Most of the major initiatives primary schools reported in the NZCER national survey in 1993 were related to property, not teaching and learning. This is not surprising given the poor state of many schools' physical structures at the time of *Tomorrow's Schools*. I sometimes wonder what might have happened in these important formative years of school self-management if school property had been in better shape when boards and principals took over: if their energy could have been able to focus more on teaching and learning, on evaluating what was happening in classrooms, on developing parents' role in learning as well as in governance.

But school trustees' knowledge and confidence were more likely to include dealing with buildings and grounds, with many getting their own hands dirty in working bees. Sprucing up a school yielded a tangible sign that the board was now making its own decisions. It could also make a school look more attractive to prospective students and their parents. With operational funds and teaching positions decided by roll numbers, this was important. Just a few students more could also improve the principal's role markedly if they tipped the number over the threshold for the principal to become non-teaching, and therefore better able to balance the demands of school management with educational leadership.

Property management at the national level appeared to be no better in the new system, which was most evident in the lack of planning that left some Auckland schools overcrowded and some students with no local school available to them. A 1997 Deloitte report included in its criticisms of the Ministry's property management "an organisational culture which did not encourage joint problem solving, shared responsibility and consultation within the Ministry" (Deloitte Touche Tohmatsu, 1997, pp. 39–40, cited in Boyd, 1998). This report led to some reconnection of policy and operations (schools funding) within the national office, and in the property and operations work at the district level. Even so, in 2001 the Controller and Auditor-General thought that the Ministry risked another build up of deferred maintenance by schools (this had cost $500 million in the 1990s) if it did not regularly review board plans, monitor actual maintenance, and undertake or have boards undertake physical inspections (Controller and Auditor-General, 2001, pp. 17–19). Boards were not property experts; they needed "practical and timely advice and support" (ibid., p. 13).

Freedom to allocate operational funding certainly made principals and their boards more aware of costs, and increasingly frustrated by plans they could not afford and erosion of the funds they did receive. In 1990 only 20 percent of primary principals thought their government funding was inadequate. By 1996, after operational funding for schools had declined by around 10 percent in its purchasing power from 1989, 73 percent thought so. Though schools learned early caution around spending, 8 percent ended up in deficit for 3 years in a row over the 1991–94 period.

By 1995 locally raised funds—including the voluntary school fees (many of which were increased in the early days of *Tomorrow's Schools*), fundraising and, in secondary schools, fee-paying students from other countries— amounted to 8 percent of the total income received by primary schools and

12 percent by secondary schools. The number of foreign fee-paying students tripled between 1992 and 1997 and they became vital to the budgets of those secondary schools that could attract them.

The 1996 education budget recognised the shortfall and began a gradual increase in operational funding for schools. But it was not enough to make up for the underfunding of the initial years of *Tomorrow's Schools*, or to cover the increasing demands on school budgets. By 1999, 87 percent of primary principals thought their government funding was inadequate. Only a quarter of the primary trustees taking part in the 1999 NZCER national survey said their board had not faced financial issues or problems in the last 2 years. Administrative support staff numbers had had to increase, as did their skills, if the principal was not to spend hours on spreadsheets ('I didn't come into education to be an accountant' was a not infrequent comment from principals in the NZCER national surveys in the early 1990s), and dealing with the increased enquiries and correspondence from government agencies, businesses selling services and resources, and colleges of education and other providers of professional development, which came with schools making their own decisions.

The new curriculum statements that started rolling out in 1994 also brought new costs, as did the new secondary assessments. Computers became must-have: first for administration, then for teachers and students. Installing computers usually required cabling and rewiring. They needed maintenance and created additional printing costs. Many schools relied on internal knowledge and willingness to add new roles to existing responsibilities:

> In conversations with friends who are in business, they say they'd employ a computer systems person to do all this organisation, then they'd just dump it all on them. But we don't have those people here—we have people like the HoD [Head of Department] Maths, who's running around getting as much as he can done [setting up computer systems and keeping them running], but he's still got to be the HoD Maths. (Deputy Principal, secondary school, quoted in Murfitt, 1995, p. 193)

Each school was left to conduct its own analysis of needs and find its own deals. The result would be a patchwork of computer equipment and software that would make it difficult for schools to share resources or information between themselves, or with the Ministry of Education.

# Competition between schools

There was competition between schools before *Tomorrow's Schools*, but it was not relied upon to improve the system as it was in the 1990s. The nature and effect of competition between schools depend on the wider framework in which it occurs. Michael Fullan, one of the world's leading writers and advisers on school and system reform, describes the gains for learning that occur with "collaborative competition", whereby schools are part of the same district, supporting one another to improve, but also wanting to do as well as they individually can (Fullan, 2010, p. 38). In New Zealand, schools experienced competition in the absence of this shared purpose and work. They were not competing to improve student outcomes within a supportive environment, but to increase or maintain their own student numbers. Competition of this kind was not a useful policy lever. Instead, it often diverted school leaders and trustees from a focus on learning, and added obstacles to improvement for schools that found themselves at the bottom of the local competition, even though on an objective scale their quality of education could be as good—or had been as good—as those that fared better. Without some district oversight there will always be a school at the bottom of the local pile, a school that has more than its fair share of students who are harder to teach.

Some schools particularly suffered because of the cumulative effect of other schools' decisions. From 1991 to 1998 a school could decide its own enrolment criteria once it had the Ministry's agreement that it could impose limits to enrolments to avoid its roll going beyond its maximum (decided by the number of students its buildings could accommodate). The number of enrolment schemes leapt from 70 in 1992 to 422 in 1998. Such schemes could be used to signal desirability: here is a school that not everyone can access. It was a useful marketing tool. Schools could devise enrolment criteria that gave them the discretion to allow them to choose students who would bring the school credit, or be undemanding, or to simply take as many students as they could, without the limit of a geographic zone.

Although competition among schools was the desired outcome of student choice of schools, in reality some schools had the upper hand—as they do in most choice systems. Unless school choice is carefully framed and regulated, it does not make educational opportunities more equally available (Musset, 2012). By the mid-1990s the Ministry faced media stories and complaints about children not being able to enrol in their neighbourhood school. It was also seeing under-utilised space in schools, while being faced with increased costs to support the expanding schools. Legislation in 1998 set out a number of principles that schools' enrolment schemes had to comply with, and enrolment schemes now had to be agreed with the Ministry. The principles included the "desirability of students being able to attend a reasonably convenient school" and enabling "reasonable use of the existing network of schools" (Breakwell, 1999). But individual schools were still devising their own enrolment schemes and the Ministry was approving them individually. There was still no forum for discussion between schools in an area to arrive at criteria that seemed fair to all, as they had done before *Tomorrow's Schools*. This middle ground did not arise naturally now. The Ministry addressed the issue through guidelines for self-managing schools, but it was not able to group schools together. It could not challenge the supremacy of self-managing schools as the fulcrum on which policy had to pivot.

By the time the Ministry did provide this framing for school decisions, damage had been done that left a continuing legacy and increased costs the Ministry had to bear: money that could well have been better spent. Some schools, particularly in Auckland, had used the additional property and operational funding gained from taking students from what had been other schools' zones before *Tomorrow's Schools* to build up large schools with attractive resources. Schools serving low-income communities within striking distance of schools with a higher socio-economic intake that could offer better-resourced facilities (such as computers, sports grounds, music) suffered, particularly at the secondary level. There was also 'white flight' in some areas, with some evidence of increased ethnic polarisation. Some parents took note of the decile ratings assigned to schools for funding reasons, with somewhat higher per-student rates for low-decile schools serving low-income communities and higher proportions of Māori and Pasifika students. Low-decile schools were twice as likely as high-decile schools to have suffered significant roll decline between 1993 and 1998 (Minister of Education, 1999). By 1998, decile 1–2 secondary schools' average roll was 419 students, just over half the average roll of 789 in decile 9–10 secondary schools (Harker, 2000). That made it harder for the low-decile schools to provide sufficient curriculum options to cater for all their students, let alone the extracurricular activities that are so important in student development, such as the ability to mount school productions, run a choir or orchestra, or offer a range of sports.

Competition between schools for students could result in deliberate targeting. A school would find its roll dropping if another school offered students free bus transportation (in one notorious case, taxis were used). Competition could also involve a combination of location and publicity. Small country schools that were just beyond cities could erode the rolls of larger city schools that could not match the attraction for some parents of small schools, often with smaller classes and the promise of strong community.

Some schools were more adept at marketing themselves than others, through placing stories and photographs of student success or completed school amenities in local newspapers and presenting a smart façade to passers-by.

Secondary qualification rates did not improve in low-decile schools: instead, they slipped somewhat. Competition simply made it harder for the schools serving the students who were to be the particular beneficiaries of *Tomorrow's Schools* (Fiske & Ladd, 2000; Lauder & Hughes, 1999; Pearce & Gordon, 2005; Wylie, 1999). There was no coherence between this policy mechanism and one of the key aims of the reforms. The New Zealand experience with school competition has not resulted in gains in student learning for the system as a whole. This absence of gains is consistent with the cumulative international research evidence that competition between schools has, at very best in a few contexts, only limited and uneven positive effects. Competition is not reliable as a systemic means to improve education (Lubienski, 2009; Waslander, Pater, & van der Weide, 2010; Wylie, 1999, 2006).

As the Ministry realised by 1998, there were costs to this competition between schools for the system as a whole: it meant more money having to be spent on buildings rather than, for example, on directly improving school capability through well-designed professional development. There were also the costs of entrenching the *self* part of self-management, of putting one's own school first, as if each school was indeed separate from others, not part of a national, publicly funded system that has to be greater than the sum of its parts.

# Development of the governance role

School boards are legally Crown entities, falling within the same general legal framework as large organisations such as the Tertiary Education Commission or the Accident Compensation Corporation, whose boards comprise people appointed by the relevant government Minister. But trustees put the Ministry of Education and the Government at the bottom of their ranking of who they were responsible to (Wylie, 1999, p. 178). In most schools the partnership between parents and the teaching professionals was seen by trustees as complementary. Most trustees saw their role as supporting the school, making common cause with the professional leaders to gain what they needed in the way of funding and a good review from ERO. Their sense of who they were responsible to, like the professionals, was first to the students in the school, then to the school, the parents and the teachers.

Few trustees had taken on the role because they sought major change in their school. Most were also sceptical that they needed the 'logical completion' of self-management through bulk funding. Bulk funding was the term used in the early 1990s to refer to the Picot taskforce recommendation that to give boards total flexibility over their government funding, it should cover their staffing costs as well as other costs. Several working groups had looked at this proposal without finding a persuasive answer to the issues of inequity between schools and for teachers in different schools that appeared likely to ensue. These groups included the Schools Consultative Group 1992–1994, which brought together the sector organisations under the independent chair of Sir John Anderson, then CEO of the National Bank, to advise the Minister of Education on school funding and staffing.[5] Anderson's concluding individual advice to the Minister was that bulk funding could have perverse effects on the *Tomorrow's Schools* goal of improving the more equal provision of educational opportunities. He also thought there was considerable variability in the capability of school governance, and that "not all boards of trustees would be capable of managing such a system without considerable support" (Anderson, 1994, cited in Pearce, 1996, p. 252). Indeed, he thought that a much more pressing matter for government attention was sufficient resourcing and support for the new curriculum and qualifications frameworks.

Trustees largely did not want to take on a full employer role, which could erode the partnership they had with their school's professionals. They foresaw future difficulties if they could not afford the teachers they wanted to keep or attract. They also foresaw increasing differences between schools due to differences in the amount of funding schools could raise themselves, with schools in poorer areas losing ground because they could not offer comparable pay, or increase their teacher numbers.

Nonetheless, the National Governments that held power from 1990 to 1999 continued to adhere to their belief that this is what school self-management needed in order to be fully realised. The school boards' national organisation, the New Zealand School Trustees Association (NZSTA), was also initially

---

5   The Schools Consultative Group operated independently of the Ministry of Education, a deliberate political decision. But this meant that the Ministry's own stream of policy work, including a trial of bulk funding in volunteer schools, operated separately and was seen to be competing (Pearce, 1996). The Schools Consultative Group ended without consensus and Anderson made his own report. A Ministerial Reference Group was set up not long after, bringing sector group leaders and the Secretary of Education and senior managers together at regular intervals for discussion. Sometimes these discussions were fruitful; sometimes they were simply used by the Ministry to inform the sector of new policy, of decisions already made. There was no programme of ongoing joint work associated with them.

in favour of bulk funding as a logical completion of school self-management. But because the majority of trustees—who were the ones who would carry the actual responsibility in schools—were largely opposed, it had to shift from this stance to one supporting individual board choice of bulk funding.

Teacher opposition to bulk funding was strong (Grant, 2003). Trustee reluctance to take on even more responsibility, and their mistrust of the claims for the benefits of bulk funding, also played a significant part (Wylie, 1995b, pp. 71–72) in government decisions that led first to a trial and then to a series of non-mandatory offers. This approach culminated in a particularly attractive offer that was still only taken up by 24 percent of primary schools and 20 percent of secondary schools by the end of 1999, when the Labour Party returned to power and ended bulk funding.

The final bulk funding offer, called 'full funding' to remove it from the negative image bulk funding now had, funded teaching positions at the top of the national salary scale, not the average. That made it attractive to schools if they had a good portion of teachers who were in their early teaching years and not paid at the top of the salary scale. Schools could also opt out if they thought the full funding option was no longer to their advantage. It was only the additional funding they received that made bulk funding worthwhile for schools and allowed them to allocate resources in new ways. How sustainable this policy would have been long term if made mandatory for all schools is highly questionable. The likely pressure on the education budget would have squeezed even further the already limited funding for the connective and developmental infrastructure that is needed by schools.

The novelty of making decisions about the school was the main source of trustee satisfaction with their role in the early years. By 1999 their main sources of satisfaction shifted to seeing progress at the school, doing things for children, and positive relations at the school. What they disliked increasingly was the paperwork that came with their role.

Much of the support for the trustee role came from school staff, particularly the principal (legally a member of the school board). Initially, trustees also used NZSTA field officers serving local areas and funded by the Government. Despite protests from boards, funding for this vital role was cut by the Government in 1994 on the grounds that schools should choose their own support services. Once again, the principle of choice was elevated over considerations of the need for connection through services that could build a shared knowledge base and develop it further. Such a network had enabled the NZSTA to produce 'the black book', the practical handbook on school self-management and what schools were legally required to do that many found invaluable through the 1990s. When government funding for this support of school governance and management was cut, the NZSTA surveyed its members (88 percent of boards subscribed) to see if it could cover the cost of field officers and maintain a national network that offered local presence. It could not: the pressure on school funds led most boards to put their support for such a service at the end of the priority list.

The NZSTA did remain contracted by the Government to provide training, though not at a level that met all boards' needs, and to provide personnel and industrial relations advice. In 1997 close to 70 percent of boards had used the latter service and 80 percent wanted the NZSTA to have a similar contract to provide them with a general support service. The same proportion wanted one outcome of a forthcoming review of ERO to be that ERO would play a more supportive role for both school boards and their teaching staff (Wylie, 1997c). It was not just the professionals who had known a different structure of support and challenge who felt something was missing in their work. Those who governed schools also wanted more from those who had expertise, who could bring into their school useful knowledge and discussion.

Many principals found themselves undertaking much of the work of their board, and if there was a high turnover of trustees, having to start afresh every few years to educate them about their role, about the school, about education. Boards usually meant well but often did not have the capacity to provide all the challenge as well as support that school self-management in the New Zealand model was relying on them to provide. Their strength was in the quality of their links with the school community and their understanding of its needs, and in their networks and individual expertise. These networks were important to tap sources of funding or in-kind support for the new management responsibilities of schools, such as advice on financial management or solving employment issues.

Board–staff relations were usually good, but this could change quickly. Things could deteriorate if the board tried to manage rather than govern, or it lost faith in the principal; if there were personal relations that soured; or if there was an issue at the school that divided the school community. My estimate in 1999, drawing on the six NZCER national primary school surveys of the decade, was that around 12 to 15 percent of primary schools would be experiencing some problem in board–principal, board–staff or internal board relations at any given time. In some schools these problems persisted and contributed to school decline. In most cases individuals would leave the school to solve the difficulty if they could not get the advice and support that helped them work together, or that resolved acrimonious disputes such as personal grievances taken by the principal or a teacher. Beyond personal networks, boards' and principals' sources of advice were often the NZSTA and the unions and principals' associations. The Ministry of Education was usually not much help: it lacked the ongoing relationships. It was set up to fund schools, not to know or support them.

The one sanction the Ministry of Education had when a school's issues appeared to be beyond the capability of the school was to temporarily replace the body legally responsible for the school, the board of trustees, with a commissioner. Only five commissioners were appointed in 1992, the end of the reforms' first 4 years. The numbers then increased somewhat; for example, 11 commissioners were appointed in 1994 (Butterfield & Butterfield, 1998, p. 234), but replacement of a board remained a rare occurrence.

Some boards got to the point of asking the Ministry to replace them, though one of the people I spoke to in 2011 recalled a desperate board whose cry for help went unheeded:

> There was a very divisive person on the board who every time something happened that he didn't agree with, he threatened to get his lawyer. The board never ended up doing anything. It just couldn't do anything. And then there was a complication when this man started having an affair with the principal's wife and so it turned to animosity and hostility. They realised that left to themselves nothing was going to happen, so they went to the Ministry, and said, 'Look we're completely stuck. We need help, would you please appoint a commissioner.' And the Ministry said, 'No, because it's quite clear that if you can organise yourselves to come in an organised group like this you're not totally dysfunctional.'[6]

# Cautious reconnections across temporary bridges

It was clear to the Ministry of Education after the first 3 years of *Tomorrow's Schools* that a strict model of separating policy and operations was not feasible. It could not remain hands-off from schools. There were too many stories in the national media about "a growing number of problems between boards and their communities; there were boards in financial difficulties,

---

6 Interview, July 2011, with former secondary teacher, inspector, and ERO and Ministry of Education official.

schools under stress, principals not performing" (Boyd, 1998, p. 163).[7] The unions were also giving them evidence of school issues that were beyond the voluntary support that the unions and other groups were giving to individual schools that had sought their help.

In a telling indication of how little was understood at the centre about the value of ongoing connections, national Ministry of Education managers wondered "why have we got district staff if all the problems are coming in here?" (Boyd, 1998, p. 163). But they had not given their district staff the numbers or roles that would enable them to nip issues in the bud by working with schools. Some small strengthening in the district staff role occurred in the 1990s, but it was not until 1998 that they were given some limited discretionary funding which they could allocate more quickly to schools under the Schools Support project. One of the prime tools of the inspectorate was found to be useful again, albeit much reduced in scope and tending to be focused on issues of school management rather than curriculum or pedagogy.

Support for schools that had run into difficulty began as a national office project in 1994, but not as a new policy. Funding for this work was not included in the Ministry of Education baseline budget until the 1999/2000 financial year. Schools Support began with a small number of "Safety Net" interventions, involving fewer than 30 schools by 1996. These were intended to run for a limited time only: to be interventions, not connections. Nonetheless, a report on the Ministry's management capability, commissioned by the State Services Commission in 1996, urged it "not to get into the direct provision of advice and support (unless it is essentially explaining the consequences of policy change to providers)", and to continue to contract the role of advice and support (Laking, 1996, p. 83, cited in Boyd, 1998, p. 166).

This caution seems to be partly because advice and support were perceived as tempting officials into action that might undermine school self-management. Warning was given against "muddling the provision of support with the power of coercion" (Boyd, 1998, pp. 165–166). It was as if it was inconceivable for the Ministry of Education to work together with schools, to make a middle ground, even though it was the government department ultimately responsible for national educational quality and performance. The principle of school self-management was more important. Separation had to be preserved. Yet

---

7   Ross Boyd's paper offers a candid look at the way the Ministry of Education developed and worked in the 1990s, including experiences and observations from other Ministry employees. I don't know of any subsequent account of changes in the Ministry as an organisation, and suspect that such an open and independent account is unlikely to appear in the now much more hierarchical and overly risk-sensitive culture of the Ministry and the wider public sector.

it is separation of the government agencies and schools, the absence of the middle ground and shared responsibility, that made and still makes it difficult to harness and use all the knowledge and actions needed to keep developing the quality of New Zealand education. Somewhat ironically, this same report noted the difficulty the Ministry had in leading policy because of the number of separate government education agencies and the ambiguity of its responsibility.

So Schools Support was not launched with the aim of providing a permanent connection between schools and the Ministry of Education. The Ministry was not offering in-kind or in-house support. Formally, its role was more of a broker, though in fact individual officials with relevant expertise did find principals and boards looking to them for guidance. There were four levels of action, and most occurred at the lowest level. "Informal action", as this lowest level was named, was a potentially creative response to the new environment. Schools Support at the national level, under Mary Sinclair, had brought the sector groups—the unions, the Principals' Federation, the Intermediate Schools Association and the School Trustees Association—into an External Reference Group: a way to build some knowledge together as well as have the groups' support. This national group was echoed in the Ministry's regions with regular meetings between the Ministry and representatives of both education and community organisations "to discuss what is happening in schools in that region". The sector groups also provided support for individual schools that came into the Schools Support ambit, using their different roles and knowledge to work with school leaders and trustees to sort out their problems.

Some of this action had already been occurring, with the sector groups taking the initiative when problems were raised with them. Much of the effectiveness of this approach depended on local capacity and expertise, and the quality of relationships and trust. The joint work was limited to work with the individual schools that raised their hands for help or that came to notice. It was a safety net for individual schools only. In the separated world, it was difficult to develop these local networks into something more strategic, which could have identified issues occurring across the area's schools and planned ways to share and build knowledge and connections to improve the schools' capability as a whole—to prevent rather than react.

Schools Support was a separate project within the Ministry, with no remit to develop anything formally that could be part of all schools' operating environment. It was only for some schools. The need for more resourcing than the standard formulas could supply individual schools may have been part of this cordoning off. It is interesting to see how Howard Fancy, Secretary for Education from 1996 to 2006, felt the need to explain that this non-formulaic funding of individual schools was limited:

> School support is not a soft way to get extra resources … I see it as quite a legitimate concern to ensure that additional spending is being used to develop capability, to improve educational outcomes and to minimise the prospects of a problem re-occurring. Not to require such disciplines would effectively penalise the 90% of schools that manage without school support. (Fancy, 2000, p. 19)

Additional funding was to be temporary and cast in a contract form, with specified sums for specified goals. These goals were within projects identified and 'owned' by the school and its board, which contributed some of its own funds and management of the project. Project participation was intended to leave the school in sufficient shape to carry on like other schools: largely on its own.

# Safety-net intervention

By late October 2000, 242 schools, around 9 percent of the country's schools, had experienced a 'safety-net' intervention, many lasting just over a year but some lasting several years or longer. Most of these interventions were the low-key "informal action". The process was more demanding for schools with complex issues. Funding plans on which the schools worked with liaison officers in the regional Ministry office needed multiple sign-off within the national Ministry office. Some business plans involving substantial expenditure also went to Treasury and the Minister for Education. Processes of negotiation and approval often took longer than those in the schools and the Ministry liaison officers working with them thought was warranted. Board chairs found themselves being the squeaky wheel with the national office to try to get faster decisions.

Expertise that schools needed was also not always readily available, able to be contracted, or able to grasp quickly the complexity of schools. This was particularly true for schools whose very existence was on the line. "They lack the knowledge of the education sector so we have to teach them as we go each time," said one official of the contractors they had had to find to prepare and see through business cases (McCauley & Roddick, 2002, p. 73). One wonders whether it would have been more efficient and cost-effective for the Ministry to use the knowledge it had and work directly with the schools. Such direct work would also have enabled an accumulating knowledge base available to schools.

The system for getting support was not quick or straightforward. Indeed, it lacked the 'flexibility' that was one of the Picot keywords for the promise of the new system. District staff were not in a position to maintain a watching brief on the schools in their area. They were not going into schools on a regular basis, maintaining connections. Ministry staff with different roles were not meeting regularly to pool their knowledge. It was harder for them to connect schools with each other so that one school could learn from another. This was not just because of the competitive edge to school relations. The local Ministry officials who were going into schools were all too often going into schools with marked problems, not those that were flourishing, so they may well not have had the knowledge base needed to connect schools productively. Too much would depend on the personal networks that Schools Support liaison officers, generally former principals, brought with them to the role.

Ministry identification of schools that might need Schools Support appears to have been an *ad hoc* process. A sequence of ERO reviews that were supplementary (more frequent than the regular 3-year cycle) was a prime trigger. Large roll declines and budget deficits, and major concerns about a principal's leadership, were also major triggers. Schools themselves were hesitant to put up their hand for help: in the self-managing schools model, seeking help could be seen as an admission of failure. Principals would wonder how this would look if they were applying to another school board for a job, because the help was named, not part of an ongoing relationship. And not unlike the State Services Commission, albeit from the perspective of schools now used to doing their own thing, they also feared that inviting the Ministry of Education into the school would result in it wanting to be "prescriptive and controlling" (McCauley & Roddick, 2002, p. 70).

Ministry officials found themselves walking a fine line in seeking change in schools that had to make their own decisions. Yet when things had got bad, schools often wanted the Ministry to be "more assertive", more initiating of action that could speed things up and avoid the disharmony and stress often experienced in schools that struck difficulty. Schools could feel helpless:

> The school was in crisis such a long time. ERO and the Ministry knew, and no one did anything. Staff morale was low, teachers were leaving. I wasn't sleeping. No one knew where to get help, and staff were vulnerable. Parents went to the Board and the Ministry wanting help. The Ministry must've had a huge file on the school. I think they'd been wondering when to intervene. (McCauley & Roddick, 2002, p. 15)

Thus problems were likely to have deepened by the time schools did get some support, and to cost both the schools and the Ministry more time and money to work through than if there had been ongoing relations between them. Hidden costs included distraction and loss of energy. Teaching and learning were affected by the attention that was needed to resolve issues of school management and governance, or by roll declines that were sometimes due to these same issues but sometimes to the now hands-off approach to school organisation and enrolments in a given area and the resulting competition between schools.

There were 15 Schools Support liaison officers by mid-2000, some working part time. Liaison officers could be working with up to 20 schools at any one time, some of which needed much more attention than others. Along with other regional staff, they were also responsible for communicating national policy changes to schools, which sometimes took priority over their work with individual schools, and later, clusters. I wonder whether there would have been more schools identified as needing Schools Support had the process been more systematic. Even so, there was probably not the capacity to cater for more work with individual schools, possibly one reason for the greater emphasis that began to go on schooling improvement clusters. Indeed, by 2001 need was outstripping Ministry capacity, in terms of both the number of people and the sharing of knowledge between the national and regional offices so that individuals were not having to re-invent the wheel or find themselves unaware of what another level of the Ministry of Education had agreed with a school or cluster.

# Holes in the safety nets

In the new contractual environment, support was often framed formally. It had to be delimited in relation to a specified plan of action and outcomes, and regular milestone reports made. This gave an additional layer of work to the Ministry of Education, schools and those contracted to provide support. Milestones too often seemed to take priority because they were affixed to set dates. The Ministry saw the milestone reporting as having a double value. The Schools Support project needed the reports in a certain format to give both it and the wider Ministry the information (or reassurance) it needed for its own quality assurance processes. But regular reporting against goals and targets should also develop individual school capacity for self-review. Evaluating its own progress against the goals in the funding agreement would build on the needs analysis done at the start (with help) to gain the Ministry's support.

Self-review meant standing back and asking whether something was making a positive difference and how it could be developed further. It meant having information about what you were doing so you could make that assessment. It meant looking at how coherent the work was: whether, say, new computer equipment was being used for the curriculum areas where performance was of most concern, and whether funding priorities matched curriculum priorities. But by now many schools associated anything the Ministry required them to do with legal requirements, with 'compliance' rather than their own development, particularly if it had to be done by a given time. They were also careful about what they shared on paper, and what they specified. Milestones could not have the developmental value for schools that the Ministry intended.

Ministry of Education support for schools as a time-limited 'intervention' also struck snags. By 2001 "Ministry respondents acknowledged that there was an element of naiveté in early expectations that individual Schools Support projects would be completed within three years" (McCauley & Roddick, 2002, p. 58). Both schools and the Ministry officials working in Schools Support thought that their relationship should be ongoing after the funding agreement came to an end, the connections maintained so that the school continued to have a source of support and advice. Once they were spending time in schools, Ministry people could see that substantial changes were often needed, changes that were not realistic for the existing capability and knowledge in these schools. Some could also see that new knowledge was needed for schools to make progress.

There was talk of long-term partnerships "supporting collaborative initiatives that develop local education infrastructure" (McCauley & Roddick, 2002, p. 59). In the new era, here was some realisation of the importance of a middle ground on which schools and the Ministry could meet and work together. But the means for building the local education infrastructure would be hampered by the centrality of school self-management and its entrenchment in the first decade of *Tomorrow's Schools*. Any sustainable infrastructure would need a recasting of roles and responsibilities, and shared work that went beyond putting together cases for funding.

# Schooling improvement: Attempting some reconnection

As the Ministry of Education worked more with schools in difficulty, and as ERO identified areas where there were more than the usual proportion of schools struggling to meet student need or getting tangled in the requirements of school self-management, there was an expansion of the Schools Support project into "preventative" schooling improvement, based on grouping schools into (mainly) geographic clusters. By 2001 around 10 percent of schools were in a Schooling Improvement cluster, working with 14 Schools Support staff, members of a national office team stationed in local Ministry offices. There was some overlap between the two forms of Ministry support for schools, so probably around 15 percent of schools would have been involved in one or both at the same time, and probably around 20 percent of all schools had had some support through the Schools Support project up to 2001. Not all of the schools in the Schooling Improvement clusters were struggling or distracted by issues of management and governance; some were included in a cluster simply because they were located in the area. Cluster membership and ongoing commitment were voluntary. The attraction was additional resourcing and the opportunity to interact with outside expertise and other schools.

Why clusters? There seems to have been some awareness of the costs that could accrue to schools left on their own. The Ministry had to keep its distance in the overall policy framework and was in no position to work consistently with individual schools. Some of the first clusters arose from ERO area reviews, which indicated common issues. There would presumably be economies of scale in hiring people to work on those issues across a number of schools. If the schools could be brought closer together, through making decisions together and shared professional development, they would form peer relations.

But the cluster approach would prove patchy, again dependent on the expertise that was locally available, the use made of it and, even more, the composition of the cluster. What it also highlighted was the need for better processes to share the knowledge that schools needed in order to change their practices, and new approaches to professional development.

It often took a year or two for these clusters to reach the first stage of developing a plan. Inter-school competition for students interfered with the openness and trust needed for real sharing (McCauley & Roddick, 2002, p. 32). Also, clusters were usually governed by the schools' principals. The principal is where 'the buck stops' in a school. Cluster meetings often had at least one principal missing as one of the group dealt with something more urgent, often issues of student welfare or behaviour, but also with things going awry with the school's buildings or systems: the property and finance twins.

So cluster understanding and plans often had to be revisited or renegotiated. Cluster work could feel more like 'talk' than 'walk'. There was little a cluster could do if one of its members made empty promises and then gradually faded from involvement.

In the *Tomorrow's Schools* model the board of trustees of a school is the body that is legally responsible for the school. ERO reports are addressed to the school board, as is much of the Ministry correspondence. The Ministry's Schooling Improvement model included trustees—and sometimes other groups with a stake in the schools—as 'partners'. This was particularly important at the start of cluster work. But it was not a simple matter for everyone to be able to get in the same room, physically or conceptually. Trustees had paid work and family commitments, for example. Where the cluster arose from one of the highly critical ERO area reviews, there was often considerable anger and pain to work through before there was even the glint of a preparedness to trust the Ministry. For iwi groups and others, issues relating to their children's quality of education were not solely the responsibility of the schools involved. The Ministry also bore responsibility. Iwi groups sought greater involvement, and a number of innovative long-term iwi–Ministry partnerships were formed.

None of the Schooling Improvement clusters were formed in middle-class or wealthy communities. Low-income communities, where Māori and Pasifika students were most concentrated, were the clusters' domain.[8] Schooling Improvement clusters were the Ministry's prime response in the mid- to late 1990s to the inequalities of educational opportunity that had fuelled the impetus for the *Tomorrow's Schools* reforms, and which continued—and, indeed, often appeared to worsen—when schools had been 'freed' to self-manage.

Self-management was proving problematic for schools in low-income areas, small schools, and rural schools: these were over-represented among the schools that had difficulty staying in ERO's regular review cycle. They were also the schools "where the risk of teacher shortage is constant" (Ministry of Education, 1996), as was the case in the new kura kaupapa Māori. They were the schools that found it more difficult to attract experienced principals, and to find the knowledge and skills needed for a board of trustees. Low-

---

8   Here is the list of Schooling Improvement clusters in 2001: Far North (78 schools), Gisborne (41), SEMO [Mangere Otara] (32), Tuwharetoa (23), East Coast (19), AIMHI [secondary schools in South Auckland and one in Porirua] (9), Paerangi [Māori boarding schools] (6), ICAN [a Porirua cluster] (8), the SMAD [(Schools Making a Difference) cluster in Christchurch] (7), West Coast (5), Wairoa West (5), Flaxmere (5), Waiau (2), Ohai (3), Taita (2), Kelston Van Asch (2).

decile schools had more trouble attracting and keeping teachers. They had to re-advertise positions more often, and more often had to employ overseas-trained teachers, who sometimes brought more rigid approaches with them that did not sit well with New Zealand students.[9] They also employed beginning teachers more often, but then lost them more often to other schools with fewer demands, once they had completed their 2 years and gained the certification they needed from the school's principal to become fully registered.

Constant staff changes, and staff starting with less experience, made it more difficult for many of these schools to build and sustain strong school cultures and systems that shared knowledge among teachers, and that provided the learning organisations schools need to be if they are to make a positive difference to student learning. There were some notable exceptions, but an education system needs to produce more than exceptions if it is to produce overall improvements in learning and achievement.

The exceptions included clusters where there was a deliberate effort to undertake collective knowledge building of how better to improve learning opportunities and outcomes for disadvantaged groups. Joint work in schools over time brought researchers and professional developers together with educators and the Ministry, and sometimes boards, so that what came out of one phase of work could be used to build the next phase of work. This iterative joint work and ongoing connections not only provided knowledge

---

9 Nationally, teacher numbers were too low to adequately staff all primary schools from the mid- to late 1990s. This was due to a combination of improved teacher:student ratios and large increases in the number of young children, partly due to increased migration to New Zealand which the Ministry's predictions had not been able to encompass. Primary school rolls rose 10 percent overall in the 1990s. Finding enough teachers to staff their school was beyond the ability of many schools, though it hit the low-decile and rural schools hardest. Teacher shortages also attracted newspaper headlines. Teaching supply was not originally included in the Ministry's programme, such was the faith in the new freedoms granted colleges of education to cater for as many students as they wished, and in school self-management.

The difficulties schools were having led to the restoration of teaching supply as a central government function in 1995/96, with a multi-pronged approach that: gave additional money to teachers taking positions in remote areas, all decile 1 schools, and low-decile schools in the north and east of the North Island; increased the number of students that institutions could take for initial teacher education; extended eligibility for this funding of new places to a wider number of institutions (increasing the competition between them); and encouraged 'compressed' courses for university graduates. Waivers on work permits for teachers recruited from overseas were introduced. Included in the Ministry's 1996 outline of the measures that would improve teacher supply were recent increases in secondary teacher pay, and slowing the introduction of new curriculum—an acknowledgement of the workload in schools.

in ways that changed school practice for the better, but also fed into some policy changes. The SEMO and AIMHI clusters would prove particularly fruitful (Annan, 2007; Annan, Fa'amoe-Timoteo, Carpenter, Hucker, & Warren, 2002; Hill & Hawk, 2003; McNaughton, 2011). Both these clusters were prompted by critical ERO reviews.

## ERO: The watchdog and scold

In the early days of *Tomorrow's Schools*, ERO reviews were focused on school compliance with legislation, through assurance audits that were largely paper based, checking school policies and paper trails. ERO shifted to 'effectiveness' reviews in late 1993, asking schools to demonstrate the difference they had made to their students' learning in terms of the school's expectations. ERO had no formal relationship with the schools. It relied on the publication of its reports and schools' knowledge that these would be available to community and media scrutiny. "Moral suasion and the creation of public pressure" were its main tools to improve schools (Ellis, 1996, p. 11).

By 1994 the Chief Review Officer during the 1990s, Judith Aitken, felt in a position to provide some sharp assessments of the *Tomorrow's Schools* system. Board ignorance of legal obligations and changes in national policy were "surprisingly common" (ERO, 1994, p. 7). There was an "extremely wide" variation in the quality of curriculum that schools provided (p. 9). Few schools were using student achievement and engagement information to continuously monitor and improve their programmes. But then, she noted, "there are only very limited support and advisory services available to principals and teachers interested in systematic assessment of achievement" (p. 9), and few reliable qualitative and quantitative assessments nationally available.

There were "repeated demands for the Office to provide more advice to schools" (p. 13). The Chief Review Officer made it clear that she thought that schools were not making sufficient use of ERO's national evaluative reports or their own ERO reviews. They were not reflecting on the reasons for the questions they were asked during the course of a review, from "an external perspective on a school from a wide knowledge base of the comparative performance of principals, teachers and schools as a whole" (p. 13). But, as principals thought (Wylie, 1997b), and an ERO reviewer at the time noted, the expertise of ERO reviewers was variable:

> There was a significant unevenness in the staff. I felt some of us could actually have a serious conversation with a principal or an HOD or a syndicate leader which was

> a conversation of educational peers, and it worked *because* it was a conversation of educational peers. The sort of conversation I'm thinking of is: Look Sarah, I think there's some great work going on in this syndicate but actually have you thought about X, Y, Z, Q? You don't think that would work? Tell me more about that? Why did you think that wouldn't work? Well actually I could connect you. I'm pretty sure if I rang a couple of people for you and got them to ring you—you know there's a productive conversation worth having. These people are doing something in this line that I think would work here.
>
> As opposed to 'it's for us to know and you to find out' kind of low grade evaluation that some of my colleagues specialised in. It was because they actually didn't have a lot of educational experience or depth themselves before they went into that role.[10]

Aitken thought that school managers could improve the quality of advice they received from others by taking a contractual approach: specifying outcomes and the price they were prepared to pay. Her comments in 1994 include concerns about the quality of education for Māori, and issues relating to the quality of governance that affect the quality of education in "less affluent areas". Shortages of te reo Māori-speaking teacher graduates are noted. But the self-managing schools framework itself is unchallenged, with one marked exception. There were too many poorly performing rural schools, with pockets on the East Coast, the West Coast and north of Auckland:

> These communities need assistance to upgrade radically the quality of education available to their children … Ways must be found, in partnership with State agencies, to establish more effective schools in many rural areas. It is doubtful whether, on its own, a simple increase in operating funds will be sufficient to effect positive improvements in areas where economic growth is likely to be very sluggish and such problems are endemic. (ERO, 1994, p. 18)

Two years later, with no sign of any action on the Ministry of Education's part (it was still in the early stages of developing Schools Support, working only with individual schools on limited project funding and taking care not to cross the self-managing schools boundary), ERO resorted to using a megaphone to reach the Ministry and the education sector. Media coverage of its first report on an area where it saw systemic failure certainly jolted the Ministry into action. ERO's first such report was not, however, on these rural pockets. It was on Mangere–Otara: that area of urban poverty whose disadvantage had only deepened with the economic reforms of the 1980s, followed by the welfare cuts in the early 1990s. Current students in Mangere–Otara included those whose parents had been the young people Peter Ramsay and colleagues

---

10 Interview, July 2011, with former principal, ERO reviewer, Ministry official and consultant.

wrote about in 1981, saying it was already too late for them to have had the education they needed.

## *Tomorrow's Schools*: Still too late?

The test of the new system was surely whether it could make a better fist than the previous system of improving student engagement and achievement in Mangere–Otara, and in other areas of high poverty or with a history of finding little purpose in education. The 1996 ERO report on Mangere–Otara schools indicated that school self-management was not making a positive difference. ERO's measure was the building block of the new system: each school on its own. By ERO criteria, only seven of the 45 schools serving this mainly very poor area were performing effectively. These seven effective schools did not include Nga Tapuwae, the secondary school where David Lange as the Minister of Education had been powerless to intervene, and whose board's resistance to any involvement by the Department of Education had led to the provision in the new era for boards to be replaced by a commissioner. Nga Tapuwae, along with two other secondary schools and one primary school in the area, were now receiving safety-net support from the Ministry.

ERO made a set of strongly worded recommendations that would have resulted in more connection between the schools and the Ministry. But the form of connection it recommended would not have generated new knowledge and understanding through joint work between partners sharing responsibility. It was consistent with the more segmented approach of the 1990s. ERO recommended connection through the hierarchical form of a tight contract, reviewed and renegotiated annually with each school.

ERO did note that in terms of improving their work, the schools were not well served in terms of advice, training, services such as principal appraisal, or support, describing these in the new public sector language as a "market vacuum". Infrastructure for the area was recommended, along the lines of the area resource that Peter Ramsay and colleagues had suggested. But in the new regime ERO could conceive only of the area resource as a broker of services, not a provider, and not the joint developer of knowledge to better serve the area's students that had been recommended in *Tomorrow May Be Too Late* (Ramsay et al., 1981). Central funding for this area resource was to be time limited. In a few years it should largely pay its own way, through schools using their operational funding to buy its services. Where schools continued to perform poorly, ERO recommended that they be required to "purchase an appropriate package of development or restructuring services" (ERO, 1996, p. 16).

Although the ERO report makes much of the fact that some schools in these disadvantaged areas had teachers who had "the margins of skill necessary to bring educational opportunities and outcomes for their students closer to that of the national average" (ERO, 1996, p. 26), there is no suggestion that these schools could be sources of sharing knowledge. There is no sense in the ERO report of the value of collective work over time, within and across schools, enlisting other expertise as well, to build and share the knowledge needed to make the schools more engaging and productive for students and teachers alike. ERO's evaluation and recommendations confined themselves to the underlying assumptions of *Tomorrow's Schools*, which positioned schools as best performing when operating separately.

Growing competition for students had led primary schools in the area to recapitate (extending the year levels they catered for), with knock-on effects as the intermediate schools, losing some of their student base, extended into middle schools. ERO thought these changes were more about preserving school funding and staffing than about improving the quality of education. This was probably true in most cases, though not for the innovative Clover Park middle school, which offered a bilingual programme that was producing notable improvements in Māori school engagement and achievement. ERO was certainly right when it noted that "there appears to have been little consideration of the likely impact of middle schools on the resource base and curriculum structure of local secondary schools" (ERO, 1996, p. 18). But it did not depart from the centrality of school self-management. It did not recommend collective work on planning for the area to make the best use of the government funding available.

The lack of infrastructure that could improve education in Mangere–Otara had not gone unnoticed by its principals. Ironically, just as the ERO report came out, the Otara Principals' Association, working with Charmaine Pountney (then teaching a course on school leadership at the University of Auckland, which some of the area's principals attended), had put in a bid for one of the Ministry of Education's management development contracts:

> We decided that what the area needed was innovative centres of educational excellence, not imitations of existing mediocre practice elsewhere. We wanted, for instance, to set up a centre for language education and research, and a centre for technology education, involving tertiary research staff and business sponsors as well as the best teachers available. We had all kinds of exciting ideas, and a wide network of talented people available to help … The Ministry of Education declined our proposal, awarding funding instead to a Hamilton human resources firm for work with some Waikato schools, and spent several months struggling to respond to ERO's report. (Pountney, 2000, p. 130)

I wonder whether the section of the Ministry of Education that decided this contract was narrowly focused on management, a generic approach that a human resources firm could supply. But schools need more than generic approaches. Pountney suggests that some of the ideas in the Otara principals' proposal resurfaced when a different section of the Ministry, the Schools Support team, put together a response that did in fact go much further in situating school self-management within a more developmental frame than ERO had recommended.[11]

ERO's report sparked anger, defensiveness and pain—among the community as well as the schools. But it also spurred discussion and then a commitment by the Ministry to work with the schools and community. Out of the hurt came a set of initiatives under the umbrella Strengthening Education in Mangere and Otara (SEMO), explicitly casting this as a "three way partnership". At the start, "the Ministry's capacity to interact in educational discussions with representatives from schools and communities was minimal ... building educational relationships was extremely difficult" (Annan et al., 2002, p. 64). But time and additional resourcing made possible the joint work and ongoing connections that—with much dedication to continued learning from the inquiries undertaken through joint work—did result in some real changes for student engagement and achievement in schools in these clusters.

## Missing connections

The SEMO experience shows just how vital for school development are interconnections focused on joint work and knowledge building, and how limited is any national policy that relies on self-managed schools left to themselves. Even so, SEMO was limited. It lacked the authority to take an area-wide view of teacher and school supply, or to reduce some of the costs of competition between schools. Sir John Anderson was already warning the Government in 1994 of systemic issues arising from the *Tomorrow's Schools* reforms that were creating "a degree of inertia and uncertainty in schools" (Anderson, 1994, p. 244) and that were impeding progress and the achievement of equality of educational opportunity. He did not think the latter was possible if schools remained stand-alone competitive units. He noted that New Zealand was unique in the OECD countries in having no intermediary structures between schools and the centre, and suggested that

---

11 She also suggests that the ERO recommendations were similar to the Otara group's proposals, but I cannot see that.

"many functions such as property management, equity funding, sharing of best practice, risk management and dispute resolution could well be managed in regional support units" (Anderson, 1994, p. 244).

But the 1990s saw school self-management entrenched as stand-alone, rather than broadened through also working collectively. It was difficult for the Ministry to envisage ongoing relationships with individual schools because it was first and foremost set up as a policy ministry, its primary relationship being with the Minister. It was also operating within a public sector model that separated policy and operations and preferred to specify what it funded through contracts, not models of shared responsibility and ongoing joint work. Its own organisation was becoming more siloed, and it lacked effective ongoing connections with the other government education agencies. Anderson noted "confusion and chaos" in schools as a result of "the existence of over five central bureaucracies with no overall effective co-ordination of the various policy strands" (Anderson, 1994, p. 244).

The Ministry did seek to encourage schools to work together, through the lever of cluster funding. Such funding was attached to particular policies or support, such as the sharing of administrative staff in rural schools or using computers in schools. Evaluation after evaluation of each new policy clustering would show that schools appreciated the additional resources or professional development clustering had enabled them to access. But often what was gained stayed inside individual schools. Many clusters dissolved once their funding ceased for a given policy initiative: this mechanism was not sufficient on its own to connect schools in collective support.

Some clusters built sufficient trust over time to keep going. For example, some of the rural school administrative support clusters went on to develop cases for new cluster initiatives they were offered, such as ICT or the literacy and numeracy innovative funding pools. They formed (often useful) networks and in some cases produced new knowledge to improve learning. But many schools joined clusters simply to access additional resources. Some clusters were cosy clubs, or sessions of superficial sharing. There was no clear authority in them that could provide the combination of challenge and support that leads to change, and no systemic processes to share the new knowledge further. Clusters could not resolve the issue of how best to meet the needs of an area's students, free of any loyalty to a particular school. Schools that felt in direct competition with each other were unlikely to form a cluster together.

There were, as always, exceptions that grew from existing strong ties and joint work. The West Auckland Principals' Association co-ordinated professional development and support for their schools, emphasising the importance of ongoing learning and strong collective school cultures. Dunedin secondary principals collaborated to provide a programme for students with behavioural issues so that one school did not end up with all the students who were hardest to teach. But clusters that endured, that had their own momentum over and above any Ministry funding, were rare.

The interconnecting roles that inspectors and other officials had played were not able to be filled by individuals who were, in any case, largely preoccupied with the new responsibilities of self-management, focused on their own school. The system became reliant on sporadic professional development funded by the Ministry, individual contacts and sector organisations. Primary teachers missed the opportunities they had had to learn more by visiting other schools. Subject associations gave secondary teachers some links across schools, though the associations were not as strong as they had been. Principals were reliant on personal networks built through their previous colleagues, sharing professional development, or conversations at local principals' associations meetings or national conferences. The education unions, NZEI and PPTA, NZSTA and the Principals' Federation, all established help-lines. Principals and teachers volunteered their expertise to provide help through their organisations, giving time to support their peers who reached the limits of their confidence, knowledge or energy. It was a system that circulated some knowledge. But it was not a system that could keep steadily advancing knowledge of how better to provide learning opportunities in different circumstances, and ensure that schools, principals and teachers most in need of changing their practice were enabled to do so.

Most principals, teachers and trustees thought schools needed more support or advice from the Ministry. By 1999, after a decade's experience of operating as self-managing schools, and without ongoing connections with the Ministry as a matter of course, only 53 percent of primary principals, 39 percent of primary trustees and 28 percent of primary teachers were satisfied with the level of Ministry support or advice for schools. The vehicles that could have been used for ongoing connection—the school charter and the annual report of the school's activities relating to the National Education Guidelines and National Administrative Guidelines (tellingly often referred to as "the NEGs and NAGs")—were rarely used. "All I got every year was a little letter back" said one experienced principal.[12] The district offices were

---

12 Personal interview, June 2011.

not staffed to have regular discussions on school development. Their role was largely reactive, not initiatory. They had no role in developing the capability of all schools in their area. ERO's role was not to discuss or advise, but to evaluate and report.

People in primary schools, whether they were governors, managers or teachers, also felt left out of the Ministry's prime function: policy. Only around a quarter were satisfied with the involvement of the education sector in policy development and change in 1999 (Wylie, 1999, p. 179). That was at a time when the current government was looking to further reduce the national infrastructure available to schools by cutting the advisory services. Schools did not think they were sufficiently resourced, but they preferred to keep some infrastructure that had some national connections rather than have the funding for the advisory services transferred to school operational grants.

It was not that principals and boards had not come to grips with their new roles. They enjoyed making their own decisions, seeing some changes in their programmes and buildings as a result. But at the end of the first decade of *Tomorrow's Schools*, they could also see that they needed more support—more connections, not just dollars—to do the job as well as they wanted to. That was especially so when it came to the major changes in curriculum and the debates around qualifications that also preoccupied this decade. I turn next to what those changes meant for students and schools, and why the lack of interconnections, joint work to design national frameworks for teachers and learners, and ongoing knowledge building made it difficult to see any gains at the national level.

Chapter 6

# Piecemeal changes: Teaching and learning in the 1990s

## Seeds falling on shaky ground

The National Government that came to power in 1990 was keen to introduce a national curriculum framework and tackle secondary qualifications, developments that had been disrupted by the earthquake of *Tomorrow's Schools*. But these developments did not build directly on what had been outlined in the mid- to late 1980s. Nor would they be undertaken through new versions of the former processes of joint work, which had brought together different expertise and had used a series of trials to secure wider understanding and a sense of ownership among teachers. Lack of these processes would make the large change that both developments entailed more difficult.

In addition, as the Ministry noted in its briefing to the new Minister, "Effecting national curriculum change is now more difficult, given the greater autonomy and funding given to educational institutions" (Ministry of Education, 1990, p. 48). The Ministry would have fewer levers in its work with schools and the sector. It was not funded to provide the interconnected infrastructure of development and support that these changes would need. Priority in educational funding was going to schools' operational grants. It no longer had a strong curriculum division to anchor and lead the development required. Curriculum and qualifications were to be developed separately in fact, since secondary qualifications were now the responsibility of the new New Zealand Qualifications Authority (NZQA).

A lot of hard work occurred in the 1990s to make these new frameworks a reality. But lack of coherence, lack of ongoing support, absence of ongoing connections between people with different knowledge and roles, and a limited number of opportunities for joint work to bring that knowledge together resulted in changes in teaching that were at best uneven, and that could not have a marked effect on student achievement overall.

The curriculum roll-out was too rapid to allow consolidation. The sequential focus on one subject area after another was not accompanied by building or sharing the knowledge that would allow teachers and schools to be more responsive to student needs, to provide better learning for Māori and Pasifika. There was no building on the work of the 1980s, such as the Schools Without Failure project, or on school development that would enable schools to better harness and keep building their own internal knowledge. At a national level there was little indication of improvement in student engagement in learning, and in outcomes.

In this chapter I start with an outline of the new national curriculum to show the kinds of change to teaching practice and the way schools work that it entailed, and the limited support that was available for schools and teachers to come to grips with the new framework. After touching on what the policy makers found a disappointing lack of change in primary student achievement in the 1990s, I focus on four significant areas to show why teachers and schools had not been able to do more: why the disconnections of the *Tomorrow's Schools* system did not address the fundamental knowledge and skills that teachers needed to change their existing repertoires. These four areas are literacy and maths in primary schools, science, and Māori learners.

Changes to secondary teaching and learning were well overdue, as described in Chapter 3. But while there was a lot of activity aimed at improving secondary education in the 1990s, secondary student achievement did not improve. In the second half of this chapter I describe this activity, and why it was that the disconnections in the system meant that progress in secondary education was more erratic than cumulative.

# The new curriculum development

The new curriculum framework was introduced as a discussion document by Lockwood Smith, the Minister of Education, just 6 months after the change of government (Ministry of Education, 1991). For the first time in New Zealand, different curriculum areas were brought together within a common framework to provide a seamless education, both across subjects and through time.

Seven areas of knowledge, "essential learning areas", were identified. To be woven through each of these were new objectives: "essential skills". These included 32 specified skills under the broad headings of communication, problem-solving, decision-making, self-management and social skills; as well as numeracy, information, and work and study.

These essential skills were not well developed, nor were they well threaded through the seven essential learning areas. Indeed, each of the latter was tackled separately, making the new curriculum less coherent than it could have been. "Working at breakneck speed to satisfy political timetables" (Capper, 1992, p. 19), separate contracted groups of experienced teachers and subject experts developed curriculum statements. First up were three of the four "basic [compulsory] subjects": mathematics, science and English. The original timetable would have seen an annual succession of curriculum statements: technology (the fourth basic subject), plus social studies, the arts, and health and physical education.

Such a pace proved unrealistic, either to develop a sound outline for each curriculum area or for schools to take on board the new curriculum framework and the curriculum statement for each area. The early contracted groups could often draw on previous work in the 1980s, with relatively strong networks in areas where there had been recent curriculum revision work, such as in science. Some of these networks included people who could also contribute knowledge from research and practice related to (some of) the essential skills, but others did not. There was no overall group working with the separate contracted groups bringing knowledge of how to include these essential skills.

Development of the new curriculum was also impeded by the now patchy institutional memory within the Ministry of Education (Eppel, 2009).[1] Officials who worked on curriculum were no longer anchoring national networks of subject experts. Teacher unions were no longer able to provide some of the connective infrastructure because they were largely excluded from the development processes. This loss of anchorage and interconnection contributed to the particularly thorny development of the social studies curriculum. Social studies needed particularly astute anchorage and joint work. It has always been a vexed area because what it should cover raises questions about social values and beliefs, and what matters most. It stirs more political interest than other curriculum areas. This curriculum took three drafts to reach a generally accepted compromise.

---

1   Elizabeth Eppel played key roles in the Ministry of Education from 1989 to 2006, and her chapter provides some frank insight into the difficulties in the 1990s of developing curriculum and assessment.

However, the development of the arts and physical education and health curriculum areas benefited by being left to last: more time was taken, with a more iterative process, using the learning from one cycle of work to start the next cycle. It was also more inclusive of teachers.

To provide a seamless education means that students should not find themselves going over the same ground twice, or be asked to undertake work they do not have the knowledge and skills to tackle. So the new framework provided something new: a generic template of achievement objectives and essential skills to be covered by students as they progressed through an eight-level sequence, covering student learning from new entrants to the end of Year 10. This curriculum sequence was not tightly aligned to expectations of particular year levels. It preserved the individual student-centred focus embedded in New Zealand education, recognising that students do not learn at a uniform pace. In a Year 3 class, for example, different students could be working at curriculum levels 1, 2 or 3.

But Warwick Elley, the assessment expert, cautioned that this eight-level sequence was an artificial construct that would not fit every subject. As an example, the constructors of the draft English curriculum had identified 33 different achievement objectives, but had not been able to specify eight different curriculum levels within each of these achievement objectives. Again, "politically-driven deadlines" had meant that not enough teachers were involved in the mapping of achievement objectives against the levels, and trials were sparse. No-one really knew how realistic these were to include in a programme, or how they would or should be used by teachers to improve student learning.

The linear progression implied in the eight-level structure—you need to master *a* before you can do *b*—worked best for maths. But even in maths, the development of knowledge, skills and understanding in different achievement objectives was not consistent for individual students. Not all of a student's work would be at the same level. Strategy use that met, for example, a level 4 objective might be exercised alongside knowledge that was only at level 2. Progress was not a straightforward matter of placing one solid building block upon another. Students learnt through "irregular spurts, sidetracks, inconsistencies and misconceptions", as well as applying mastered skills and knowledge (Elley, 1994, p. 38). The students were part of the learning material: they were constructing something of themselves. Elley expressed scepticism that an "outcome-driven rather than interest-driven" teaching would be more effective (pp. 39–40). Teacher interpretation of student interest was probably often not as well gauged as it could be in our schools, as noted in Chapter 3, but providing teachers with what appeared to be a blueprint to which every student should conform would create misleading understandings of a different kind.

## Making sense of the new curriculum

Schools were not left to make sense of the new curriculum on their own. Contracted professional development was available for each new area as it came out. This was largely provided by the Schools Support services run by the colleges of education (most of which were also distracted by amalgamation with education departments in the universities during the 1990s). Professional development for a specific curriculum area was offered for a limited period only and did not reach every school. The advisers themselves did not have much time to come to grips with the new curriculum. By the time examples of how schools were using the new curriculum in promising ways had emerged, it might be too late to share them more widely, even if they were known to advisers. Other schools would be moving their focus to the next curriculum area to be introduced.

What difference did the new curriculum framework make to what happened in classrooms, to students' everyday educational opportunities? Piecing together what was said in surveys, qualitative studies, ERO reviews, the 2002 Curriculum Stocktake report (Ministry of Education, 2002b) and reflections in interviews in 2011[2] suggests the following:

- Many teachers were thirsty for professional development and for the opportunity to work with others beyond their own school. They therefore welcomed what came their way with the new curriculum if it brought them new knowledge or practical ideas they could easily use.

- Many teachers and schools mapped what they were already doing onto the new framework of levels and achievement objectives, probably tweaking rather than redesigning. This was possible because the curriculum outlines had built on previous work and were not tightly prescriptive.

---

2   Sources include: Aikin (1994); Hill (1999); Mansell (1999); McGee et al. (2002); McGee et al. (2003); Ministry of Education (2002a); Renwick and Gray (1995); Thrupp, Harold, Mansell and Hawksworth (2000); the NZCER national surveys, particularly Wylie (1997b) and Wylie (1999).

## 6   Piecemeal changes: Teaching and learning in the 1990s

- Tweaking rather than redesigning was also common because the framework underpinning each of the areas was not clear at the start (perhaps because it had not been trialled, and there were no illustrations or stories to share from actual schools putting something into practice, as there would be if there had been good trialling).

- Many were unsure what the 'broad and balanced' curriculum they were supposed to provide actually looked like in the new framework, so they continued their existing allocation of time to each subject area.

- Many teachers and principals made efforts to cover every achievement objective in every essential learning area, particularly since ERO reviewers looked for evidence that they were doing so. This led to concerns of superficiality, with the curriculum sometimes treated as a matter of compliance rather than exploration and innovation.

- The new curriculum became synonymous with increased assessment, planning and reporting. Assessment was likely to be linked with reporting—a ticking of boxes rather than evidence to inform learning. Sometimes this led to an over-emphasis on teaching objectives that were easily assessed. Quite a few teachers did think, however, that the increase in assessment gave them a better idea of individual students' learning needs. But, overall, teacher understanding of the fruitful role that good assessment can play in learning was not marked, and was not tackled by Ministry of Education professional development contracts until the late 1990s.

- By 1999 fewer than half of primary teachers thought that their assessment and curriculum resources were good, and around half were not confident that they could assess students against the curriculum.

- Most teachers were developing their own assessments.

- Many teachers felt burdened by the paperwork of more explicit and specific planning, and recording of assessment evidence.

- The new curricula were associated with increasingly high workloads. By 1999, 41 percent of primary teachers thought their workload was excessive.

- In quite a few schools the curriculum documents spurred more review of what teachers were doing, and greater alignment of programmes and resources across classes and within subject departments to match the curriculum.

- Overall, the impact of the new curriculum was highly variable, and it did not result in richer and more robust learning across the board. Some subjects in secondary schools, particularly those taught mainly at the senior level (such as history),[3] remained untouched, creating an unevenness between subjects and within schools.

None of this unevenness seems surprising given the absence of trialling to see how teachers made sense of the curriculum statements, and therefore what they would need to successfully use them. For the statements to work as intended, teachers would need to be able to draw on well-trialled guidance and resources, including assessments that were not mere checklists. And this new approach would have benefited considerably from ongoing processes to share learning from schools and advisers as schools worked with the new curriculum, to identify common issues and make improvements.

# Mixed messages on the purpose of assessment

The relentless pace of the change, the absence of worked examples or linked assessments that could be used in learning, and the lack of any overall coherence made it difficult to grasp the underlying possibilities the new approach represented. ERO's literal approach to the achievement objectives segmented the curriculum and encouraged assessment for recording rather than learning. One highly experienced principal who had had good professional connections with other principals and advisers, and would have thought herself well informed as she worked with the new curriculum, looked back on the 1990s with frustration at the lost opportunities because of the lack of clarity around the purpose of the framework:

---

3 *Tomorrow's Schools* significantly disrupted what had been the promising development of a new history syllabus, with related well-designed resources that would have given the prominence needed to New Zealand history (Fountain, 2008; Sheehan, 2010). As it was, history teachers tended to stick with what they knew. It is only recently that there has been more interest and confidence in teaching our own country's story and complexities. It also undermined the development of resources for Pacific history study, including the loss of a unit on Samoan history in the Samoan language, when materials left on the desks of officials were thrown out in the weekend transition from the Department of Education to the Ministry of Education (Fountain, 2012). This was not the only curriculum resource or curriculum or system knowledge lost in that transition. Little archiving of material occurred, probably a sign that in the scramble to make rapid change, archiving so that knowledge could be easily retrieved was not seen as one of the essentials; as if there could be no learning or building in the new era from what had gone before.

## 6 Piecemeal changes: Teaching and learning in the 1990s

> It was an appalling roll out of the first curriculum framework, because we never understood it. We could have made it work better if there had not been such accountability. 'You will do every Achievement Objective etc.' I only got the framework after three curriculum statements.[4]

The Ministry did fund the development of assessments that could support student learning, but these were not widely taken up, largely because they were not presented within professional development or ongoing learning that showed schools how to make the most of them.

These new assessments included school-entry tasks in reading, maths and oral language. While informative, they were time-consuming, and their use gradually declined.[5] The ARBs (Assessment Resource Banks) for maths, science and English, curriculum-levelled tasks that could be used within classroom learning, were developed by NZCER, building on teacher-devised assessments. They were liked by the minority of teachers who used them. Teacher use appeared to depend on the recommendations of those with more expertise, within their school or in the advisory (Schools Support) service. But there was no systematic way to get them used in every school: no ongoing networks of those with expertise who could develop and share good knowledge of how to use the assessments to improve learning (Gilmore & Hattie, 2000).

The largest government investment in assessment was not primarily for teaching and learning but to provide national monitoring of student performance. Many of the National Education Monitoring Project (NEMP) tasks were released for teachers to use after they were employed to provide a national picture of student performance in Years 4 and 8. Not many teachers used them. Again, there were no ongoing connective processes through which they could have been recommended and their use supported. NEMP did attempt to contribute to the development of teacher assessment capability. It had an annual intake of around 150 practising teachers, who administered the assessments to children and groups of children, or who marked the assessments using criteria they had formulated themselves with

---

4  Interview, June 2011, with highly experienced principal, active in principal professional development and support, and with some Ministry of Education experience.

5  Schools could voluntarily send individual school-entry assessment scores to the Ministry for national collation to gain a national picture of the performance levels of school entrants. Some 30,000 scores were received and analysed in 1999/2000, showing much lower average scores in maths and reading for students in very low-income communities: children in decile 1 schools had early reading scores that were on average almost half those of students in decile 7–10 schools. Māori and Pasifika students were also starting school with lower scores than Pākehā or Asian students (Davies, 2001).

guidance from the NEMP team. Teachers who took part were positive about the opportunity to see other classes in a range of different schools, to gain understanding about how to shape assessments designed to probe children's thinking as well as knowledge, and to work with other teachers (Gilmore, 1999). Some came away with a definite appreciation of the value of schools having their own moderation processes and benchmarks so that there was both a shared understanding among the school's teachers of what achievement and progress looked like and a way of identifying common aspects of the curriculum where students might be struggling.

This inclusion of teachers in the NEMP work benefited a small number of teachers each year, and probably some of their schools. But it did not create an ongoing network of teachers who could share their work in particular curriculum areas, or undertake inquiry into aspects of common interest, such as developing units of work that were designed to improve student skills and knowledge in areas the NEMP assessments showed were weak. NEMP was not funded to make or sustain such connections. The furthest it could go was to report its results and present them at conferences. Comments from its sector advisory group discussions on the results were later posted on its website after each NEMP round. But NEMP was not systemically linked with the School Support services' advisers, who were the ones most likely to go into schools and work with them. Even had it been, the advisers were not funded to maintain teacher networks to progress new practice knowledge. Thus there was a real gap in what could be learnt from the NEMP results and built on to improve student performance. Like too many projects and initiatives in the 1990s, the lack of systemic interconnections made NEMP less useful than it could have been.

# Question marks over primary student performance

In his otherwise optimistic take on the introduction of *Tomorrow's Schools*, Lyall Perris (Acting Secretary for Education 1995/96) noted greater social stratification of schools and some evidence that "children in the least-advantaged schools are receiving a poorer education than they might have done" (Perris, 1998, p. 24). Despite all the effort put into the new curriculum statements, he thought that the reforms were likely to have brought "no significant change" for many students.

## 6  Piecemeal changes: Teaching and learning in the 1990s

Our maths results in the 1994 Third International Mathematics and Science Study (TIMSS) were described by Wyatt Creech, the Minister of Education in 1997 when they were published, as "mediocre" and "disappointing". Overall, we were performing at about the international mean. We did well at the top end of performance—20 percent of Year 5 students performed at the high benchmark—but we had 22 percent performing below the low benchmark.

Four years after the implementation of the new maths curriculum statement, with its associated professional development, some improvement was evident in the 1998 TIMSS maths results: 24 percent of Year 5 students were performing at the high benchmark and 19 percent below the low benchmark. Māori students' average score improved from 427 to 445, but Pasifika students' score improved only from 412 to 416.

In science, whose curriculum statement was implemented in 1995, with some professional development to accompany it, our average Year 5 score increased from 505 in 1994 to 514 in 1998. Māori student scores also improved, from an average of 457 to 478; Pasifika student scores were unchanged.

Our Year 5 reading scores overall in the IEA 10-Year Trends Study were much the same in 2001 as they had been in 1990/91. We continued to have one of the widest ranges of scores among students (Ministry of Education, 2003). Māori average scores were lower in 2001 than in 1990 (445 and 458, respectively); Pasifika average scores were slightly higher in 2001. Māori students were more likely to attend rural schools: ERO had voiced concern about the quality of rural education in 1994, and rural students' reading scores slipped between 1990 and 2001 (from an average of 518 to 484).

The new national monitoring of student performance through NEMP showed a mixed pattern. Fewer students had word recognition scores that were below the range for their age in 2000 (12 percent of Year 4 students, down from 19 percent in 1996). But reading comprehension scores, more important than word recognition, did not improve over the same period (McNaughton, 2011, p. 44). Between the first and second rounds of NEMP (1995–98 and 1999–2002), Year 4 achievement gaps between Māori and other students did not narrow in reading or maths, though they did in science. Low-decile school students lost some ground in reading, but not in maths or science (Flockton, 2003).

None of these measures of student achievement corresponded exactly with the new curriculum statements and their myriad achievement objectives, which were teachers' preoccupations in this period.

There are mixed signals in the performance data about gains over time, either overall or for the groups who had previously been underserved in education. The international assessments showing substantial proportions of low performers began to undercut satisfaction with our proportion of high performers. There was certainly no evidence that either school self-management or the new curriculum were able to bring about rapid improvements in primary student performance. Where improvements seemed evident, as in maths and science, one could link it to recent professional development and the opportunity for teachers to gain some new understanding and practical knowledge. Without systematic national investment in ongoing support for teaching and its development it is hard to make marked progress. This is exemplified in the recommendations of the 1999 Literacy Taskforce, and in the challenges facing the teaching of maths and science that lay behind the "disappointing" mathematics and science performance of New Zealand students.

# The 1999 Literacy Taskforce

The Literacy Taskforce was set up in 1999 to provide advice for the Government's goal that "By 2005, every child turning nine will be able to read, write, and do maths for success" (Literacy Taskforce, 1999, p. 2). Principals and teachers "who are working successfully with those children considered most at risk of failure" formed most of the taskforce (p. 3). Working with them were researchers, professional development providers, ERO, and Ministry of Education curriculum policy officials. Two literacy researchers and academics on the taskforce joined eight of their peers on a Literacy Experts Group, which fed into the main taskforce.

This return to a joint working approach marked a significant turning point: a realisation by policy makers of the need to have all these roles and expertise in the same room, identifying the underlying issues, coming to a shared understanding and a commitment to the path forward. The taskforce was to give advice on how to define the broad government goal, how to measure progress towards it, and how best to support literacy learning. It did not work in isolation: the members were asked to take the issues identified out to their "colleagues" for discussion. Thus the report was well informed and the issues widely discussed, bringing them back to priority for some educators. The report was generally well received. It would eventually lead to a new approach to professional development to improve reading and writing. However, the more coherent infrastructure it recommended, to counter the variability of learning opportunities available in New Zealand schools that was impeding progress, was only partially followed.

The Literacy Taskforce noted the wide variation in skills and knowledge among teachers and in schools. It was concerned that schools were choosing programmes that were not effective and were not evaluating their use. It also noted that not enough was known about good practice in New Zealand schools: what teachers whose students were doing better than one might have expected were doing. It recommended the development of a professional development "package", along the lines of the successful ERIC approach of the 1970s and 1980s, which could bring best practice into schools through videos as well as written material. It recommended "a nationally co-ordinated service" to support schools to develop literacy leadership, and "materials and opportunities" for principals to be updated on literacy learning so that, for example, they would not allocate a beginning teacher to a new entrants class, which needs particularly skilled teaching (Literacy Taskforce, 1999, p. 14).

All these recommendations point to the need for a stronger infrastructure for teaching and for the management of schools, for links across the system that would share and generate knowledge. But this was still a step too far in the context of the pervasive framework of self-managing schools. At the time the Literacy Taskforce was meeting, the National Government was proposing that the advisory service be disbanded and its funding dispersed into the per student operational funding received by each school. The taskforce expressed its concern at this move.

It also tackled the greater needs of students in low-decile schools by recommending that Reading Recovery funding be prioritised to these schools. This recommendation was ignored. Once resourcing is given to all schools on a per capita basis it becomes difficult to take it away. The eligibility criteria for Reading Recovery were also set in relation to the *school* average reading level at age 6. The combination of the way it was funded and the eligibility criteria meant that many students with low reading levels who attended low-decile schools missed out: their school did not have sufficient Reading Recovery funding or the ability to supplement it. To use the Reading Recovery resource to really make a dent in the underachievement of students from low-income homes, and thus many Māori and Pasifika, one would need to change the eligibility criteria in relation to national rather than school reading levels, and be prepared to have district or national allocation of some dedicated funding. This would mean a government prepared to move away from a purist self-management model and prepared to prioritise any new money secured for education to those most in need, along with the infrastructure to support improved teaching and learning, rather than keep dissipating it in slight increases to each school's operational grant.

"One size does not fit all" became a phrase often heard in education circles at this time, after Howard Fancy, the Secretary of Education 1996–2006, kept using it to emphasise the need for "local solutions for local problems".[6] But funding formulas have remained one-size-fits-all, centred on individual schools. This would continue to make it hard to develop the infrastructure needed to make the most of self-managing schools, to change how schools worked to ensure they had robust grounds for local solutions.[7]

## Maths: The costs of an insufficient infrastructure

The 1994 TIMSS results for maths and science exposed some long-standing systemic weaknesses that should not have been left to individual schools to solve on their own. In Robert Garden's analysis of the results (Garden, 1997), he noted that primary teachers, particularly of junior students, were less confident teaching maths and science than teaching reading and writing. Although the New Zealand curriculum covered more topics than most other countries taking part in TIMSS, primary teachers gave much less time to maths and science than they did to reading and writing.[8] The new curriculum statements had only intensified the expectations of topic coverage. But

---

6   For example, in the Ministry of Education's Annual Report for 1999, p. 7.
7   This one-size-fits-all approach to school funding meant that the Ministry could not provide the additional funding to Te Aho o Te Kura Pounamu (then The Correspondence School) that would have allowed all schools to build on this school's development of an e-learning platform in the early 2000s. This platform would have provided a system to maintain a learning record for each student, identifying next steps for their learning that would be shared with students and their families. The Ministry could not see that The Correspondence School could and should play a more nodal role in networking schools, because it was also a school and should not be treated differently. I was on the board of The Correspondence School at this time and heard this reasoning first hand. This was another significant and efficient system-building opportunity missed.
8   However, Scott (1997) found that while junior school teachers were not organising many lessons around science, observations showed they were in fact providing more opportunities in other lessons for students to learn science that fitted into the science curriculum, through discussion of points that came up in reading and writing, for example. This was more likely to happen in the junior school. This often-unplanned approach (whose usefulness would be dependent on teacher knowledge), and the availability of science-related topics in the reading material that students could access in, for example, school journals and the holdings of their class library, may point to the absorption of some knowledge and ideas while students were 'reading' rather than doing 'science'. This might be one contributor to the better performance of New Zealand students at the secondary level in the international science assessments. Garden (1997) also notes that secondary teachers of science usually have a science degree (unlike primary teachers). The New Zealand curriculum made science compulsory in Years 9 and 10.

"implementation of them in the manner which is intended demands considerable expertise in subject matter, pedagogy, and assessment" (Garden, 1997, p. 187). He doubted this expertise was sufficiently present in New Zealand primary schools, developed in initial teacher education, or supported with professional development, curriculum guides and curriculum-related assessments that would give teachers and students accurate feedback on their performance. The coherent national infrastructure that was necessary to improve maths learning was simply not present in the system. As well, many New Zealand primary teachers spent little time on professional development and professional reading, two activities associated with higher student scores in TIMSS.

One study of primary student teachers found that over half had negative attitudes to maths, and most had not studied maths at secondary school beyond Year 11. Many did not understand basic mathematical concepts. Yet their 3-year degree would have only one and a half courses focused on mathematics teaching (Biddulph, 1999, pp. 27 & 80). In 1996 ERO noted that the autonomy of each of the institutions providing initial teacher education, coupled with the absence of any "one agency with an interest in, or responsibility for, the effective operation or outcomes of the pre-service teacher training system as a whole", meant there was variation in selection and in courses across the country (Cameron & Baker, 2004, p. 19). The institutions were competing for students, even in 1996, when there was a teacher shortage. There was no common ground where they could work together and take a concerted national approach to the issues being identified with lack of teacher knowledge and confidence. With separated and competing initial teacher education institutions, and the Ministry's role in supporting and developing teacher capability limited to short-term work on the introduction of the new curriculum statements, the New Zealand system had no mechanism for the kind of coherent approach needed to achieve a real sea-change.

Problems with our level of maths confidence and performance were not new. Maths had been identified as an area of weaker New Zealand student performance in the TIMSS predecessor, the Second International Maths and Science study, in the mid-1980s. At about this time, primary schools were starting to receive the first of the *Beginning School Mathematics* (BSM) resource from the Department of Education. BSM started on its rather lengthy development road in the late 1970s through the joint working group process, including teachers' college lecturers, advisers, inspectors, experienced principals and teachers working with curriculum officials. The BSM resources had been thoroughly trialled. On the surface, here was something that should have improved mathematics learning, though it was not without its critics. By the time it was ready, there was new research showing that young children could tackle numbers earlier than had been thought, or supported through the BSM resource.

The BSM resource was still being introduced when *Tomorrow's Schools* came in. It was not mandatory, though most schools used it because it had the authority of the Department of Education and because it was called a 'resource' rather than a 'programme'. Many teachers did not use it exclusively. Most who did use BSM were positive about it, but several lessons can be learnt from the BSM experience in terms of what is needed to support teachers to change their practice:

- Just like the new curriculum framework of the 1990s, this set of modules covering mathematics in the first 3 years of school came to schools piecemeal, making it hard for teachers to grasp the underlying principles and the resource as a whole.[9]

- Advice on and support for the introduction of BSM was uneven. Teachers were divided in their views on the quality of the advice and support they had had (Bennie, Henry, & Ratcliff, 1990). Much of this advice was school-based. In some schools no-one had had any advice and support on how to use the resource.

- Teachers were tending to "follow instructions accompanying the resource religiously", and in doing so missed the intention of the resource to tailor teaching to individual children's strengths and weaknesses. The same lack of teacher confidence was evident in 1991, resulting in conscientious coverage of everything in case students missed out. This often resulted in slower student progress.

ERO would later criticise teachers for having low expectations of students. I don't think it is that simple. The frameworks teachers use play an important part in what they think is possible. What they include in their teaching may not be framed just by what they think individual students are capable of, but also by what they think students need to 'cover'.

---

[9] The reason for the piecemeal introduction was the need to ration the funding available. BSM was highly dependent on equipment for children to use, which was supplied by the Department through a budget-limited pipeline, staggering its introduction to one school year level after another.

Without sufficient guidance it was all too easy for conscientious teachers, particularly if they lacked knowledge and confidence, to take written resources literally, to try to cover everything—as they would do when it came to the achievement objectives in the 1990s curriculum. If we want to improve the rate at which students learn—to tailor learning tasks to the 'zone' where learning is most likely to occur, where a particular student will feel both confident and challenged—then our written curriculum frameworks, guidance and resources need to be designed coherently, with 'road' trials to test that what is intended is what is actually understood.

Overcoming teachers' literal conscientiousness was one of the prime achievements of a professional development contract undertaken in 1991 to work with teachers on their use of BSM (Higgins & Hendry, 1992). Teachers who participated became more confident that they could match children's knowledge with the tasks that would challenge them at the right level, and thereby increase the children's knowledge and skills. These teachers were supported to work with their own school colleagues, so that schools would have their own collective approach to improving children's mathematical learning. They had also become connected to their counterparts in the other schools taking part. Imagine being able to build on this!

But this professional development could only include and connect 20 of the 200 primary schools in the region served by this particular contract, and only for a year. It did not lead to a regular programme that, over time, could have improved the capability of all the schools in the region, establishing strong networks of teachers who wanted to keep developing their practice, anchored in the college of education. There was no mechanism for learning from the success of this approach, to use it to strategically develop a more systemic approach. Such a systemic approach was problematic in the new contractual environment that came with *Tomorrow's Schools*, because it largely funded professional development as a one-off activity rather than as part of an essential infrastructure that should also continue to build knowledge across the sector. In the 1990s there was essentially no methodical support and development of the kind that was so sorely needed for maths.

## Science stagnates

The Ministerial Task Group Reviewing Science and Technology Education in 1991 was taken aback by how little professional development science teachers had at both the primary and secondary schooling levels. In addition, it noted that

> Given the low priority accorded to science, and the general lack of qualifications of primary teachers teaching the subject, it is unlikely that schools most in need of support will be able to recognise the need for, or be prepared to allocate funds to, teacher development in science. (Ministerial Task Group Reviewing Science and Technology Education, 1992, p. 33)

Its surveys found heavy reliance on the advisory services by both primary and secondary teachers, services that then seemed as if they would be cut. The task group recommended the retention of science advisory services and tagged funding for schools to ensure at least 5 days' annual professional development in science for every science teacher. Clearly this group, which included businessmen, did not think that boards and school managers would make the best decisions on funding allocation just because they were physically closest to the students.

The science advisory positions the task group saw as essential were also subject to individual institutional decisions and priorities, this time the colleges of education and universities. Contracts with the Ministry of Education to provide professional development associated with the new curriculum statement helped maintain science advisory positions through the 1990s. But these positions were not sufficient to undertake the ongoing work with schools which the task group saw as vital if New Zealand students were to improve their scientific knowledge, skills and understanding.

Professional development accompanying the new science curriculum statement was available only for a limited period. Small schools, schools without a strong internal community of sharing and development, and schools that experienced high turnover or were reliant on beginning teachers (likely to be those in poor and rural areas) were largely on their own if they missed out or were not organised enough to get themselves included in the contract. Some schools had sufficient funds and gave science priority so that all their teachers (if they were primary) or all their science teachers (if they were secondary) attended—the most likely foundation for school-wide change to occur. Others could not afford to do so and were reliant on individuals to bring back new knowledge. This meant the new knowledge could be filtered or distorted by individual messengers, and by how well led the school was to ensure there was time set aside for sharing and ongoing discussion and work together. Most schools did not have the strong collective cultures needed to ensure the new knowledge was sustained and built on:

> In the mid-1990s, when the new science curriculum statement came in, you'd go into a school, it was all happening, and then you'd go back, and there was no sign of it, because the teachers had all left, and there was no more professional development, because it was rationed. It was typical of the weakness of many of the educational initiatives. We pay attention for a few years, then—nothing. We make no allowances for staff changes.[10]

Most of the professional development contracts to accompany the new curriculum statements left teachers wanting more. In science, the Ministry-funded programmes consisted of three 1-day sessions, with school visits by the professional development facilitators between sessions. Teachers felt they could come to grips with the new approach of the new curriculum in this time, but needed more time and support to translate this understanding into practice (Bell & Baker, 1997, p. 7). As with maths, there was no follow-up, no building on the new knowledge. The contractual time-limited approach was limited in its effectiveness. It was also inefficient.

Competition between schools also eroded the vital sharing of resources and experiences that often improve both resources and teaching. Principals might sense competition most intensely with neighbouring schools, but it is interesting (and sobering) to note that the new sense of competition and self-regard that came with *Tomorrow's Schools* also dampened communication in previously wider networks, which had been more directly focused on what happened in classrooms:

> And there might be a resource book, in Science, for example, the experiments you could do. We could modify them, but the basis was there. And you knew that most people in most of the other parts of the country were doing similar sorts of things. You'd get feedback, exchange information and so on. But now we're almost in a competitive environment, that is, people aren't sharing as much as they used to, and I think that's detrimental. (Intermediate science teacher, quoted by Thrupp et al., 2000, p. 108)

In science, as in other subjects, secondment of experienced teachers to work in the professional development contracts, or to work with the Ministry on the curriculum statement and guidance, was not as easy as it had been before *Tomorrow's Schools*. Some boards of trustees were reluctant to lose their good staff even temporarily. Some boards were also reluctant to have the knowledge of their teachers used to improve the capability of teachers in other schools, because of their sense of needing to retain a competitive edge in what they offered.

---

10 Interview, May 2011, with ex-ERO reviewer, ex-Ministry of Education official.

Progress in science teaching stalled after the brief period of professional development associated with the new curriculum statement. There was no strategic national investment in supporting science teaching. Priority went to literacy and mathematics at both the national and (often) the school levels. The recommendations of the 1997 Mathematics and Science Taskforce, a response to those "mediocre" TIMSS results, paved the way for the development of the nationwide Numeracy Programme, a major source of professional learning which also encouraged more collective approaches in schools. But the taskforce's science recommendations were only partially realised. The Ministry funded the development and publication of new resources that were consistent with the new science curriculum, but not always the professional learning that needed to go with them. As a result, well-designed units and material, using solid knowledge on good science teaching practice, would languish unused in school storerooms.

No surprise, then, that in 2011 the Prime Minister's Science Adviser would express alarm at the state of science teaching and learning in New Zealand schools (Gluckman, 2011). Nothing had changed fundamentally because we had not provided science teaching with the infrastructure it needed. The need for all students to leave school with a good scientific understanding is inescapable in a society and world facing increasingly complex and difficult decisions. The need for New Zealand to (re)build its scientific and technological strengths to provide a better economic and environmental base is also inescapable. We had been at the start of a promising turn in science teaching development (Bell, 1991). *Tomorrow's Schools* left science teaching mainly treading water. It left too much to individuals (who were also working more in isolation), and too much to enthusiasts who had insufficient national anchoring. There has been no dedicated ongoing science curriculum position at the Ministry. In 2011 Ministry national office support for science was down to a half-time role, filled by someone who had not taught science. We are in sore need of strategic investment focused on the kind of science teaching and learning that is relevant to the 21st century (Bull, 2011; Bull, Gilbert, Barwick, Hipkins, & Baker, 2010) if science education in New Zealand is to play its vital role.

## An absence of useful focus: Schools and Māori learners

Although the goal of improving Māori student learning outcomes was present at the national level, incorporated into Ministry of Education strategic goals, it was not well integrated into the professional development focused on curriculum, on the heart of classroom life. Professional development in the 1990s funded by the Ministry was focused on each particular curriculum area, which meant it did not necessarily address some of the wider pedagogical issues of how to better engage students in learning. Only 33 percent of teachers thought their professional development in the English curriculum had provided adequate support for them to improve the achievement of Māori students in their classroom or school. The figures are even lower for maths: 24 percent, and science: 16 percent (McGee et al., 2002, p. 84; McGee et al., 2003, pp. 55 & 197).

Addressing Māori students' needs was among the areas where English-medium school principals felt least satisfied with the advice available to them:[11]

> The NEGS and NAGS—schools had to engage with their Māori communities—they told us we had to do it but provided no support, no guidelines on how it would be done, just that it would be done.[12]

Looking back in 2011, an experienced principal I spoke with recalled that, despite the marked emphasis at the national level on raising Māori student achievement, schools were more likely to focus on adults, on external relationships, on governance: "we saw it only in terms of role models, awareness of the Treaty of Waitangi, and partnerships. Things like getting a Māori trustee on the board".[13]

Schools were keen to employ Māori teachers, but there were insufficient numbers. In secondary schools, as well as teaching their own subject, "teachers who are the only Māori teachers on staff feel the exigencies of being 'on call' for all Māori-related activities" (Gardiner & Parata Ltd, 2008, p. 38).

Popular emphases such as taha Māori (the inclusion of aspects of Māori culture, as teachers understood them, in school and class life) and other approaches which meant well often did not in fact address the core of Māori student disengagement with school, did not sufficiently focus on pedagogy, on achievement. As one educator looked back ruefully:

---

11 In the NZCER national surveys, Māori issues consistently appeared at the end of the list of current national policy issues and day-to-day school work on which principals felt they had access to useful advice. See, for example, Wylie (1999. p. 50).

12 Interview, August 2011, with Māori researcher, developer of innovative and highly effective approaches based on student and whānau voice and participation that have improved Māori student engagement and achievement at both primary and secondary levels.

13 Interview, June 2011, with highly experienced principal, active in principal professional development and support, and with some Ministry of Education experience.

> I think that schools often equate Māori community, Māori students as needing to participate in a particular way, and that way being a culturally appropriate way, so that in some schools I've seen they almost need to define who the child is in terms of their Māoriness, because we've looked for solutions around the edge of a discourse that says these Māori students have lost their identity, therefore we've got to give their identity back to them, teach them about being Māori. So insulting, Māori kids know they're Māori, they get treated differently, so why shove it down their throat and make that another problem that they have to deal with? I look back on all the initiatives for Māori students including taha Māori, and I feel really bad about some of the things I did as a teacher under their name because that's what we thought was going to be the right thing.[14]

Māori-medium education grew markedly in this period and had attracted 20 percent of Māori students by 1996. But kura kaupapa Māori also faced difficulty finding sufficient teachers. On top of this, as pioneers they had far fewer curriculum resources and far less advisory support to draw on as they created programmes that also utilised knowledge important to individual kura whānau.

There was no improvement in Māori educational achievement over the decade. In both 1993 and 1999, 43 percent of Māori school-leavers achieved the equivalent of NCEA Level 2 or better, the level that has recently become the benchmark for school success. In 2000, 36 percent of Māori students were still leaving school without any qualification, twice the rate of the student population as a whole (Statistics New Zealand, n.d.).

In 1997 Te Puni Kōkiri criticised the Ministry of Education for its lack of any notable progress in improving Māori student outcomes, citing a lack of focus in its work and the lack of sufficient capability and capacity (Hamilton, 1998, p. 238). Simply including "increased participation and success by Māori through the advancement of Māori education initiatives" in the NEGs that all schools should follow and in the ERO reviews, and reiterating the importance of improving Māori schooling success in numerous Ministry written communications, was not enough.

ERO also kept a focus on Māori student achievement in its annual reports and showed increasing frustration that policy at the national level, and the Ministry's own strategic goals and the outcomes on which its performance was supposedly measured, were not reflected in marked growth in schools' capability and capacity to better serve their Māori students. But the Ministry

---

14 Interview with Maori researcher, August 2011, developer of innovative and highly effective approaches based on student and whānau voice and participation that have improved Māori student engagement and achievement at both primary and secondary levels, interview.

was not backing the policy and strategic goals with a consistent strategy to build on existing knowledge of how best to engage Māori students in learning, to develop that knowledge further, and to thread it through the professional development it funded.

# Particular challenges for secondary schools

The lack of improvement in Māori student qualification success was mirrored in the lack of improvement in student qualification success overall. In 1990, 63 percent of secondary school-leavers had the equivalent of NCEA Level 2; in 1999, it was 64 percent. *More* students left school without a qualification in 2000 (19 percent) than in 1991 (16 percent). Why could school self-management, the new curriculum and the stirrings of changes to secondary qualifications make so little difference?

For a start, there was little incentive for schools to work hard with students who were disengaging. Instead, it was the reverse. Competition between schools coupled with schools' ability to readily suspend students saw a marked increase in suspensions and expulsions, and in the number of early-leaving exemptions granted to those who wished to leave school before the end of compulsory schooling. Some students also saw attractions in post-school tertiary or work-related training options that offered a different learning experience, one where they felt treated more like independent adults, able to learn through doing, through projects.

And as secondary schools entered the 1990s they were not well positioned to make fundamental changes in how they worked and what they offered. Capper (1994) found the 12 low- to mid-decile secondary schools in which he had hoped to follow the development of more collaborative professional school cultures as they made use of the greater flexibility of school self-management poorly equipped to work in new ways. Change was something done *to* them, from outside the school, rather than something they could shape, to improve things for the students and the school. Even in schools that had been working towards more "participative decision making" for some time, the tendency was to add committees alongside existing hierarchies, increasing workloads rather than changing direction. Although there was some knowledge at the time about the value of more collaborative working, what stands out in hindsight is how few of these committees or new structures appeared to address issues in teaching and learning; how little they were connected to what happened in classrooms.

Lack of coherence was also apparent in how the schools approached budget setting: as administration rather than based on analysis of school priorities. Lack of understanding of the importance of coherence is also apparent in the absence of systematic ways in which individual schools could learn from their own experiences. For example, only one of the 12 schools used its historical data on student assessment results in self-review to see what might need attention and priority. Only one school kept data related to student engagement in school, such as attendance, disciplinary action or vandalism. There could be no analysis of patterns over time or across students or courses, and no checking of assumptions people had about what was going on, if the data were lacking. Self-management was starting without the information and evaluative habits it would need to keep developing in ways that put student engagement with learning and achievement at the centre.

Even in the one school that did keep student engagement data, there appeared to be no sense that student views would also be a valuable check on how school policy actually worked in practice and whether it achieved its aims. Students surveyed in Capper's (1994) study were generally positive about their schools. However, they were alert to strains in staff relationships and to any inconsistencies between the stated values of the school and their own experience, or inconsistencies in how different teachers treated students or followed school discipline rules. Inconsistencies led to disengagement, and disrespect for teachers: not what you want from a school discipline policy. But few teachers in the study were aware of student views in their school. Student views and information about how they experienced classes compared to what teachers thought they were providing would prove to be a powerful means to start to change teacher practice in the AIMHI (Achievement in Multicultural High Schools) cluster later in the 1990s, through the involvement of researchers working with the schools. But when *Tomorrow's Schools* began, schools were on their own, without useful and robust tools and examples, without the ongoing support and challenge that are needed to make real change. Many secondary schools would remain on their own throughout the 1990s.

Increased management workloads were already isolating the principals and senior staff in the early 1990s. Their credibility as educational leaders was reduced rather than enhanced. Secondary principals and senior staff talked of "telescoped deadlines" and of "mind-blowing" increases in information coming into the school (Hill, 1992, p. 17). Their attention was taken elsewhere by the new framework for school self-management. It is no wonder, given what secondary school culture was like at the start of *Tomorrow's Schools* and the absence of systemic knowledge or support to change it, that it was difficult for secondary schools to work differently. They remained 'subject' rather than 'student' centred, even when the new qualifications were calling for the latter.

# Changes to secondary qualifications: Promises and pitfalls

The hugely ambitious and radical approach to qualifications outlined by NZQA in 1991 brought school qualifications and vocational qualifications gained in a polytechnic or apprenticeship onto a single eight-level national certificate. Where you learnt and for how long were to be less important than *what* you learnt. Building blocks for the new qualifications would be standards-based units that students could be assessed against when they were ready to meet the criteria of the standards, not in terms of how many years' schooling or apprenticeship they had served. The model was more like a driver's licence than an exam at the end of a year's course. Although the new national certificate would initially run alongside School Certificate and Bursary examinations, it would share 'units of learning' with Bursary examinations, suggesting that these examinations, geared to students intending to go on to university, would also use unit standards and would eventually be placed on the national certificate. This modular approach to learning and qualifications had the potential to lead to major changes in how teachers taught and how they assessed. It could mean real changes to the structures of secondary schooling, its timetabling and course structures.

Capper, who had advocated the need for fundamental change to the secondary curriculum and qualifications, nonetheless warned that the qualifications changes first outlined in 1991 were coming too fast on the heels of *Tomorrow's Schools*, which had left secondary teachers weary (Capper, 1992). It certainly did not help to have two such major reforms in such a short time-frame. But it was not just the competition for energy and attention that weakened the move to the new qualification framework. It was not sufficiently coherent with the new curriculum: they were developed separately. The new NZQA did not engage sufficiently with the sector, so that teachers and schools would feel some ownership of the new qualification. Nor did it provide sufficient infrastructure for teachers to make the most of what should have been a more flexible framework.

The infrastructure that was needed for the new qualifications to also change teacher practice had been evident in the results of the trials of achievement-based assessments that took place in 1987-89. This was part of the work on qualifications the Department of Education had noted in its 1987 briefing papers as likely to improve the ability of schools to in turn improve Māori student achievement. The 1990s' trials of the new unit standards, a form of achievement-based assessment, confirmed this knowledge. Had this knowledge been used systematically it could have eased and made more productive the introduction of the new qualification.

## What standards-based assessment needs in order to shift teaching and learning

What could have been learnt from these trials? They showed that linking assessment more closely to teaching objectives often led to more engaging courses for students, in which they had to play a less passive role (Eng, 1992). We don't know if this linking improved their performance, since these trials of a more integrated approach had to take place within the existing norm-referenced Sixth Form Certificate qualification. Individual student grades remained dependent on their school's available range of grades, which were decided by the School Certificate scores achieved by that school's Fifth Form students (not necessarily the same students) the previous year. So students could be producing a higher standard of work in the Sixth Form while being penalised by lower standards of work achieved in the Fifth Form the year before. This mismatch between the new assessment and the way it was translated into qualifications also shows that trying to gauge the effects of changes in teaching practice is difficult if the measure of student achievement used is not relevant.

The 1987-89 trials did show how a shift to standards-based assessment meant that teachers had to be much clearer and focused about what students should gain from their learning and how student work could demonstrate this. Where standards-based assessment led to greater clarity for both teachers and students it could shift practice. The results of these trials help explain how it was possible for the introduction of NCEA in 2002 to finally start to shift New Zealand secondary student performance upwards. NCEA would use standards-based assessment, and it would be free of any norm-referenced limitation to the measure of student achievement. The measure would be relevant.

It was also clear from these trials that it was not enough to simply publish standards-based criteria. Standards are not like batteries that can be inserted to power a machine. They need interpretation, thinking, discussion and experimentation (Hipkins & Robertson, 2011). Some trials of achievement-based assessment simply gave teachers written criteria for assigning grades; others included professional development and moderation between schools. These differences provide a natural experiment to see what works better to improve student learning.

Teachers who had professional development that gave them knowledgeable support to integrate the kind of assessment that was likely to improve teaching and learning into their courses, and who took part in moderation, could change their practice far more than those who only had written guidance. Such change to their practice often meant some changes to the content of those courses as well as to how they were taught.

But the further development of achievement-based assessment and its support was blocked by the *Tomorrow's Schools* earthquake. NZQA inherited the standards criteria developed in these trials and used some in national course descriptions, but most were published "informally", for "experimentation" (Lennox, 1995, p. 19). The work was not entirely wasted. It showed teachers and subject associations what was possible. It also showed the value of teachers working together. Moderation of student work (comparing judgements to ensure consistency) through teachers' interaction, anchored through work with regional or national moderators, increased teacher knowledge and confidence. It was a powerful way to give real life in classrooms and schools to national frameworks designed to improve student learning.

Moderation was used in trials for the new National Qualifications Framework. But its use was limited, because in the new system there was no way to pay for the infrastructure that would meaningfully link subject teachers across schools and with the national moderators. In this separated world, NZQA felt it could justify some moderation costs through the use of the fees students had paid to enter for qualifications; students, as consumers, were entitled to consistent standards. But NZQA did not feel it could use these fees to fund moderation as professional development for the production of useful guides for teachers: "for effects on teaching and learning" (Strachan,

1996, p. 5). There is more than a certain irony in this, though one can also understand the logic, with everything sheeted home to users to pay for. NZQA was supposed to retrieve many of its costs through charging providers, including schools, for accrediting their courses and assessment and charging those entering for standards and qualifications. But a user-pays model taken literally, in a context where the users have limited funds so that charges must remain low, cannot fund the investment that is needed to change practice, to improve student success in these qualifications. NZQA processes could not align with the Ministry's objective of improving student achievement because they were dependent on this limited policy model.

## Costs of fragmentation

NZQA was not sufficiently funded to support schools to implement the new qualifications, to work with them to develop capability at the individual, school and system levels. The new approach was undercut from the start by this lack of government investment. But, just as importantly, NZQA and the Ministry operated separately, which meant there was insufficient coherence in what was developed. And the schools were self-managing. There was simply no way in the new fragmented system to build in or sustain the kinds of connections that would not only allow teachers to come properly to grips with the new possibilities but also keep building on them.

In 1994 Sir John Anderson had told the National Government that there was a need for central policy direction:

> The existence of over five central bureaucracies with no overall effective co-ordination of the various policy strands has created confusion and chaos in schools. Implementation of the curriculum and qualification reforms must be professionally managed by a dedicated unit which is able to place other proposed changes within this context. (Anderson, 1994, p. 244)

Curriculum development and qualifications development should have been hand in glove. Instead, they were separate pieces of work. The Ministry contracted curriculum development. NZQA undertook or contracted qualifications development. Both incoherence and too swift a pace led to strong criticism from a wide range of educators and assessment experts, and a further undercutting of this visionary attempt to change the nature of qualifications in New Zealand. The unit standards were criticised as too cut and dried, too modular, too divisive of knowledge and skills to fit many subjects or to support deeper learning (Hall, 1997; Peddie & Tuck, 1995).

## 6 Piecemeal changes: Teaching and learning in the 1990s

David Hood, who led NZQA from 1990 to 1996, thought that technical issues relating to assessment were the 'froth' of the public debate over the National Qualifications Framework, and that the real source of opposition to it was in the paradigm shift it proposed. Schools that were accustomed to the old framework and did well on it did not want to change. He noted that prestigious, often private or boys', schools had "considerable political influence which they use to good effect" (Hood, 1998, p. 108). Retention of the three-tier examination system (in which these prestigious schools had done well) led to a dual system of assessment which was too costly of teacher time, building teacher resentment to the change. The dual system made it "impossible to meet the needs of the consumer, as external examinations based on time serving courses of fixed length makes flexibility of preparation impossible". Teachers, he lamented, were not changing their approach, citing a 1997 study that found "Students report that unit standard assessment practices mimic the old practices" (p. 108).

Teachers were not using the new assessments to develop skills that were not subject-specific, such as communication, self-management and working well with others, the sorts of skills that employers value. Ironically, these very skills were part of the National Curriculum Framework, among the 'essential skills'. But given the absence of a national infrastructure that would build and demonstrate the kinds of unit standards that Hood was thinking of, integrating knowledge with these abilities, it is not surprising that many teachers continued to use their existing knowledge. Perhaps because of the rapid roll-out of specific curriculum areas, the essential skills were not given a spotlight of their own or developed along with the curriculum areas.

Not every subject used both unit standards and the existing qualifications. Some subjects with a more vocational focus used only unit standards, some of which were derived from industry organisations. This two-tier system did little to bridge the hierarchical divide between the academic and vocational subjects, as intended in the original outline of the National Qualifications Framework.

Even for the enthusiasts, the lack of infrastructure, or cumulative ways of sharing and building knowledge, created problems:

> I recall with some sadness in the 1990s going back to schools that I'd visited 2 or 3 years before, and there was a period there where I never saw the same HOD [head of department] two visits in a row because they were the people who were being 'killed off' by unit standards. We've had so many false starts and restarts and there are some people who are just so keen to be, well not left behind but in the forefront, and they wear themselves out with every false start. A lot of people are quite keen to do things

without the proper preparation having been made, or even the proper assurances that if they do it, it will still be worthwhile in 2 years.[15]

Added to this, in 1991 staffing cuts were made in secondary schools through the reduction of 25 percent 'preparation time'. This led to increases in class size as well as loss of non-class time, the kind of time that is key if teachers are to come to grips with substantial changes in curriculum and assessment frameworks.

Even with these cut-backs, shortages of secondary teachers became evident from 1994. Secondary teachers thought that the introductions of the curriculum and qualifications frameworks were not sufficiently resourced for the changes they asked for, particularly in assessment and course structure. In part they thought this was because both had been developed too quickly, with insufficient involvement of the teaching profession through its national organisation, the Post-Primary Teachers Association (PPTA). Twice during national negotiations on teacher collective contracts the PPTA called on members not to undertake any work on the new national curriculum or qualifications (Alison, Cross, & Willets, 2003; Grant, 2003). Once again, haste and exclusion in the developmental stages of those who would need to make something work had an unfortunate cost in what eventually resulted. It meant that it took longer than it should have for New Zealand to move to a qualifications structure that would eventually offer a better chance of increasing student engagement and outcomes than the former structure. It also compounded teachers' and principals' suspicion of the new government agencies, particularly NZQA.

The PPTA was sufficiently perturbed to launch an independent inquiry into the qualifications framework in 1997. This inquiry brought together two of its former presidents, Peter Allen and Shona Hearn, the assessment expert Terry Crooks, and Kathy Irwin, a Māori education academic. The aim was to provide a set of principles on which to base a secondary qualifications system that drew on the experience with the National Qualifications Framework and tried to avoid the difficulties encountered. This teacher-organisation-initiated inquiry was later said by Ministry officials to have provided the grounds for the development of the National Certificates of Educational Achievement, NCEA (Alison et al., 2003, p. 5). It also paved the way for the re-inclusion of PPTA representation in that development, including a consultative road show jointly led by the Ministry and the PPTA.

---

15 Interview, June 2011, based on experience as an ERO reviewer in the 1990s.

The development and introduction of NCEA marked a generally more positive turning point in the enduring quest to develop the quality of secondary schooling, for all students, as I shall explore in Chapter 9. Here I want to point to flaws that marred its introduction, lessons from the 1990s that were either not evident to policy makers and politicians, or could no longer be realised in the fragmented environment produced by *Tomorrow's Schools*. The Ministry and NZQA still operated separately, though by the end of the 1990s the Ministry had regained leadership of the policy framework for secondary qualifications and NZQA's role would be to implement it. There was insufficient joint work undertaken during NCEA's development, work that would have brought educators, researchers, assessment experts and officials into the same room to consider all the relevant knowledge, allowing a co-construction of understanding and a commitment to change. NCEA and the revision of the curriculum were not undertaken in tandem. There was still insufficient planning for the challenges that a new qualification framework brings simply because it calls into question former ways of judging performance. There was not even any professional development allowed for in the initial planning: the PPTA had to argue strongly for two 'Jumbo' days that brought teachers of the same subject together for much-welcomed coming to grips with the new standards.

## Lessons from the 1990s

School self-management that left schools on their own, coupled with a separation of government functions and lack of national infrastructure to the degree that we had it, made New Zealand unique. So in 1999 it was difficult to draw international comparisons when I was concluding the report on the latest NZCER primary national survey with a reflection on what we had gained, lost or maintained over the first decade of *Tomorrow's Schools*.

In some key respects little had changed. Parents' satisfaction with their children's education remained high. Teachers' enjoyment of their work with students, and their pride in seeing them achieve, was undented by the structural changes. Yet student performance on the measures available showed no marked improvement. Teachers' desire to keep learning themselves for their students' benefit was as marked as ever. But their desire for ongoing professional learning was not matched by their opportunities.

What would allow us to make gains instead of treading water, given our self-managing schools system? I found two pertinent studies. The first was more in the way of a warning. An English study found that most schools made no gains in student achievement within that country's self-managed school framework because they focused too much on administrative changes, or took on too much at the same time (Gray et al., 1999). I could recognise that same pattern in New Zealand. Schools that had managed to improve in England had usually had very good support from their local education authority. But we no longer had the equivalent.

The second study, of schools that were self-managing in the United States, found that only 10 percent had managed to make real change in their programmes (Calhoun & Joyce, 1998). What these schools had that the other self-managed schools did not have was external support, student learning at the heart of school development work, substantive staff development that cohered with their school development work, and regular time for staff to reflect, analyse, plan and review their work together. This set of conditions would be proven time and again in international studies of school and system improvement undertaken in the 2000s. They would be evident, too, in the valuable joint work that was undertaken in New Zealand in the 2000s through knowledge-based approaches to professional learning and support that in their turn produced new knowledge of how to produce gains for students.

But in New Zealand at the end of the first decade of *Tomorrow's Schools* we had these conditions in self-managing schools only in patches. Often schools would have some of these necessary conditions for change for limited stretches, such as the length of a professional development contract. It was not enough to embed more coherent practices and ways of working together. Indeed, only 30 percent of primary teachers had any regular non-teaching time to work together in 1999, and that was less than the 35 percent who had had such opportunities in 1989.

The 1990s showed the shortcomings of introducing new curriculum and qualification frameworks to schools that were stand-alone, only temporarily connected. It also showed the shortcomings of developing these frameworks rapidly, without bringing different knowledge—of teachers, researchers, advisers and professional developers, curriculum and assessment experts, policy makers—around the table to work together, iteratively building on consistent evidence. It showed the shortcomings of treating curriculum and qualifications as things to be implemented, things to be ticked off: things that would therefore seem to many schools more a matter of compliance than excitement or spur for real change.

The new curriculum and qualifications framework depended on schools working more collectively, both internally and externally, operating as inquiry or learning organisations. The 1990s showed the shortcomings of not working with schools to change the way they worked at the same time. It showed the shortcomings of putting self-management ahead of learning: student learning, adult learning, system learning.

A change of government in late 1999 would see some willingness to learn from the first decade of *Tomorrow's Schools*. There would be a much greater emphasis on improving the capability and capacity that needed to go into those "local decisions" of self-managing schools. In the next chapter I look at what was done to focus school leadership and governance more on student learning and engagement, and the moves towards more joint work between schools and between educators and the government agencies. The second decade of *Tomorrow's Schools* would see some much-needed gains in capability and student qualification achievement. It would also expose the limits of a system based on separation, on self-managing schools framed as stand-alone units, without sufficient interconnecting infrastructure.

# Chapter 7

# Trying to 'steer at a distance'

There was always an expectation in the *Tomorrow's Schools* reforms that the link between schools and the government agencies would be through the accountability school boards had in return for their funding and flexibility. Actual experiences of this link in the first decade of self-managing schools, as described in Chapter 5, were not of a two-way connection that could make this accountability play a strong active role in schools. School charters and the annual reports related to them were not the basis of useful discussions about ongoing school development, related to the Government's educational priorities, nor were they to the fore in ERO reviews.

This chapter is about the actions the Ministry and ERO took in the period 2000–11 to improve schools' capability to exercise self-management, in line with the original expectation of the reforms that school self-management would improve educational opportunities. In the 2000s the government agencies could not, or did not try to, change the division between policy and operations that kept them at a remove from schools, that overarching framework for *Tomorrow's Schools*. But they did work on finding new ways to 'steer at a distance', as Howard Fancy put it, not encroaching on what sometimes seemed to me to be the new sacred cow of self-management, but by setting schools on the path that was needed if the school system as a whole was to do better by its students.

I start with changes to the framework for school planning and reporting, how they were received, and how they did lead to some improvements in school self-management over time. Yet this was not enough to make a real improvement in the unevenness of school leadership and governance, and in the ability of schools to use their self-management. The schools that had most difficulty with self-management—for whom it was not enough to meet all the challenges they faced—often continued to be the schools serving students whose educational opportunities needed most to be improved. But difficulties with self-management were not limited to these schools, which was an important limitation of the *Tomorrow's Schools* system. Persistence of unevenness in school capability raised questions about what was being asked of school boards, and principals, and how well they were being supported. First, more support for new principals was developed. This was followed by a new framework for school leadership, based on research synthesis, that could give both principals and the Ministry a stronger platform for what best to focus on to improve student learning.

Funding of education, though it improved over the 2000s, could still not match expectations and needs at both the school and the system level. The National-led Government that came to power in late 2008 after 9 years of Labour-led Governments has responded to the continuing recession by holding or trimming public spending. Education, like health, has always been a priority for voters, and government funding for education has not been cut, unlike some other public services. School operational funding has in fact increased. But this increase at school level has been at the cost of some important investments in the essential infrastructure for education. Some of the key professional learning programmes have been axed. New connections between individual schools and the Ministry were heralded in 2010/11, focused on school charters and annual reports. However, these new Ministry–school connections are occurring in a more mistrustful context, without ongoing joint work at the policy level, and with considerable reduction of such work in professional learning. It is unclear whether the new Ministry–school connections will be able to bring to schools the challenge and support they need to keep developing in ways that will improve student learning.

## Getting inside schools' heads

Changes to charters that were introduced in legislation in 2001 show the officials' unease about whether what was now a disconnected system could improve student learning. They are also a testament to the continued reliance on school self-management to achieve those improvements. The Ministry was not in a position to challenge the very assumptions of the *Tomorrow's Schools* system and build new ongoing connections of support and challenge, with responsibility shared in a real way between government and schools. But it had the authority, with political backing, to frame how schools reported their work. In doing so, it could influence how they approached that work.

The deliberately named Education Standards Act 2001 specified that school charters should now be strategic plans. These strategic plans should have goals for improved student achievement over the following 3 to 5 years, improvement targets for the current year (the annual plan) and the "activities" planned to reach the strategic goals—what allocation of resources in expertise, materials, time and money the school would make to improve student performance. Schools' annual reports would include analysis of the progress made towards their student achievement goals. These annual plans and reports would be "lodged" with the local Ministry office (Ministry of Education, 2002c, p. 2). "Lodged" is an interesting term. It honours the self-management principle by avoiding any implication of a hierarchical relationship, of schools reporting to a controlling authority.

Nonetheless, even with such a carefully chosen term, schools were accustomed to doing things on their own. Some now equated school self-management with autonomy, and some principals and boards reacted negatively to what they saw as an imposition on this autonomy. But the Ministry's intention was not to tell schools what to do and how to do it; nor was it to add something that schools would see as mere compliance—something to be ticked off and put aside once done. Tim McMahon, who spearheaded much of the Schools Planning and Reporting project, told regional seminars around the country that its purpose was to change teachers' practice in classrooms, otherwise there would be no change to student outcomes.

How the Ministry hoped to change teacher practice was through instituting in schools "a continuous improvement culture" (Ministry of Education, 2002c, p. 1), through annual cycles of self-review, based on student achievement data, which would assess a school's progress against its strategic goals and annual targets. It was asking schools to use student assessment and performance data as the litmus test for decisions on how best to use staff and money, and to keep reviewing these decisions, shifting resources where the needs were greatest. Such linking of analysis, action and budget allocation should build more connections within the school programme, more coherence in what people put their energy into. It should lead to more sharing of knowledge within the school and the building of knowledge and shared purpose, as teachers at different year levels tackled a common target; for example, to improve the reading comprehension levels of Māori boys.

The inclusion of long-term strategic planning, with goals 3 to 5 years away, was intended to encourage cumulative effort and knowledge-building, to move away from the periodic spotlighting of a curriculum area or school level that had dominated the first decade of *Tomorrow's Schools* (largely, it has to be said, because of the swift succession of new curriculum guidelines rather than schools' own desires).

Schools were given free rein to set their own goals and targets, and to decide which measures of student achievement they would use: these measures could be qualitative as well as quantitative. The NAGs did become more specific: statements about the need to improve student outcomes now included a priority on improvements in literacy and numeracy achievement, particularly in the first 4 years of school, and on working with Māori communities to "plan, set targets for and achieve better outcomes for Māori students" (Ministry of Education, 2002c, p. 3).

Schools were encouraged to have a trial run before 2003, when they were legally required to use the new planning and reporting framework. They were supported in coming to grips with it through the now usual array of guidance on paper and on the Internet (the Ministry's main channels, unless individual schools approached Ministry officials) and advice from school support services and NZSTA. The time taken, the guidance and the advice combined to successfully convey the message that this new framework was aimed at raising student achievement, not reducing school initiative (Hipkins, Joyce, & Wylie, 2007).

At the start, strategic planning was often a "smorgasbord of things the school hoped to achieve or focus on" (Cain, 2009, p. 5). But over time this framework did provide many schools with a more cohesive approach to what they were doing, underlining the value of continual development and openness to change. It also had important aspects in common with the framework for the revised *New Zealand Curriculum*, which was re-crafted through a carefully designed development process from 2002. The 'revision' of the New Zealand curriculum was a process that would leave teachers and principals with a strong sense of ownership of the new curriculum framework when it was available in draft form in 2007 (Ministry of Education, 2007), with mandatory use by 2010; along with great respect for the Ministry officials involved, particularly Mary-Anne Mills, and Mary Chamberlain, who spearheaded the work and took it around the country.

The revised *New Zealand Curriculum* positioned schools as actively constructing their own curriculum emphasis. They would achieve this through working with their communities to identify a core set of values, within the national framework, that would be the touchstone for their priorities and work. Schools were not to simply "implement" a set of separate curriculum statements. They would need to grasp the whole intent of the New Zealand curriculum framework and plan a coherent programme for students' learning, both in each year level and across time, using assessment as an essential part of teaching and learning. Assessment was now inside the curriculum, a touchstone for ongoing inquiry about where students were on their learning journey and what they would need for the next stage. Inquiry cycles were laid out for teachers. Inquiry was also emphasised in building student ability to evaluate their own learning in the light of their goals.

Like the planning and reporting framework, the revised New Zealand curriculum framework nudges schools towards more collective ways of working, with more self-awareness, more weighing of action and achievement against purpose. At both the national level and the school level these two frameworks have given New Zealand education much needed coherence. By 2009/10 the majority of primary and secondary principals in the NZCER national surveys were saying they would use the planning and reporting cycle, or something like it, even if it was not mandatory.

But planning and reporting did not reconnect schools with the Ministry, despite the indications in the initial outline of the new framework that

> By analysing the information that schools provide in their Charters and reports, the Ministry may be able to help schools identify challenges and opportunities, and help them to plan and implement programmes that produce better outcomes for their students. (Ministry of Education, 2002c, p. 8)

Although regional and district office staff numbers rose, they were not increased sufficiently to work more closely with schools on an ongoing basis, and they often had to give priority to new national initiatives or national office enquiries. Regional offices were also too frequently restructured to provide continuity.

The regional and district Ministry of Education offices were not given any clear mandate to work with individual schools, other than checking that their plans and reports covered what was in the legislation. They don't seem to have been reading them systematically to give feedback on the content: on whether, for example, a school's strategy was likely to achieve its desired goal. They were not reading them to see whether there was continuity in the goals: whether school knowledge and capability were in fact building, whether there were gains over time for students. Without knowledgeable feedback, many schools could continue to see their sharing of their charter and reports as largely about "compliance without purpose" (Cain, 2009), rather than working together with the Ministry to keep improving student learning.

Nonetheless, by 2007, 60 percent of primary and 54 percent of secondary principals were saying that they would like to have, or had had, professional discussions with the Ministry of Education on their annual plan and targets

(Schagen & Wylie, 2009). They could see value in such discussions and did not see them as undermining their self-management. Most primary principals were also interested in working with their local Ministry of Education office to establish local priorities for action. But the local offices lacked any clear mandate to put together a picture of the collective strengths and needs of the schools in an area so that there was a useful basis for collective thinking and action. Such a picture would have taken time they often did not have, particularly with schools using different measures and targets. One regional office did use regional-level NCEA achievement data to challenge those at an annual sector organisation regional meeting of school leaders for what they saw as complacency about lifting Māori student performance, but strategies to improve things had to be left to the individual initiative of those in the audience. The regional and district offices were rarely in the position to provide the ongoing hub needed to connect those grappling with the same issues. There were also gaps between the regional offices and the national level of the Ministry, with little evidence of the two-way flow of information and joint work that would have helped the development of both policy and operations.

# Can ERO improve school self-management capability?

After two government reviews of ERO's approach, arising from persistent sector unease that ERO reviews were primarily judgements of compliance rather than supports for improvement, ERO reviews from the early 2000s included specific suggestions for improvement. They also included some areas the school itself nominated, as well as the areas of government priority for the year a particular school was reviewed. Some feedback on school plans and annual reports occurred, usually within the context of the school review as a whole. Suggestions from ERO reviews fed into what schools included in their planning, or had already included.

But for most schools these reviews are only once every 3 years. Indeed, from 2010 a school could be judged as doing so well that it did not need to be reviewed for another 4 to 5 years. This government decision seems like a throwback to the 1990s, when it seemed important to separate government agencies and schools: when we did not know what we know now about the importance of good connections of challenge and support for schools.

Even schools that appear to be solidly performing can hit snags. The former chief inspector of OFSTED, the ERO equivalent in England, also voiced disquiet when the government there exempted 'outstanding' schools from further regular inspection. OFSTED monitors information on student achievement in these schools. In 2011 it found that 40 percent of outstanding schools that it went back to on the basis of that information had declined in overall performance, usually because of a change in school leadership, loss of teachers or a change in the student intake (Ofsted reveals how its star exemptions fell from grace, 2011). In its annual report for the year ended 30 June 2000, ERO reported on analysis that "indicates that the greater the time that elapses between ERO reviews of a school, the greater the probability that ERO will find unsatisfactory performance that requires a return to the school to carry out a discretionary review" (ERO, 2000, p. 24).

In the 1990s ERO and compliance did seem synonymous to schools, and most would probably have welcomed longer stretches between reviews. But with the generally more positive perception of ERO in the 2000s, as ERO reviews became more focused on the development of each school, disconnection from external feedback is hardly an appropriate reward for doing well.

Principals I spoke with in 2011 included those whose schools were now in the 4-to-5-year review cycle. They were certainly happy to have a longer interval before they would need to assemble all the paperwork, the proof of what they are doing, that ERO requires. It is a solid exercise that takes substantial time (and photocopying). But they also thought that *all* schools need more regular feedback from ERO, or at least from a source that usually had a wider overview than the school could access through its own knowledge and networks. Indeed, most principals want *more* feedback than they are currently getting, from either ERO or the Ministry, provided it is well informed and able to provide useful new understanding that is relevant to the school.

Just under half the primary principals in NZCER's 2010 national survey expressed a preference for ongoing discussions on their school's annual plan rather than the current ERO review, improved though they find it. Most of the rest were unsure whether they would prefer ongoing discussions or the current form of ERO review, probably because it would depend on the quality of these discussions. Only 10 percent were happy to stick to the current ERO framework. This may be because, while ERO reports are used by schools somewhat more than in the 1990s, there is still uncertainty among principals about whether ERO reviews are a reliable indicator of the overall quality of teaching and learning in a school, and whether the results are consistent across schools. Though ERO has made available lists of its evaluation indicators, it is not clear how they are actually used in ERO review judgements. Its reports on the quality of teaching at the national level have also lacked information on how teaching is assessed, raising questions about the validity of the judgements and national figures. However, the national reports do describe good and, more recently, poor practice, and it would be interesting to know whether school leaders then use these as benchmarks to look at their own practice. But what the ERO national reports are not able to provide is advice on *how* to change practice.

Since 2010 ERO has offered more post-review assistance for the schools that fall short of the criteria needed to remain in the 3-yearly review cycle, indeed calling this category "longitudinal". Later in this chapter I look at the disappointment one principal experienced when ERO could not provide the advice she needed.

ERO has also sought to strengthen schools' capability to make the most of their self-management by developing a set of self-review guidelines, which also encompass strategic planning and the wise use of achievement and engagement information. Schools' desire for such knowledge is evident in the popularity of free workshops on these guidelines that were requested throughout the country in 2009/10.

# Whose responsibility?

Around 16 percent of schools reviewed each year in the mid- to late 2000s would be told at the end of their ERO review that ERO would be back within a year, or soon after, because it had found "cause for concern about the education and safety of students" (ERO, 2010). As in the first decade of *Tomorrow's Schools,* the same cluster of school characteristics showed that the schools that struggled most included those serving students for whom school self-management was supposed to work best: Māori, those in low-income communities, and rural and small schools. Most schools to which ERO returns within 1 to 2 years address the most pressing issues identified and return to the normal 3-year cycle. But around a fifth of all schools slipped out of this normal 3-year cycle at least twice from the mid-1990s (Wylie, forthcoming), indicating that improvements were not sustained: the schools had not been able to develop stronger school cultures, attract good leadership and governance, use professional development well, or make good funding decisions.

Last year I heard the highly experienced principal of a small rural school talk about what he had inherited when family connections prevailed upon him to return to the educational fold. In the 6 previous years 10 principals went through this school. Teacher turnover was also rapid. The school had five ERO reviews in those 6 years when two would be the norm. Its roll dropped by two-thirds. Student learning was badly compromised for the mostly Māori students who remained. Their turnaround principal was passionate about the neglect he saw:

> Where was the moral purpose in those principals? They used it as a springboard—their first principalship, then they could move to a larger school. Where was the New Zealand Principals' Federation in this? NZEI? ERO? The Ministry of Education, which annually approves school charters?[1]

This is an extreme example of what can happen in a system based on schools operating autonomously. ERO's responsibility was limited to review, identifying actions the board needed to take to meet its legal responsibilities (such as regular teacher appraisal) and recommendations. The Ministry of Education appeared to have provided financial advice but did not appoint a limited statutory manager (perhaps that would be too expensive for a small school; perhaps the tide looked as if it would turn with each new principal). No-one had the authority to work with the board to recruit or appoint a new principal, to gauge their capability and commitment. No-one beyond the school had the clear authority to work with a principal over time, providing the support and challenge that principal may have needed to halt a slide and turn a school around.

The professional educational organisations can and do offer advice and support to their members, but they cannot tell boards whom to appoint, and they cannot work or keep working with a principal who does not want their advice and support. Other schools in the area are competitors. They were not unhappy to see some of this location's students come their way. The schools in the area lack the incentive and resources to work together, to share responsibility for the wellbeing of all the area's schools and students.

The local community of this school eventually used its networks and moral suasion to recruit the skilled leadership needed to revive their school, which is now flourishing again. Other schools facing difficulty keeping or attracting

---

1   Doug Hales, presentation to the Wellington branch of the New Zealand Educational Administration & Leadership Society, 14 November 2011.

knowledgeable and capable principals—still most likely to be located in rural or poor areas—are often not so lucky. It is hard to see how we can make progress overall if we remain reliant on good luck to keep a sizeable proportion of our schools in good health.

# Governance becomes more focused, but no simpler

The school planning and reporting framework also started to shape what school boards focused on in their meetings and consultation. Providing strategic direction for the school and scrutinising school performance were increasingly identified by trustees as key elements in their role, alongside support for the school.[2] However, board expertise was still more likely to be found in relation to finance and property than it was in strategic planning.

In 2007 ERO judged that 40 percent of schools needed to improve their school governance. Most of these would benefit from the "regular, targeted training to build trustees' capability to govern more effectively [which] has often been recommended by ERO as a way of addressing the governance issues identified during a review". Seven percent of the boards needed much more: they needed "targeted intervention" (ERO, 2007, p.2). In 2008 the Audit Office concluded that although the Ministry of Education provided a good level of general training and support for school boards, it should get more systematic information about board needs from the organisations it contracted to provide this support, to better meet these needs. The Ministry should also more systematically monitor board performance itself, including reviewing school charters to identify boards in need of support.

Variation between regional Ministry offices was noted in terms of the support they offered to boards 'at risk', with "no overall guidance available to help Ministry staff to decide when and what support they should give boards at risk" (Office of the Auditor-General, 2008, p. 35). It was unclear, therefore, whether all the schools that might need such support were getting it. ERO's picture would certainly suggest that they were not. The Audit Office also found there was no knowledge in the Ministry of how effective the 227 completed statutory interventions since 2001 had been in improving the ability of those schools to self-manage (Office of the Auditor-General, 2008).

---

2   Trends in governance were drawn from the NZCER national surveys over the decade: primary in 2003, 2007 and 2010; secondary in 2003, 2006 and 2009.

What the Audit Office was pointing to was the absence of any mechanisms for ongoing evaluation and learning within the Ministry itself in terms of its support for self-managed schools.

Since this report, the Ministry of Education has tightened its contracts with providers of training and support to boards, including the NZSTA (New Zealand School Trustees' Association), and its processes for identifying boards needing support. It has set up a register of people accredited to undertake statutory interventions. It has updated its guidance to trustees, including more of a focus on the role of boards in improving student performance.[3] How effective these moves have been is yet to be documented. The sharper guidance for new trustees is cast in more readily approachable language, but would still need interpretation and fleshing out for many trustees. Anecdotally, I have heard of frustrations with the new processes of contracting support, which involve more layers of people and time.

School governance has turned out to be no simple role.[4] Indeed, the NZSTA now bristles at the description of trustees as volunteers—which is how they are often self-described, and how school governors are generally described overseas—because of the complexity of their role and their joint accountability to both the school community and to the government. In the NZCER surveys, trustees do see their role as it has been framed by government, but they do not see themselves as government agents. Indeed, several hundred boards initially held back from using the recently introduced National Standards after consulting with their communities. While there was some talk of 'sacking' boards that did not comply with the legislation that made their use mandatory, it would have been unrealistic—and not as cheap as having a school board—to sack all these boards and replace them with school commissioners. Instead, compliance was brought about through close inspection of individual school charters for the first time, with the Ministry withholding its required approval until it was satisfied that the National Standards were adequately used in school targets. Without Ministry approval of their charter, schools would be ineligible for the carrots of access to Ministry-funded professional development and additional support for students. Nor could schools be rated within the 4- to 5-year ERO cycle, however strong their student performance on other measures.

---

3   *Effective Governance: Working in Partnership* came out in 2010, half the size of the *Working in Partnership* guidance it replaced. It is much more focused on the actual role and practice of governance than the previous guidance, which was framed more by legal and policy outlines.

4   For further description of the role, its demands and inconsistency in operation see Wylie (2007a), and New Zealand School Trustees Association (2008).

Trustees would generally like more support from the Ministry for their role. The NZSTA unfavourably contrasted the 2008 annual budget of $4.5 million for trustee professional development with the $200 million for teachers' and principals' professional development.[5] One estimate I heard around this time of what it would take to provide boards with sufficient training and support was more like $13 million a year: money that is unlikely to ever be found. And this estimate did not include the additional costs for schools that had reached the stage of needing a statutory intervention, often for reasons related to governance.

One of the most difficult questions I have been asked over the years is whether we should retain school boards. Good boards I have encountered have certainly added value to their schools. There is the obvious value of additional resources, making good use of trustees' own employment and community contacts. Good boards bring community knowledge and their own expertise to the table, which complement the educational expertise of the principal and senior staff and widen their perspective. A good chair of the board lightens some of the inherent loneliness of the principal's role, giving the opportunity for ongoing discussion of what is happening and how it can be developed. Good boards are (generally) able to select a good principal when making an appointment. They respect the educational expertise of the staff and support its further development. The iterative cycle of continual development included in the planning and reporting framework, framed by core values the school community has discussed and understood, makes sense to them.

But the system we have cannot ensure that this complementary partnership between educators and trustees will occur at every school. It cannot ensure that it will continue where it does exist. Unevenness of the expertise that boards can bring to their schools continues, without any easy answer. Principals in schools whose community cannot supply all the complementary expertise they need to undertake a complex role continue to carry their boards rather than being supported and challenged by them. Often these are the very schools where the student needs are greatest: where principal and senior leadership energy is needed most to work with teachers and students, not distracted by the work needed to make school governance work.

And even the good boards cannot substitute for the educational knowledge that schools need to improve student learning. This is the prime missing

---

5 'Secondary union clutching at straws', NZSTA media release, 17 December 2008, was released in response to PPTA comments on the financial crisis at a secondary school, which questioned the responsibility asked of school boards.

connection in our unique system of school administration. In overseas systems that have been effective in improving learning (examples are given in Fullan, 2010, and Levin, 2008), principals' immediate accountability is to administrators who have educational expertise. *Tomorrow's Schools* uncoupled this important link, first, by standing schools alone, and second, by putting most weight on the staff–board partnership, while separating operations and policy, disconnecting the schools from the Ministry.

I suspect that if *Tomorrow's Schools* were designed today, with the knowledge we now have, we would not ask so much of school boards. We would also not stand schools alone, without being part of a school district through which schools can have ongoing challenge and support while contributing to the collective wellbeing of the district's schools and students. I believe school boards are here to stay, and schools and their communities need this ongoing connection. But the time has come to reframe their role, and to reconnect schools with the Ministry in ways that strengthen both. I recommend ways to do this in the conclusion (see Chapter 10).

## Growing school leadership

Around half the principals appointed by boards are fresh to their role (Robertson, 2011). In 2002 the Ministry began funding the first systematic programme to equip new principals with the knowledge they need. As well as the opportunity to get to grips with the big picture of their role, participants in the First-Time Principals programme start to use the inquiry process, identifying a goal or challenge at their school, which they tackle with the advice and support of an experienced principal mentor. They are connected as they make sense of their new role with someone who has a good understanding of the day-to-day reality of the principal role. But not all new principals gain these connections: the programme remains voluntary, the decision to take part left to individuals.

Business leaders and professionals who have come to know something of the principal role, perhaps through serving as the chair of a school board, are often struck by the diversity of demands on principals, a greater diversity than they experience themselves in their own leadership roles. Along with this diversity, principals are often interrupted. Their plans for what they will accomplish by the end of a day or week can easily be thrown out of kilter by things that need an immediate response. The buck really does stop with the principal, particularly in smaller schools, usually primary, whether it is stepping in to take a class because no reliever can be found or the school is trying to save money, arranging for the repair of blocked drains, or finding psychological help for a child who has had a dramatic meltdown in the playground. A quarter of primary principals in 2010 were also teaching a class every day.

Fortunately, most principals relish the responsibility and variety in their work. They like solving problems for children and adults, seeing students and teachers flourish. They generally enjoy their role. But a 2005 study of principal wellbeing, initiated by the New Zealand Principals' Federation because of its growing concern with the size of the role, found that principal stress levels were high compared with other occupational groups, GPs excepted (Hodgen & Wylie, 2005). Stress levels were still high in 2010. Principals with the highest stress levels had fewer professional connections with other principals and felt poorly supported by the Ministry. They were more likely to experience tensions in their relations with their school board, and to spend more time on management aspects of their role than educational leadership.

Even principals without high stress levels experience an ongoing tension between the different aspects of their work. This tension is most marked when it comes to the emphasis they would like to place on leading the continual development of teaching and learning, working with others to provide what is now known as 'pedagogical leadership'. It is this leadership that is essential in schools, and that is needed if our education system as a whole is to keep developing. But for many principals it must be weighed against their responsibility to manage finances and property, to find more money and support for the school, to maintain the school profile in the school's locality, and to provide the Ministry of Education and ERO with what they ask for in the way of information and documentation. The attention this kind of leadership should have is up against the crises that students bring or create in school, that disrupt their and often others' learning. It is up against responsibilities associated with staff employment. None of these are likely to go away in the present system.

# Growing the knowledge needed for effective school leadership

"Strong Professional Leadership" became one of the Government's priorities for action in 2007. Included in the Government's plans was a significant turning-point in the development of useful and shared knowledge that could enable principals to work smarter, not harder. This was an Iterative Best Evidence Synthesis, focused on the research evidence on the links between school leadership and student outcomes, and a companion description of effective leadership in New Zealand, *Kiwi Leadership for Principals*. These two bookends for framing the principal's role were the result of joint work by two Ministry sections, bringing together operational and policy perspectives and involving experienced principals, researchers, professional developers and education groups in a process that took several years.

The innovative Iterative Best Evidence Synthesis (BES) programme began in 2002. Spearheaded by Adrienne Alton-Lee, a former teacher and academic before joining the Ministry, the BES programme aimed to identify practices and principles that were effective in improving student performance, through a rigorous scrutiny of existing research. The results would provide resources that schools, professional development providers and advisers to schools could use to decide how to make the best use of their never-sufficient time and money. Such knowledge is essential if schools are to be able to make wise use of their self-management. By 2007, five of these syntheses had been produced.[6]

In 2007 the Ministry section responsible for principal support had recently recruited a former rural adviser, Darren Gammie. He had seen how much principals and those in advisory roles like his own needed the understanding that a BES could produce. He helped make the case to invest some of his section's funds into a Leadership BES. Sound New Zealand expertise was available for the synthesis itself: Viviane Robinson, who had played a key role in the First-Time Principals programme, and Margie Hohepa, who had researched and supported Māori-medium schools, led a University of Auckland team.

The BES process is a demanding iteration of analysis and discussion, with each phase producing the platform for the next. The Leadership BES had a rocky start. Disquiet among New Zealand principals expressed itself forcefully as an initial draft was underway. Would this analysis take into account the full width of the unique New Zealand principal role: their responsibility for the school finances, property, employment, and partnership with parents through the board of trustees? Would it produce a checklist of perfection that principals would never be able to meet, but that would be used to judge their performance?

---

6   The BES programme's home page is http://www.educationcounts.govt.nz/topics/BES. It provides access to the full reports, summaries and exemplars of particularly effective teaching practices that accelerate student progress.

In addition, *Tomorrow's Schools* had asked schools to focus on what made them distinct, to think of themselves as separate entities. Over time, this resulted in principals often describing their schools as 'unique'. For some principals this seemed to mean that broader frameworks were not applicable and that the value of external knowledge was limited. This is school self-management taken too literally.

Difficult though the iterative process was initially, it provided a valuable forum, with key players finally in the same room, learning to find common ground because they focused on one strong shared purpose: a desire to support and develop school leadership that would work well for New Zealand students. Like the iterative processes that had been used before *Tomorrow's Schools* to develop curriculum and resources for school development, and that had been revived in the revision of the New Zealand Curriculum just concluded, this opportunity for ongoing discussion and contribution within a deeply shared purpose led to a greater level of shared understanding and commitment to what emerged. What emerged was more useful because it had been through those discussions.

The Leadership BES contains not just a synthesis of research, but illustrations of principles at work, vignettes, descriptions of 'smart tools' that schools can adapt to their own context, and questions schools can use to think about what they are doing (Robinson, Hohepa, & Lloyd, 2009). It shows that effective school leadership is not about the principal as a single heroic figure (not a sustainable reality), but about the way schools can work more coherently and collectively. It is about the way schools can run learning for adults through the 'management' processes of meetings and performance appraisal, and timetabling so that teachers have time to work together, to share their knowledge and analyse student progress to see if they need to make changes to what they are offering students and how they are relating to them. It frames school leadership as leadership of an organisation that is continually learning and inquiring. It is of a piece with the iterative planning and reporting framework and the teaching as inquiry cycle outlined in the New Zealand Curriculum. Indeed, the teaching as inquiry cycle used in the New Zealand Curriculum originated in work for the social studies BES (Aitken & Sinnema, 2008) and was further developed in discussions around the BES on professional development (Timperley, Wilson, Barrar, & Fung, 2007).

Finally, almost 20 years into *Tomorrow's Schools*, I could see coherence in the key policy frameworks for school self-management. There was certainly much more progress needed to make that coherence a daily reality, which raised questions about the need to rethink how schools and government connected, how schools were supported in ongoing rather than one-off ways.

## Thwarted connections

In their foreword to the Leadership BES, Ben Levin, who was pivotal to the recent and notable improvements to the performance of the Ontario school system,[7] and Michael Fullan wrote after praising it that

> The challenge for all partners in New Zealand (and beyond) will be to make sure that the lessons and implications of this synthesis leap off the pages and become part of the fabric of education. This means much more than creating some professional development events or new resources. It means considering how the findings herein can be reflected in school and national policy … This BES report on leadership will be for nought unless there is a concerted plan to develop the core capacities of effective leadership in all New Zealand schools. (Robinson et al., 2009, p. 14)

Such a plan had been developed by the Ministry by 2009 through an iterative process and joint work with an ongoing advisory group[8] carrying on from the Leadership BES work. It was a pleasure for me to be part of this group, because it was a forum for genuine open discussion about how to improve and support school leadership, and it did start some useful action. It brought together the Ministry of Education, union and professional association leaders, the NZSTA, academics (who also provided leadership professional development), and me, a policy researcher. There was sufficient continuity in the membership for trust to develop, enabling that open discussion. Here were the connections with a shared purpose that we needed if we were to make progress.

The leadership dimensions and skills and dispositions identified by the Leadership BES and included in *Kiwi Leadership for Principals* provided the coherence needed to support good school leadership.[9] They were used in new professional development for around 300 principals in 2009/10 as part of the

---

7  His account of how this occurred, and the importance of focusing on capacity development within a coherent and focused approach that aligns schools, school districts and the equivalent of the Ministry of Education in purposeful, knowledgeable and respectful ways, is highly readable and important (see Levin, 2008). It should be required reading for Ministry, Treasury, State Services Commission and Department of Prime Minister and Cabinet employees, their Ministers, education organisations, and lobby groups.

8  Initially called the External Policy Group, it became the Professional Leadership Forum in late 2009.

9  More information about New Zealand school leadership and policy related to it can be found in Wylie (2011c).

Ministry's plan to develop strong leadership in every school. They went into the new standards for principals, which boards should use in their annual appraisal of their employee. Viviane Robinson and I developed a 'smart' tool, an electronic survey that would simultaneously serve both individual schools and the national level. Schools get a picture of the leadership practices that are most related to gains for students and decide what they want to develop further. The survey and reports have proved to be a useful and stimulating process for schools. Collating the school pictures provides a national picture. The first national picture—the baseline for monitoring what the national needs are for supporting leadership development—was completed in mid-2011.[10]

What is missing now is an ongoing forum to discuss those collated school results, to put them in the context of what is being done to support the capability of school leadership and gauge whether that is enough to keep developing teaching and learning in schools. The leadership advisory group that had given me some optimism that the divisions between the Ministry and the sector were finally being bridged had what turned out to be its last full meeting in early 2010. There was not much optimism expressed at that meeting. One of the group summed it up: we were looking at a rapidly approaching 'perfect storm'. Political haste and unwillingness to have real dialogue and undertake joint work with those who need to make policy succeed were stoking opposition to the introduction of National Standards in literacy and maths in primary schools. NCEA standards needed to be revised to align with the revised *New Zealand Curriculum*, along with other changes to NCEA, increasing secondary teacher workloads substantially at a time when Ministry funding for many secondary subject advisers was to be withdrawn. And in difficult economic times, teacher and principal collective contract negotiations lay ahead.

The new professional development for existing principals, which used the national frameworks to identify and support local needs and showed what could be gained by having well-grounded national frameworks, came to an end. Leadership and management advisers, who were also using the new frameworks, lost their positions as the Ministry retendered all the school support services. Some have found positions in the organisations that won the new contracts, allowing some continuity. But a lot of momentum and connections seem to have been lost in the transition, which also involved restructuring in the

---

10 The *Educational Leadership Practices Survey* and the baseline picture are given in Burgon, Ferral, Hodgen and Wylie (2012).

Ministry and with it the loss of key people. Currently, there is no clear way to keep building on what was achieved in the work the Ministry led.

None of the ratings given the Ministry of Education in its 2010 Performance Improvement Framework Review by the government troika of the State Services Commission, the Treasury and the Department of the Prime Minister and Cabinet were at the highest level, 'strong'. Its strategic leadership of schools, and its provision to schools of services and infrastructure, were all 'needing development'. So, too, was its progress on the goals of Māori enjoying success as Māori, and the Youth Guarantee policy, aimed at providing better options for secondary students. While Ministry staff "have a strong commitment to helping achieve a better education system", there was insufficient openness to external input, particularly from the sector and those with expertise, and insufficient "active learning" within the Ministry itself. Too much "risk aversion" was making the Ministry too slow and creating uncertainty for schools and those working in education beyond the Ministry. It needed to have more "effective engagement with those stakeholders who are key to progress on the most significant issues". Its work would provide better value if it sought and used knowledge of the cost-effectiveness of educational practices, programmes and structures, and shared this knowledge with the sector so that it could spend its money wisely. It needed to work with the sector better if the prime focus of educational leadership was to be "increasing student achievement and the effectiveness of the education system" (State Services Commission, Treasury, & Department of the Prime Minister and Cabinet, 2011, pp. 8–10).

In its post-2011 election briefing papers to the Minister of Education, the Ministry notes the importance of "buy-in" to the closures of "non-essential" schools, which it envisages as one of the few ways that sufficient savings can be made to fund growing educational needs. "Successful improvements in the schooling system can only be achieved if we take those working in the sector with us" (Ministry of Education, 2011a, p. 24). 'Buy-in' and 'taking with us' are a long way from 'working together'.

The leadership advisory group was not the only Ministry–sector–researcher group to come to an end in 2010. There seem now to be far fewer ways for this kind of ongoing working together to achieve the shared understanding, sense of shared responsibility and willingness to act that are needed more than ever. One notable exception is the work the Special Education section within the Ministry has done in relation to student behaviour, developing the PB4L (Positive Behaviour for Learning) strategy, through joint work starting with the 2009 Taumata Whanonga, which discussed existing evidence about effective behaviour management to develop a shared action plan. Without such ongoing connections focused on a shared purpose, the Ministry's difficult challenge of needing to make the education dollar go further while achieving marked gains in student learning will be far harder.

## The new local links: Grounds for hope?

Ministry restructuring has, however, included a greater focus on the local level, with the aim of forging closer Ministry–school links.[11] ERO has also begun to offer schools that did not make the 3-year cycle more regular advice to help them return to the 3-year cycle, and the two organisations are likely to communicate more about their work with such schools.

What sorts of support are called for? Last year I returned to talk to the principal of a school whose progress over the past few years had been notable. In one of the poorest and most vexed communities of Auckland, this school had a long history of unstable leadership and too-frequent ERO reviews. Finally it was given a statutory adviser, who used personal networks to find a leader who saw a moral obligation to this community and its children.

This Māori principal had worked in low-decile schools, with Māori and Pasifika students, with good results. In this school she needed to tackle change on a number of fronts, but with minimal resources. The school was in debt as the result of previous principal and board decisions and inaction. A school–community garden, which she instigated, served a number of purposes in terms of children's learning, nutrition and building the home–school links that are important for children's learning. Behaviour improved with thoughtful, positive framing. She situated the school within wider health and social services networks, garnering more of the support the children needed. She tackled the low quality of teaching she first encountered, using her own connections to recruit an experienced lead teacher to help her start to shift teaching practice, and making it clear to others that their practice needed to change—resulting in those who did not see the need to change leaving the school. Good-quality literacy professional development from involvement in a school improvement cluster augmented the knowledge she and her lead teacher had.

---

11  The Ministry has 11 offices, situated in four regions. Special Education, the largest section within the Ministry, providing specialist services for schools as well as policy development, maintains a larger network, using 16 districts, with between one and four centres in different locations in each district (a total of 40 offices).

But all of this was not enough to lift all the children's learning consistently. Her experienced lead teacher followed her partner to another part of the country, and it proved difficult to sustain the teaching practices they had introduced. Like many low-decile school principals, she was over-reliant on young teachers and immigrants. These new teachers often leave once they have gained teacher registration, seeking out less demanding schools or schools that are a shorter commuting distance from where they live. Where low-decile schools have a strong backbone of committed and knowledgeable teachers, working in a strong collective culture, such turnover of new teachers need not be undermining—though it certainly adds to the workload. But in this small school it continually eroded the work being done, and the continuity of teacher–student relationships that is particularly important for children in such schools.

When I spoke with this principal in mid-2011 the optimism I had seen during the previous few years of progress was almost gone. She had exhausted her own connections to recruit the knowledgeable staff the school needed to both teach the students and work with the beginner teachers. She worked with them herself, and rejigged the timetable to give the beginning teachers regular planning time so that they felt more on top of their work as well as less drained by the intensity of classroom work with these students. But she still faced the need to recruit, yet again.

She had made sufficient progress in the school for it to be close to returning to the normal 3-year ERO cycle. That would have been her preference: something the teachers and community could take pride in, spurring new effort. She was not quite close enough, and the school remained in what was now termed the 'longitudinal' category of reviews. But she hoped that the new ERO framework would give her more attention: new insight and support that might break the impasse she felt she had reached. Things seemed promising initially, with a person from the regional Ministry of Education office involved as well as the ERO reviewer. But nothing new came her way:

> I invited them to put any suggestions down on the table that they had because I was more than willing to give anything a try. Up until then they were going to come every month, then they said we'll go now and we'll email you at the end of Term 3. I took that to mean they had nothing to put down on the table and that really frightens me … If you're on the bottom, the chances from what I have found here of getting off the bottom become more and more remote and harder. There has to be another way.

Although there was the appearance of greater connection between school and government agency, in fact the government officials focused only on the school's planning and self-review capability, and added little. The principal already had the capability to diagnose her school's needs: that wasn't the problem. What she wanted was not the shell but the substance: educational knowledge, someone who could observe and discuss the school's educational practices on the basis of tackling similar challenges themselves with some success. She also needed networks that could yield experienced teachers whom she could recruit to the school, who would stay committed. These officials appeared to lack both the knowledge and networks she needed. Without that knowledge or those connections, they could contribute nothing.

# Challenges for Ministry–school connections

These were the very early days of the Ministry's new local approach and ERO's assistance to schools in the longitudinal review category. One would hope that the frustrations for this principal would not be repeated. There are some challenges ahead, however, for the new approach.

The new Ministry roles at the local level pivot on the planning and reporting framework. Ministry knowledge of schools will be shaped by what schools report of their student achievement and the school's identification of priorities. Every school has been assigned a senior adviser, whose role is to discuss school progress on its annual targets and longer-term goals with the principal. Schools' access to Ministry-funded professional development will be on the basis of what the school has identified in its planning, and will be decided by a professional learning and development officer. Schools like the one described above, whose annual reports show low achievement levels, or that have rolls with substantial numbers of the Government's priority groups (Māori, Pasifika, those from low-income homes, and students with special learning needs), will be offered a student achievement practitioner. This person will work with the school to institute a change team within the school, who will work with their colleagues on new approaches to accelerate rates of student progress. By the end of 2011 there were some 50 of these practitioners, working with 300 schools.

The success of this new approach in establishing more productive Ministry–school connections, and in supporting schools to improve student achievement, relies on:

- the quality and relevance of the knowledge and connections Ministry officials can offer, including whether they have a full (rather than compliance-based) understanding of the national frameworks schools must operate with—the New Zealand Curriculum, National Standards and the assessments that contribute to teacher judgements, NCEA, as well as the NEGs and NAGs and other regulations

- whether Ministry officials bring strong evidence-based knowledge that schools can use to keep developing their practice so that students gain more from it

- the timeliness and appropriateness of Ministry allocation decisions

- how well the new contractual environment for funding professional development, and statutory advisers and commissioners, works to bring schools the knowledge they need in ways that build their own knowledge and capacity

- whether support is continued long enough for schools to embed the changes and see positive and enduring results

- whether there are sufficient connections of a knowledge-building kind between the Ministry officials working with individual schools and those they contract to work with schools

- whether schools trust the officials and the processes they use.

Establishing trust in the current environment may not be easy. Some of the first work undertaken in the new Ministry roles seemed to emphasise compliance rather than the shared responsibility, working together over time, that is needed. The advent of National Standards saw the first systematic scrutiny of every primary school charter since the early days of *Tomorrow's Schools*, and strong follow-up Ministry action to persuade boards to change their charter where it was found wanting in terms of including National Standards. Probably around 15 percent of primary schools had to be actively persuaded, where boards saw only costs rather than gains for student learning. They were not prepared to fudge their position in the careful wording used by the many other schools that have concerns about the National Standards, and about reporting achievement and setting targets while the National Standards are still bedding in, with likely inconsistency between schools in how they judge student performance against the standards.

Included in the group that had to be persuaded were schools that have been at the forefront of innovation based on the New Zealand Curriculum and sharing good practice with other schools. Schools that did not comply were faced with having a statutory manager, even if they could show that their student achievement was good on existing standardised assessments. Access to support for teaching and learning was, as always, a significant lever. Non-complying schools would not have access to Ministry-funded professional development, nor to additional support for individual students with low literacy or mathematics levels. Every school board was eventually persuaded. A cynical taste was left in many of their and their principal's mouths. Boards and principals see themselves as jointly accountable to their community and the Government. In the past that joint accountability was unproblematic. Now quite a few schools see government and their community as facing in different directions.

Schools have also been accustomed to dealing directly with professional development providers contracted by the Ministry. The new process will need to prove itself in the face of suspicion that it is an erosion of school self-management, that it will delay schools accessing what their own analysis identifies as the knowledge they need and are ready to use.

Ministry staff certainly face an uphill slog to (re)gain schools' trust. Their own educational reputation will become even more crucial to the success of the policy emphasis on improving the quality of teaching and learning. To undertake the work envisaged will require Ministry staff who have substantial experience of working successfully in schools and of bringing about change in teaching practice and student achievement, who keep abreast of new knowledge and are connected to those who are generating it.

But the Ministry has struggled for some time—and continues to struggle—to attract sufficient educators with this experience. Not a few are deterred by the Ministry's need to give first priority to serving its Minister. This priority is particularly problematic where a Minister chooses to engage only superficially with the sector and shies away from having the Ministry undertake the ongoing joint work needed to accompany substantial changes to the national frameworks intended to alter school practice, as occurred with the introduction of the National Standards in the 2008–11 period.

In addition, the Ministry cannot match the salaries many principals and quite a few senior school staff get. A hidden cost of centring educational administration on self-managing schools, and enlarging the demands on principals, has been that school managers' salaries have had to become commensurate with these greater responsibilities. But a by-product of this is the undermining of the career paths that in the past brought school operational knowledge into the local Ministry level, as well as into national policy and guidance. Educators who have served in the Ministry have often done so on secondment, to retain their income levels. Others have come in on contracts. That has another cost: too many people employed short term or not as part of the Ministry's own core teams, reducing the knowledge and consistency over time of those teams. A fast turnover in Ministry roles also makes it difficult to build on the knowledge and relationships established—a hidden inefficiency. At the national level there has been a noticeable loss of expertise in the past couple of years.

The new approach at the local level only connects the Ministry with individual schools on a one-to-one basis. This means the connections cannot challenge the fragmentation that came with *Tomorrow's Schools*. The new approach is therefore limited in its ability to develop more collective approaches to sharing and building knowledge in an area. These new connections aren't weaving a new fabric of shared responsibility for an area's students, allowing the kind of joint inquiry work, discussion, and decision making that we need more than ever if we are to make the best use of the public funding available for New Zealand schooling.

# Pressure on system funding from school self-management

In its 2002 analysis of what was needed to lift system performance, the Ministry of Education signalled the need for clear goals and priorities in education, to address education sector workforce issues and ensure sufficient resources for achieving the changes needed in education (Ministry of Education, 2002c, p. 53). Is it ironic that after Treasury scorned the Department of Education for stressing the need for more investment in education in the mid- to late 1980s, its replacement, headed by an ex-Treasury official and with other ex-Treasury officials in senior management, was having to note that the education system could not be maintained, let alone developed further, unless funding was increased?

Funding for education was indeed increased over the past decade. Until the recession there was more investment in system initiatives to improve teaching practice—with some notable successes, as I describe in the next chapter. School operational grants were also increased, though never enough to meet rising expectations and costs. The NZSTA's major, albeit unachieved, goal for the 2000s decade was to increase school operational funding by more than just changes to the general cost of living index. It also wanted the original 1989 funding formula revisited to cover the reality of the administrative costs of having each school self-managed and the now essential computers and Internet access. As early as 1994 Sir John Anderson observed that this funding formula no longer fitted what was being asked of schools. The Ministry of Education undertook a review of operational funding in 2005/06 (Ministry of Education, 2006) and included sector groups in an advisory group. Hopes that increases would be made to recognise the new costs were, however, disappointed.

By 2007 locally raised funds were contributing 28 percent of the overall money at schools' disposal, up from 17 percent in 2001 and 8–12 percent in 1996, even though it had become increasingly harder for individual schools to raise additional money (Hartevelt, 2008). Though the National-led Government elected in 2008 increased schools' operational funding by more than the rise in the Consumer Price Index, the proportion of primary schools that ended the 2010 year in deficit was 52 percent, up from 40 percent in 2006. Most of these deficits will be for a single year. Nonetheless, the overall picture is of a continuing slippage in the ability of existing government funding, coupled with local effort, to cover what schools are spending.

School leaders and boards have to give priority to financial management and raising funds. School budgets are tight, and even in well-managed schools can be thrown out of kilter by an unexpected new cost. On the whole, self-managed and separately funded schools have to take a cautious approach to innovation. They cannot be as flexible as *Tomorrow's Schools* anticipated because they cannot afford to take financial risks (Wylie & King, 2004, 2005). Understandably, they usually budget only money they are sure of getting. Schools can move faster where they have good experience to build on (whether their own or the knowledge of those they work with) and where the change does not involve substantial expenditure. Otherwise it is difficult to make major changes in their programmes unless they can attract new funding, be included in well-designed professional development, or are in partnership with research developers building and using knowledge. Most of this needs funding at the national level, as part of ongoing infrastructure.

Continued increases in school operational grants over 2008–11 were made possible by cuts in national programmes and support. This is not a wise trade-off. More than ever, schools and the system need to be sharing and building knowledge of how to better meet student need within reasonable budgets. They also need to be working more collectively at the local level, rather than grappling with meeting student needs in a piecemeal fashion, with each school trying to preserve or extend the funds at its disposal even though some across-school sharing of resources could cover more students, or better meet particular student needs where expertise cannot be sufficiently funded separately at each school.

At the system level there needs to be increased coherence so that, for example, new knowledge we have is used in preparing new teachers so that they can be effective more quickly. There needs to be more thought given to the national infrastructure schools can use. We need better connections if things are to really change, particularly when public funding for education is very unlikely to increase.

# Chapter 8

# New frameworks for teaching in primary schools

## Support for change

Significant changes did occur in many New Zealand schools and classes over the past decade. What changed in primary schools was largely due to government support for, and Ministry work on, accumulating knowledge about teaching strategies that also build students' learning strategies. The Ministry actively sought to make better use of new or synthesised knowledge about how to do this, supported by more useful assessments for identifying student strengths and needs. Professional development using this knowledge and the new assessments also focused on building school culture that would work collectively and with an inquiry focus: evaluating the effectiveness of the strategies rather than taking it for granted. You could sense a definite sea change by the mid-2000s, when the draft *New Zealand Curriculum* was circulated, further enhancing this inquiry focus in the context of an appealing curriculum framework.

As I show in this chapter, primary student achievement and engagement improved when schools were well supported and had developed good internal processes for such collective work and clear frameworks of student performance, and had good levels of curriculum expertise. But not all schools improved; not all schools changed these essential ways of working; not all schools had the support they needed to do so. The progress that was achieved showed what is possible through deliberate government work. But the uneven spread of new practices and greater capability also showed that this work needs to continue, with sustained attention and sufficient infrastructure to ensure these changes reach all schools, all students.

I start by looking at how teaching practice shifted in many primary schools in the 2000s, focusing on numeracy and writing. Then I look at the development of a culture of professional inquiry in schools: the kind of culture needed to make the most of self-management. Around half the teachers in the NZCER 2010 national survey were in schools that were working more along these lines. I also note the constraints evident in the support that primary schools could access during the 2000s, which meant this culture was still not widespread by the end of the decade.

Yet if the new National Standards framework is to succeed in improving learning, it needs every school to have such a professional inquiry culture. The overly rapid development of the National Standards, coupled with their mandated use in school charters and reports and the new centrality of those charters and reports in Ministry–school connections and allocation of support, has also raised some significant issues, which are discussed in this chapter.

If we are to see gains in student achievement at the national level, we need to see gains for Māori and Pasifika students and students from low-income homes. So my final focus in this chapter is on the challenges experienced in low-decile schools that have made substantial shifts in their teaching practice. The depth of these challenges, in schools that are working at the limits of their knowledge, energy and funding, points to the need for better connections between schools. It also underlines the importance of joint inquiry work anchored by research partners, work that can keep building knowledge that can be used across the country if open and trusting connections with the Ministry of Education are achieved.

## Shifting numeracy teaching

Out of the 1997 Mathematics and Science Taskforce mentioned in Chapter 6 came a policy commitment to better support primary teachers, mainly in mathematics. The Ministry did not try to do this alone, at a distance. What became the Numeracy Development Projects, which had reached about 95 percent of primary schools by 2009, was the result of a connected sequence of joint work, bringing together teachers, teacher educators, researchers and Ministry of Education officials. A set of networks connecting individuals and institutions, the Ministry and the sector gave the project coherence. Research and evaluation were threaded through so that there was ongoing learning, and this learning was put to use to keep improving the quality of the projects.

The programme began in 1999 with a strong research base. It brought together the evidence from NEMP and TIMSS and other assessments of where New Zealand students' mathematics knowledge and ability to use mathematics for problem-solving was weakest, the existing research on how children developed mathematical understanding, and the existing research on effective professional development and school change. The project work identified both what teachers needed to know and do differently if New Zealand students' mathematical understanding was to improve, and the most effective way for teachers to gain and use this knowledge.

Connection and coherence were key to the conception of the Numeracy Development Projects. Schools were connected to the programme through the facilitator they worked with. The facilitator was part of a team employed by each of the six school support services located at the universities. Each facilitator took part in annual national training, with national co-ordination and site visits, and was involved in the development of the materials used in the project. An annual conference shared and discussed experiences, including formal research and evaluation. The knowledge gained in this way informed the next stage of the projects as they tackled successive schooling levels until they reached teachers and students in Years 9 and 10.

Facilitators came with two powerful new ways for teachers to understand their students' needs and thus be able to respond better to them. For the first time in New Zealand, teachers had available a clearly laid-out and conceptually sound 'number framework', describing how children's knowledge of number developed. Coupled with this was a diagnostic interview, a one-to-one discussion between teacher and student that revealed the numeracy strategies the student was using: their thinking behind what they did on the page with numbers. Teachers were often surprised to find that students who performed poorly on the traditional written work and tests actually had a good grasp of solving problems involving number. Conversely, other students "who they had thought were the whizz-bangers of the class, they passed every paper test, and suddenly they were finding massive gaps in their strategies" (facilitator, quoted in Higgins & Parsons, 2009, p. 238). New resources designed to capture student interest were produced. Facilitators worked with schools over a year, modelling how to make the shift to the new approach, how to use the results of the diagnostic interview to see what a child was ready to move on to (thereby making it less likely that teachers would move too fast or too slowly), and how to structure lessons so that they were more engaging. Exemplars were provided in what became known as the "pink books", from the colour of their cover.

Demand for inclusion in the Numeracy Development Projects at any one time usually outstripped the project's resources. It certainly changed the way many teachers approached numeracy teaching. Student scores on the number framework improved substantially when their teachers took part in this professional development, which was customised to their own classroom and school and allowed them to work with facilitators who were part of a wider network, using common tools such as the number framework. These common tools also made it easier for teachers to share what they were doing with each other within and across schools.

In 2006 a sample of New Zealand Year 5 students took part in the next TIMSS round. Those whose schools had taken part in the Numeracy Development Projects had higher scores on average (Caygill & Kirkham, 2008, p. 52). But although most students' teachers had taken part in this professional development, TIMSS maths scores in 2006 were much the same as they had been in 2002. The proportion of students with low scores had reduced between the 1998 and 2002 TIMSS rounds but did not reduce further in 2006. Māori and Pasifika students' scores were lower on average in 2006 than they had been in 2002. Their average scores for the TIMSS science test also dipped over the 4 years, suggesting some other reason for lower maths scores on this international test than student experiences in maths classes—perhaps some differences between the two cohorts of students.

The Numeracy Development Projects data do not show a similar pattern: Māori and Pasifika students gained as much as any other students over the course of their teachers' professional development and in schools that sustained the momentum gained during their professional development work. Not all schools could embed and sustain the Numeracy Development Projects learning, however. Low-decile schools struggled to do so more than others and were less likely to have the mathematics leadership needed within their own staff.

# A way to go

New Zealand primary teachers and students still have a way to go in mathematics and are still in need of systematic support. The new National Standards set the bar higher than many will reach (Young-Loveridge, 2010). In part this is because the National Standards reflect new knowledge about the importance of going beyond knowing 'facts' to being able to think mathematically. One of the key contributors to the Numeracy Development Projects noted that this means asking many teachers to make a profound shift from the way mathematics has been taught in New Zealand and the way they were taught themselves in their own schooling:

> It would be naïve to think that one or two years of professional development could miraculously change teachers' attitudes, feelings, beliefs, and values as well as their understanding of mathematics. (Young-Loveridge, 2010, p. 30)

What the Numeracy Development Projects did achieve with a year's carefully designed and connected professional development was a good foundation for this next shift. Schools with at least one teacher with strong mathematical understanding and interest could use it well by putting these teachers in leadership roles to work with other teachers, including new teachers who may have missed out on the numeracy professional development. Schools that had got into the inquiry swing of the planning and reporting framework, and that were keeping good data on student achievement patterns, could also embed the new learning in their everyday practices. But numeracy could not remain at the forefront of school attention all the time. Primary schools can generally give a concerted school-wide focus to changing their practice in substantial ways in only one curriculum area at a time. So to embed the new knowledge and new practices, and to build further on them, good *internal* school connections and coherence are also essential.

Many schools have struggled here. They have either lacked a teacher with strong mathematical knowledge, or the school leadership needed to take a systematic approach, or, like the principal in the previous chapter, they have seen their efforts corroded by continual teacher turnover and the loss of expertise. Others have simply darted from one professional development focus to the next, sometimes not wanting to be left out of new initiatives—especially those involving computers.

After their numeracy professional development came to an end it was largely left to schools to contact facilitators to seek advice. Some would be prompted to do so by ERO reviews identifying issues or suggesting that the school had reached a plateau, and that external advice would help it gain a fresh perspective. But the time lapse between ERO reviews could mean that schools lost valuable momentum and would have to rebuild their capability back to the level they had before, rather than further improving. Over time, the connections between schools and the Numeracy Development Projects weakened. This made it harder to get into schools the new knowledge that researchers looking at teaching using the framework and resources from the projects were gaining about the potential for misunderstanding, particularly if teachers simply assimilated the frameworks and resources into their existing ways of doing things. For example, just as teachers took the 1990s curriculum achievement objectives as the specification of content that had to be covered uniformly, so the number framework was sometimes used as something that all students needed to go through—even if they already had the knowledge and skills. Doing so risks wasting precious learning time with unnecessary repetition.

The Numeracy Development Projects, and the networks that came with them, have now come to an end. Their legacy is evident in the shifts in many schools' approach to teaching number and in the resources available to them on the Maths New Zealand website. These have recently been augmented by the results of a follow-on project involving facilitators working with a small number of schools to accelerate students who were just below National Standards, showing some good results for this group.[1] But this seems to be the last appearance of what had been the deliberate creation of a national network of development and inquiry in mathematics teaching. Online resources and school stories are now the main channel for Ministry of Education support for the development of mathematics teaching and learning in New Zealand schools. But online resources and stories are not enough on their own.

There is a wealth of useful knowledge in the 2007 Iterative Best Evidence Synthesis of effective pedagogy in mathematics (Anthony & Walshaw, 2007, 2009) waiting for the kind of inquiry development the Numeracy Development Projects achieved. A compelling illustration of the power of putting the findings of this BES to work is given in an account of how joint work between a researcher-teacher educator and a school enabled two Māori teachers to realise how they had simply assimilated the knowledge from their numeracy professional development into their former ways of teaching mathematics, rather than using it to change their practice. The changes they then made led to a new and more effective approach (Ministry of Education, 2011b). Māori and Pasifika students in their classes in a low-decile school made several years' progress on the number framework in the course of just one year: a remarkable gain, and just what is needed if we are to come close to the aspirational National Standards. Just as importantly, because they learnt in a new way, student effort was more enjoyable and paid off, encouraging further effort. Students learnt that maths—and the thinking skills that come with maths—is for everyone.

Illustrations like this could be potent in changing teaching practice, but not if accessing them is reliant on individual principals and teachers discovering them on the Internet. If we want our teachers to be more effective, we need to locate them in ongoing networks where such knowledge is put to good use. We

---

1   This was the ALiM pilot study. Schools participating were identified by Numeracy Development Projects facilitators as ones with sufficient mathematical expertise and school systems to be able to make the most of the additional funding to relieve teachers that came with the study. Facilitators and schools worked together, and schools decided how they would use the additional teacher time with students. Gains for students were found in most, but not all, the schools. See Neill, Fisher and Dingle (2010).

need ongoing communities of mathematics learning and inquiry that maintain links between teachers, teacher-educators, professional developers, advisers, researchers and policy officials. In such a community, the approach mentioned above could be used in other schools to spread and keep building such useful knowledge. It should be used in initial teacher education so that new teachers start on a strong footing. Such communities need to be based on institutional links so that they do not rely on individuals or short-term contracts. We can't afford to lose knowledge once gained, or for the wheel to have to be continually re-invented because we are re-fragmenting our education system.

## Shifts in writing

If you were to bring a teacher who stopped teaching in the early 2000s into a writing lesson today, or into a science or social studies lesson where students were writing about the results of a project they had undertaken, they would probably find some marked differences. They would often hear more students talking. They would also hear a new language in the talk, of 'learning intentions' and 'success criteria', language shared by teachers and students to gauge progress and decide the next thing to work on.

One of the phrases that increasingly ran through much of the Ministry of Education-funded national professional development programmes, such as the Literacy Professional Development Project (LPDP) and Assessment for Learning, was "feed back, feed forward". The feed forward—teacher and student thinking of the purpose of this particular learning—was novel for many, and the feed back much more specific, much more useful in terms of improving the quality of work, knowledge and skills than the reassurance of a tick, a smiley face or 'Good work!'

The current teacher would also tell them how students can 'self-monitor' their work, because the rubrics or descriptions of what good work looks like, what they are aiming for, are shared with students. The retired teacher might then sometimes wonder why they are seeing the student's own evaluation of their work, putting evidence against the work's success criteria, with a teacher's tick alongside, rather than detailed teacher comments. But for today's teacher, what is important is that the student is equipped with knowledge once held by the teacher alone, and can use that knowledge independently to improve their work.

Teaching writing has more dimensions to it now. Teaching writing in New Zealand primary schools has for a long time been student-focused, drawing on individual student knowledge and experiences. But over the decade more commonality has been evident in schools as teachers drew on the first national writing assessments tied to the curriculum (AsTTle),[2] and then the exemplars of different grades of student writing at different curriculum levels that followed. Writing provided a major impetus for more collective school cultures because teachers began to look together at actual student writing work, to discuss what they saw in it and what they expected of students at each year level. It was an eye-opener for many teachers to realise that there was no clear pathway in writing for the students in their school. Reading had its progression, marked by increasingly complex texts. The Numeracy Framework also gave teachers a common yardstick of how students' understanding and skills grew and consolidated. Now teachers began to work with a yardstick for the development of writing skills.

Schools that chose a writing focus for their LPDP work, in the major literacy professional development of this decade, often saw marked gains in their students' writing levels (McDowall et al., 2007). This national project had a strong research grounding and inquiry framework (Timperley & Parr, 2009).[3] It offered schools the opportunity to work with a facilitator over a 2-year period, learning more about the theoretical principles underpinning effective literacy teaching and how to put these into practice, and also about what progression over time looks like—and why it matters.

Facilitators worked closely with each school's literacy leader. Part of their role was to strengthen this leader's knowledge, and their skills and confidence to work with other teachers and cross the threshold into individual classrooms to observe and give feedback. One principal spoke to me of the insight that came from using a very specific lens: aligning teaching with learning:

---

[2] AsTTLe stands for Assessment Tools for Teaching and Learning. They cover reading comprehension, writing, and mathematics. Their development by the University of Auckland, led by John Hattie, was funded by the Ministry of Education.

[3] The project was developed by looking at the evaluation of its predecessor, the Literacy Leadership professional development. The Literacy Leadership Project covered most schools, but with much less alignment of student achievement data and deliberate work with schools to improve their capability to change their practice. For example, facilitators lacked any development of their own skills to broker the work with self-managed schools. The Literacy Professional Development Project did not try to cover all schools at once; it served 386 primary schools over three cycles, with learning from each cycle used to improve facilitators' practice and the tools they could bring into schools. Helen Timperley and Judy Parr from the University of Auckland brought rigour and challenge to the research. They worked with Pam O'Connell and Learning Media's professional development expertise, and Ministry of Education officials working in literacy, who had substantial literacy expertise themselves. See Timperley and Parr (2009). Learning Media has produced a summary of learnings from the project: *Introducing the Literacy Professional Development Project: A Learning Project*, available at http://www.learningmedia.co.nz/sites/all/modules/filemanager/files/Introducing_LPDP.pdf

> We couldn't see why students weren't learning—these are good teachers, we always checked student books—but we weren't looking at the right things. Nothing was aligned. I didn't check that student writing and learning was about what the teacher delivered. I would look at student books at a different time of year than I would look at their [teacher] planning, and I'd look at their practice at another time of year. Their planning could look absolutely brilliant, but I didn't check, what did the teacher do, did students' learning match the learning intention of that lesson? It just seems so fundamental now!

## Schools inquiring

Schools that kept building on the learning they gained during their work with the LPDP facilitators did so by continuing these cross-class connections through a strong literacy leader who kept up the practice of observations and feedback to teachers. Common assessments were used by a school's teachers. This enabled student progress to be tracked over time, and trends compared for different cohorts of students. Issues and the teaching strategies that could improve student learning could then be identified and the strategies tried out to see if they made a difference (O'Connell, 2010).

This is the inquiry cycle of the New Zealand Curriculum put into effect: teachers analysing their own practice against their own success criteria. It is a more rigorous approach than in the past. It asks teachers to keep checking the purpose of their lessons and work with students in order to weigh what students should be gaining in both content and learning skills (a dimension that runs through all the key competencies of the New Zealand Curriculum). It harnesses the energy within schools. It makes teachers more productive, where it is done well, and uses sound knowledge.

Inquiry takes a range of forms in schools. Here is what it looked like in one low-decile school in 2011:

> This year, we've got professional learning communities that share professional reading and data. Everyone focuses on four students in their class, one has to be someone who's struggling, and they bring their data [about the children's performance], they talk about their programme, decide what their next steps for that student are, and then in two weeks they have to come back and report on what they had done and how that's gone. Our achievement data this first half of the year has improved remarkably. It's about giving teachers the time and the strategies and the framework to look at what they're doing in a way that is non-threatening, inside a secure and supported environment. Even our weakest teachers are doing remarkably better.[4]

---

4   Interview, July 2011, with highly experienced and well-connected principal.

# Strengthening school professional inquiry cultures

Because of this inquiry or evaluative thread running through much of the professional development in the 2000s, participation in, say, the LPDP or Assessment for Learning, could support substantial shifts in the everyday work of teachers and schools. Professional development has increasingly been customised to schools so that teachers are learning together as a school, making it easier to identify what they could do differently together, what school systems of support and ongoing inquiry would work best in their school. Working together in schools also got a much-needed boost from the inclusion of entitlement to classroom release time in teachers' collective contracts. A real spurt in school professional collective cultures was also nourished by the discussions each school staff needed to have as a whole to understand the New Zealand Curriculum and use it to give more coherence to their programmes, together with its emphasis on teaching as inquiry. A school inquiry focus also animated many projects in the Extending High Standards Across Schools (EHSAS) clusters.[5]

In 2010 the proportion of primary teachers in the NZCER national survey who said they had enough time to work together to plan and discuss their work with their colleagues had doubled in just 3 years: from 28 percent in 2007 to 61 percent.[6] Along with this gain for teachers of (finally) having time to work together went other changes of a similar magnitude. Teachers' 2010 national survey responses showed that primary schools were much more focused on improving student performance by using the kinds of attention to student achievement information coupled with looking more at what students were experiencing in lessons, which had been emphasised in the LPDP and other professional development that drew from similar theoretical pools.

---

5   There were three cohorts of EHSAS clusters. The programme ended in 2009 when the National Standards took priority in Ministry funding for ongoing professional and school development, though existing clusters were allowed to run their contracted course, on their own, without the national networking that EHSAS, with a small Ministry national office staff, had started to promote. EHSAS clusters were expected to build on existing good practice within one or more of their member schools to raise student achievement and document what they did to add to the national knowledge base. Where clusters had connections with each other, or with other inquiries and research, they did contribute to an understanding of how to change teacher practice; for example, by threading key competencies through 'subjects' as framed in the New Zealand curriculum. But most were not so connected and were not always using a sound knowledge base. Some were undertaking projects that would have needed more than the 3 years' funding for each cohort in order to bear fruit.

6   This section summarises material presented in more detail in Wylie (2011b).

More primary teachers thought they were getting improvements in student achievement in 2010 than in 2007. Not surprisingly, job satisfaction was higher. And these gains occurred without increasing teachers' average work hours. These were still high, at 51 hours a week. Around 40 percent of teachers still thought their workload was not manageable. The intensity of teaching has not diminished, but it has been tempered and made more productive, more rewarding for teachers whose schools have made good use of the new knowledge made available to them in the past decade.

# Constraints on achieving shifts for all schools

The Numeracy Professional Development projects were the only programme of this new breed of curriculum and school professional culture-building projects that reached over 90 percent of schools. Many primary schools did not have the opportunity to be involved in the several years' development offered by the Literacy Professional Development or Assessment for Learning, or the less cohesive and more variable ICT[7] and EHSAS clusters, which also offered schools the chance to build their internal strengths with external support. Making such a difference through joint work over time between a school and external expertise does not come cheaply, whether provided through a national programme or working with school support advisers, or with researchers, or with external expertise that a school or cluster has contracted.

New Zealand needed to (re)develop the capacity it had to provide schools with such useful external expertise. Each of the programmes and projects of the 2000s that showed gains for student learning also had to build in its own systematic development and support for the understanding and skills of staff who worked in and with the schools. Limits on the number of schools that could access professional development programmes with positive reputations also arose from the limited number of facilitators and providers available. Schools that developed their own capability over this period also

---

7   The ICT professional development cluster programme was the longest running, since 1999, with a succession of 3-year cohorts of up to around 40 clusters at a time. Its initial purpose included giving principals and teachers computer skills and confidence, with the focus becoming more on the use of computers and the Internet in children's learning.

became more discerning about who they worked with when they used their school funds, and here, too, demand from schools outstripped supply. Private providers of professional development that individual schools approached could also become discerning about who they would work with: not always the schools in most need, most liable to distraction.

School clusters continued to be voluntary and to vary considerably in their cohesion and focus. A school could belong to several clusters with different membership and a different purpose, making it hard to develop cohesive connections with a strong inquiry focus. Cluster funding other than for school improvement was time-limited, usually to 2 or 3 years. Often the first year was taken up with the schools building trust and working out processes for working together. The Ministry of Education offered no guidance on how to work as a cluster; self-managed schools that were unaccustomed to working collectively across schools needed guidance as well as time. Clusters could often reach the end of their funding with a sense of being cut short just when they were starting to make progress. Nor did the Ministry ask clusters to build on existing knowledge with a sound basis of what was likely to improve student learning, or provide them with some options that provided such a platform.

Although the Ministry asked clusters to provide a focus for their work that related to government priorities, few clusters were deliberately supported to provide new learning for the system as a whole. The new learning was limited to their reports to the Ministry and sometimes conference presentations. The ICT and EHSAS clusters were beginning to be more linked, but this linkage was still young when the remaining clusters were recently ended.

A strong positive tide has been running through New Zealand primary schools, particularly since the mid-2000s. It was a strong enough tide to double the proportion of primary teachers reporting that they worked in ways that are consistent with the accumulated knowledge we have about effective school cultures, in just 3 years from 2007 to 2010. Yet it has not been wide or deep enough to lift all our vessels for student learning.

Over half the primary teachers in 2010 were not working in schools that were as coherent in their approach, or as supportive of teacher inquiry focused on student achievement, taking risks and seeking to make well-grounded innovations,[8] as we need schools to be. Without strong school inquiry cultures it will be difficult to keep developing the quality of our education and to better

---

8   A 2011 ERO evaluation of how well school processes supported the 'teaching as inquiry' approach rated 26 percent of schools in its sample as giving teachers' inquiry a high level of support, and 46 percent as giving their inquiry some support. See ERO (2011, p. 27).

engage those who come from families that have not been as well served by our education system as they should have been, particularly low-income, Māori and Pasifika students, and students with special learning needs.

If we can continue the positive momentum gained in the 2000s—due to the convergence and coherence of sound underlying principles within professional development and the New Zealand Curriculum—by working with schools over a reasonable period of time, it does not seem impossible to me that we could see such strong inquiry-focused cultures in the majority of our primary schools within another decade. The big provisos are:

- how well the Government's shaking up of professional development and support for schools will utilise the knowledge gained over this past decade of what schools need in order to make sustainable shifts in teaching practice and culture
- how well we keep building the knowledge we need from the new forms of professional development and support—whether we approach and use them in the same spirit of inquiry and shared responsibility that animated and powered the gains made in the 2000s
- whether we can sustain or re-energise strong school clusters and build new connections between schools, overcoming the competitive strain so that schools can better support each other in their learning
- whether school staffing is sufficient to enable time for curriculum leaders to work with teachers across the school, for teachers to undertake continual inquiry of their own practice, and for teachers to work together to tackle the particular challenges their students experience in school learning
- whether the National Standards are used to focus on learning, or to return schools and the Ministry alike to a greater focus on compliance.

# National Standards: Trajectory interrupted or a new pathway?

In 2011 there was not much optimism in schools and among those who work with schools that the inquiry focus that was energising teaching could continue to develop, because it did not seem to be sufficiently reflected in, and supported by, the wider school policy context. The too-hasty and under-cooked introduction of the National Standards was undermining the sense of shared responsibility between schools and the Ministry that had slowly and unevenly been forming over the 2000s through the professional development projects, the development of the New Zealand Curriculum, and the clusters. The professional organisations failed to gain government support for a knowledge-building framework around the National Standards (such as first trialling them), or for the creative proposal that all schools should work in local clusters to build knowledge on the moderation judgements needed to place students in relation to the National Standards. This would include sharing results across schools within these clusters in an inquiry framework that sought to improve practice, and sharing cluster-level results with the Ministry, as a way of building shared responsibility across schools for their cluster's results.

This proposal could have provided the basis for the kinds of connections and shared responsibility we need across schools to keep building our knowledge of effective teaching and improving student achievement. With this in mind, one highly experienced principal lamented to me last year, "We have lost the best opportunity we have had in the last 20 years to really go forward as a system".

The 2000s had shown many primary principals and teachers how useful assessments could be if they were well designed and used as part of personal and school inquiry cycles focused on actual teaching practice and student learning. They had seen that students were interested to know what they needed to strengthen (Guy Claxton's description of 'learning muscles' went down well in New Zealand[9]). Assessments, review and evaluation were now seen mainly in the context of learning rather than as judgements made to assign students or ration support.

So the strong professional dismay at the introduction of National Standards following the election of the National-led Government in 2008 was not so much about the idea of a consistent national framework of assessment, but about its development and execution. Onlookers who have worked successfully with schools shared this sense of a lost opportunity to keep building on what was occurring:

> If the National Standards had been well piloted, or given more time in the articulation and planning, the Minister could have created champions all over the place for herself.[10]

---

9  Guy Claxton is an English researcher who has worked on student engagement and motivation, and has given the useful conceptualisation of learning skills as 'Building Learning Power'. He has been a popular presenter at a number of New Zealand professional conferences.

10  Interview, July 2011, with former principal and Ministry of Education official, and current leader of a professional development organisation.

It's a very bad model of implementation. It goes against everything we know about how you would implement something in the system. Like, you would impose it nationally to begin with, straight up. Like, you wouldn't do a lot of negotiation and development work with stakeholders. Like, you wouldn't build in a system right from the start of evaluation, calling it a trial or whatever, that would feed back on these issues to do with how the moderation works and whether the standards are too aspirational. So it's an incredibly bad model. The basic idea of National Standards, that's not so bad. I do get how a very effective school doing a very good job could be very resistant [to National Standards] simply because of the way that they were positioned in the implementation.[11]

Belying the seeming solidity of their name, the National Standards are an odd mix. They combine throwbacks to uniformity with sophisticated teaching practice. The main throwback is setting a standard for each year level and then requiring all students to be rated against the standard for their year, with a scale that seems more fitting for the grading of fruit or appliances than for learners: 'above standard', 'at the standard', 'below the standard', and 'well below the standard'. Benchmarks of student performance overseas generally use neutral terms such as 'basic', 'proficient' and 'advanced', thus avoiding the erroneous assumption some parents and media commentators are making in New Zealand that either a school or a student is 'failing' if a student does not reach the set benchmark for their year.

Both parents and teachers expressed concern in the (brief) consultation on the initial National Standards outline that this uniform framing of expectations of student progression over time, in such seemingly black-and-white terms, would undermine student motivation (Wylie, Hodgen, & Darr, 2009).[12] There is a long-standing emphasis in New Zealand education on motivating individual students as individuals, building confidence by pursuing things that interest, and expecting different individuals to have their own trajectories. National Standards appears to challenge this understanding of the importance of teachers finding individual paths for students (Hinchco, 2011).

What we do know now about student progression that was not so clear before is that students can often make faster progress in the early years of

---

11 Interview, July 2011, with a prominent researcher with a substantial track record of effective work on changing teaching practice.
12 Wylie, Hodgen and Darr (2009). Schools do not need to use these terms in their work with students and in their reporting to parents. However, because of the framework of the National Standards, and the initial publicity about them, these terms may now be unavoidable in such reporting. In many cases, 'reporting to parents' is in fact now a three-way conference, with the child included and often providing their own review of their progress, in line with the emphasis on supporting students to be independent learners.

school than teachers have thought, and that it is good for students to build a solid platform for their ongoing learning, particularly in the early years of school.

But we also know that not all students follow the same trajectory of development over time, and that performance levels are not always predictable. A low performance level does not lead inexorably to a later lack of knowledge and skills or failure to gain a useful qualification. Over half the children who had low levels of reading comprehension and mathematics knowledge and skills when we tested them at age 8 for the Competent Learners project went on to get NCEA Level 2 or 3 (Wylie & Hodgen, 2011, pp. 39–45). My conclusion from the other material we have in the Competent Learners project is that these students were fortunate to go on to have learning opportunities that engaged and motivated them, and teachers who worked to accelerate their learning. They were positively engaged in learning through their primary schooling and while they crossed the sometimes perilous seas of early adolescence, when growing independence can divert attention away from school.

In the Competent Learners project we also found that it was not just a certain level of literacy or mathematics performance that would lead to achieving the new qualifications benchmark of NCEA Level 2. Students also need good levels of communication, self-management, perseverance, curiosity and social skills. These aspects of the New Zealand Curriculum's key competencies are not a specified part of the National Standards. They are often instilled through the kind of curriculum experiences supporting student engagement in learning that Brian Hinchco noted as one of the strengths of the New Zealand approach (Hinchco, 2011).

The National Standards are restricted to literacy (reading and writing) and mathematics. These are the curriculum areas that are easiest to map over time as a progression of knowledge and skills, and the ones that are, as the Ministry says, 'foundational' for much of the learning in other curriculum areas.[13] What worries many principals and teachers, and others in the education sector, is that what *can be measured* will become *the measure* of student progress and achievement. Other attributes and knowledge that students need, indeed, the full scope of the New Zealand Curriculum, will be squeezed in teaching because they are not so easily mapped out over time.[14]

---

13 Literacy and mathematics dominate most countries' national educational measures; science is the other curriculum area most likely to be included when countries have national tests or standards.
14 These fears were expressed in the initial consultation, in teachers' and others' responses as the National Standards took more explicit shape, and in the 2010 NZCER primary national survey; see Wylie and Hodgen (2010).

Primary principals and teachers look at secondary schools and see how much of the secondary curriculum and learning are framed by secondary qualifications. They fear the same thing happening in primary schools, but more narrowly, in the absence of the subject range covered by the secondary qualifications. As described in Chapter 6, science was already in the shadows of primary school teaching in the 1990s, and it slipped even further back in the 2000s as the national priority went on literacy, numeracy and assessment for learning. Science learning was stimulated most within some of the environmental and healthy schools initiatives, especially where teachers and students could work with knowledgeable people who supported ongoing and authentic school projects, such as improving the ecological health of the school grounds or an area adjacent to the school. Social studies, music and art have also been dependent on enthusiasm and individual teachers' networks. Without some kind of concerted and supported joint work, anchored by both 'subject' and pedagogical expertise, it is hard to see this picture changing.

Where the National Standards fit best with the trajectory that schools were on in terms of becoming more inquiry focused, and more collective and deliberate in scrutinising and developing their teaching practices, is that they are not measured by a single mandatory national test. They need interpretation: teachers and schools need to think about their meaning and how to measure them. Teachers use more than one source of evidence about student performance to make the 'overall teacher judgement' of where the student sits in relation to the standard for their year (or age, for Years 1–3 students). Teachers in a school need to work together to check the consistency of their judgements, a continuation of the work many were doing with samples of student writing but had not done so often in reading and mathematics. An electronic 'consistency tool' will provide some guidance on the main national assessments used in schools by 2014.

To get national consistency, this same checking and discussion, or 'moderation', is also needed across schools. Potentially, this provides a new pathway for the kind of joint work we need in order to keep building teachers' capability and knowledge, particularly if it is coupled with discussion of patterns of progress over time and how these are related to teacher strategies and emphasis. Certainly in the early years we cannot expect that the National Standards will have been interpreted and judged consistently across all schools. They will not provide reliable national measures of student performance, let alone reliable school measures. Primary schools have not had the support they need to undertake this sophisticated work within such a narrow time-frame—they have had even less than the little that accompanied the introduction of NCEA. Because of the haste to get National Standards 'implemented' within a 3-year electoral cycle, what electronic and hard-copy advice the Ministry has been able to provide has not always been consistent or clear. Schools were also given insufficient time to do the work they needed to do to make sense of the standards before they had to meet government deadlines (for example, in the first use of the National Standards in reporting to parents in mid-2010).

Some 'learning networks', continuing on from those set up in 2008 to enable sharing and support between small groups of principals or schools, are undertaking moderation. Limited in number, and voluntary, it is hard to see that they will make much impact on national patterns of understanding the National Standards or achieve consistency across schools. They have not been interconnected, and it is unclear how they will support the building of knowledge for the system as a whole.

Gary Hawke, Chair of the National Standards Sector Advisory Group, has emphasised that the implementation of the National Standards should be "a journey of continual improvement" that will take "a long course of change", and that the information from National Standards should not be an end in itself: its value lies in the extent that it leads to change in teaching practice where that would improve student achievement.[15] This perspective is in keeping with the inquiry trajectory that many schools were embarked on before National Standards. The National Standards Sector Advisory Group also emphasised the importance of "interactions" between schools to foster the knowledge-building needed to use the National Standards to best effect for student achievement.

"Sector engagement is key," noted Hawke, and the group he chaired recommended a wider national forum focused on this journey of change and improvement. Such a group could accentuate this positive aspect of the National Standards and the focus it can give in-school and across-school inquiry. If National Standards are to provide such a platform for ongoing development, then a wider national group that brings together the sector,

---

15 National Standards Sector Advisory Group (NSSAG) chair's reports from NSSAG meetings of 29 August 2011, 1 December 2011 and 23 February 2012, available on the NSSAG website: http://nssag.minedu.govt.nz. NSSAG brought together the heads of the Ministry of Education and ERO, representatives of most sector groups (but not NZEI or the New Zealand Principals' Federation, who thought that NSSAG's brief from the Minister was too limited), Māori and Pasifika representatives, and some individual principals appointed by the Minister. It also included members of the Minister's National Standards Independent Advisory Group, who were primarily academics.

Ministry, ERO, assessment experts, researchers and professional development providers to undertake ongoing joint work is needed. This group would need to be able to have open dialogue on the patterns emerging as schools make sense of the National Standards, and as they report results, and analyse how these patterns relate to both school practice and Ministry support. Their dialogue would also need to be informed by ongoing research that allows the fears the sector and assessment experts have about National Standards to be tested.[16] If the New Zealand curriculum is narrowed and thinned, if students are disengaging or losing motivation, then that would strongly point to the need to revisit the framing of the National Standards.

# The low-decile challenge

Impressive gains in student achievement were made during the 2000s by some low-decile primary schools that had the opportunity to work with professional developers and/or researchers who could bring frameworks for inquiry that linked what teachers were doing with what students were learning. For example, Stuart McNaughton and others from the Woolf Fisher Research Centre at the University of Auckland worked with seven decile 1 schools with high proportions of Māori and Pasifika students in repeated cycles of 'problem solving'. These schools were able to decrease the proportion of students with low reading comprehension scores from 59 percent to 32 percent over a 3-year period, much closer to the national proportion of 23 percent achieving at a low level on this normed assessment measure. One school, with which the team worked for much longer than 3 years, raised its distribution of student scores in reading comprehension and writing until it was even somewhat better than the national distribution (McNaughton, 2011, pp. 69–71). It did so by embedding the problem-solving cycle into its everyday work and retaining teachers who had built their expertise.

In projects that were shorter and perhaps less intense, or in schools that started with less initial capability, gains in learning have often been less in low-decile schools than in medium- and high-decile schools (McDowall et al., 2007). The challenge is much harder for low-decile schools because their students are starting from a generally lower baseline. In low-decile schools, making shifts in student achievement and sustaining them requires high levels of capability, systematic monitoring of individual children's progress (with the aim of

---

16 See, for example, Elley (2010); Hattie (2009); Hinchco (2011); Thrupp, Hattie, Crooks and Flockton (2009); Wylie and Hodgen (2010).

accelerating progress so that these students are learning faster than the average gain over a given period), and checking whether that aim is evident in teacher practice and in what students learn. It requires familiarity with assessment tools that are well chosen, and knowledge of how to interpret the more fine-grained results that the current generation of assessments can provide.

Making such progress in low-decile schools also requires ongoing connections and the deliberate building of knowledge as new questions arise. The principal I quoted earlier in this chapter, who learnt to align all the planning, teaching intentions and actual learning, was pleased that after several years of hard work his teachers had fewer students achieving at low levels after their first year at school. They had learnt from Stuart McNaughton's work to look at student progress across the years to check that the gains they had achieved in their teaching were maintained over the summer break from school, and that children kept making progress rather than stalling. When they found their students were losing ground between school years, like many other students from low-income homes, they tackled it collectively. Teachers discussed student work at the end of the year so that a student's next teacher could start the new school year with no time lost, no making up the ground at the expense of progress:

> A child arrives on day 1 of the school year, and immediately they're engaged in dialogue about their level of work from November, looking at their last piece of work with the teacher: 'this is what you can do, you're addressing your audience okay. What were your learning intentions again? Your weakness? Your strength?' The kids all know the curriculum levels, and now the National Standards. We make the links—here's where you need to be now at year 5—if you want to be here [on the curriculum levels] as a college student.

This approach kept some students on a steady upwards trajectory, but not as many as the teachers and principal had hoped. They now had new questions. Was their focus on students whose level of work was just below where it should be on the Literacy Learning Progressions at the expense of those who had been tracking quite well, but whose progress now seemed to have stalled? Or was this stalling, and a plateau effect they were seeing with their Years 3 and 4 students after they had accelerated their rate of progress in the first years of school, a sign of something else? Other low-decile schools in their cluster were also finding that it was harder to keep accelerating Year 3 students' rate of progress in writing. Was this plateau simply how children developed, or was it due to an obstacle they were encountering, perhaps the curriculum demands outstripping their vocabulary, their knowledge? Was it something the teachers were doing? Or was it an artefact of the assessments they were using? This well-connected principal's reading and discussions were getting him no further, and his teachers were feeling increasingly frustrated that their efforts were not bringing them in reach of the target they had set themselves. Doubt was setting in, which can undermine the considerable effort needed to shift student learning in low-decile schools.

Finding that Year 3 students' writing was hard to accelerate, the cluster's next step was to ask their professional development provider to have workshops with teachers of Year 3 students across the schools to see if they could identify what they could do differently.

It seems to me that here was a question with a number of layers that would benefit greatly from schools with similar questions working together, with research-based support of the kind that made such a difference in the 2000s. Project clusters of this kind could build the knowledge we need by systematically sharing their experiences to explore what might be happening, to decide on the basis of existing evidence and well-formed theory which responses were most likely to progress student learning and then try them out. The cluster this school belonged to could be one node of a national network of schools connected by systematic cycles of inquiry into shared issues in student learning.

But the future of the schooling improvement area-based cluster this school belonged to was unclear, like that of most existing clusters that had formed to gain additional government funding to tackle vexing issues. It had taken several years for the schools in the cluster to build sufficient trust to share results and have open rather than polite dialogue about them. Cluster members did not want to lose this new shared platform. The gains they had made, in most but not all of the schools, made this openness and common purpose valued, something they saw as part of the way schools should be working.

However, this principal was doubtful that the cluster members on their own could afford to pay for the professional development and advice that had supported their progress, the data cleaning and analysis that had helped them size their challenges and assess their progress, and the teacher time to work together across schools. Prioritising the acceleration of student learning so that there were far fewer children lagging behind national levels of achievement meant adept juggling of demands and using the school operational funding to the hilt. Low-decile schools, in particular, need ongoing intelligent external support that keeps them developing, energetic, contributing to shared knowledge of what can be achieved and how.

## What change can we expect in low-decile schools?

We have learnt enough from this last decade's work to know that low-decile schools can accelerate student learning if all the ducks are in a row, anchored by curriculum expertise, in schools that are well connected with sufficient well-based challenge and support. We also know that even in the minority of schools that have been able to make the most of the knowledge and connections generated in the last decade it is not common for student scores to rise to the extent needed to match those of schools serving middle- and high-income communities.

If we are serious about the ambition of having most students performing at National Standards levels and going on to achieve NCEA Level 2, then we will need to give the same kind of support and connection enjoyed by the schools in the successful professional development projects to *all* low-decile schools, rather than leaving them on their own to find answers to some of the hardest challenges in education. We need to ensure low-decile schools have strong professional inquiry cultures, built further by engaging in ongoing joint inquiry so that they are respected contributors to the knowledge we need, not treated as the system's too-difficult margin.

Stuart McNaughton has done much to show that it is possible to improve the educational experiences and performance of students from low-income homes, and of Māori and Pasifika students, around half of whom attend decile 1–3 schools.[17] He describes himself as a "cautious optimist" when it comes to the challenge of changing all the schools that serve these students. For this to happen, he says, it will need long-term commitments, policy coherence, and collaboration between policy and operations: the joint work he has seen make a marked difference. He also concludes that without an "integrated approach" that reduces inequities in the out-of-school dimensions of these students' lives, "substantial and enduring gains" are not possible (McNaughton, 2011, pp. 158–160). These inequities in families' living standards were shaved back somewhat in the 2000s, but they remain large and appear to be increasing again with the continuing economic difficulties, a cost-cutting government response and the spread of lowly paid and more insecure work.

My sense is that if we are able to use the knowledge we now have of the importance of employing capable school leaders, while locating schools in networked and knowledgeable clusters that combine well-grounded inquiry,

---

17  In 2011, 44 percent of Māori students and 60 percent of Pasifika students attended decile 1–3 schools, a total of 49 percent for both groups.

support and challenge, it is very likely that we will see good shifts in student achievement in many low-decile schools over the next decade. The degree of shift will be limited by how well we achieve the infrastructure that enables these schools to change and to sustain these changes. It will also be limited by any lack of change in the wider social context to improve the quality of low-decile school students' and families' day-to-day lives.

## New promise or new divides?

The intensive effort low-decile schools have to make to accelerate student learning takes all their current levels of staffing and funding. Any loss of staffing or funding will make it harder for them to maintain the changes they have made or make further changes. Increases in teacher:student ratios, for example, may mean that it is no longer possible for a school to free up a literacy leader to work with other teachers as they teach, to give them the 'feed back, feed forward' understanding and purpose that works so well for professional learning as well as student learning. It would also be hard to sustain or make new progress if these schools have fewer resources to invest in building partnerships with students' families and their wider community. Such partnerships are needed to enhance students' out-of-school learning opportunities, the experiences that contribute to and reinforce the knowledge, skills and confidence that students attending mid- or high-decile schools often take for granted.[18]

In an era when new funding for education is very unlikely, electronic learning has appeals. However, to do it well so that it makes a real difference for student learning is not cheap. To do it well also requires building on knowledge gained over the past decade about how best to use computers for learning. Having computers and Internet access does not change learning in itself. Knowledge needs to be shared with schools so that their purchases and use of time are effective. It will not be enough to simply provide some physical infrastructure.

---

18 A recent strong example of the difference to student learning made by an effective home–school partnership approach was highlighted in the Best Evidence Synthesis (BES) on school leadership. The Reading Together programme used in the example has currently been made available to around 100 low-decile schools by the Ministry of Education. It is a capability-building approach, which also uses local public libraries. Schools can also purchase the programme guidelines. It seems to me that having 100 schools use it at the same time could provide the basis for a very useful inquiry network, as would seeing how it worked with low-achieving students in mid- and high-decile schools.

The Manaiakalani cluster in Auckland has used additional government and other funding to pursue e-learning, with some promising results,[19] but for most low-decile schools such innovations remain on the very distant horizon. One estimate is that this approach costs around $400 extra per student per year (Boven, Harland, & Grace, 2011, pp. 44, 47).[20] That is much more expensive than the professional development inquiry approach to infrastructure that was able to improve schools and learning in the 2000s.

Costs of e-learning may reduce with the forthcoming Network for Learning, a government initiative to provide a fibre link supporting ultra-high-speed broadband to the gates of almost every New Zealand school. This network promises a common gateway for sharing to support learning: sharing within the school (with some powerful examples of schools using programmes enabling co-construction and sharing this to boost professional learning), between school and home, between schools, and between schools and other organisations, including government.

But the expenses schools will have to meet are a hidden hook in the great promise of the Network for Learning. It is not free. Schools will need to cover the costs of connecting with the fibre link, buying new equipment, and then covering ongoing costs with commercial providers of broadband access and the maintenance or upgrading of the new equipment. Given the already competing calls on school funding, this will not be the easy choice that one would like. It may mean that what a school can offer its students and teachers through the Network for Learning is related more to its school community resources than to student or teacher need.

Experience with clusters and networks through the 2000s also tells us that the Network for Learning needs to provide more than just access to a common space if schools are to be able to make more efficient progress by working together. As an example, national and local co-ordination and support on the basis of ongoing inquiry have been crucial to the growth of the Virtual Learning Network in 21 clusters, enabling students in mainly rural secondary schools and one urban area to access subjects, such as physics or

---

19 The New Zealand Institute highlighted gains in student learning and engagement in the Point England and Manaia View schools to recommend e-learning as a circuit-breaker for later youth disadvantage, noting that it would need government investment and would best be done in clusters so that schools could learn together and from each other, and to achieve economies of scale. See Boven et al. (2011, pp. 31–36). For more on the recent experiences of e-learning in the Manaiakalani cluster, which has been spearheaded by Point England school, see http://www.manaiakalani.org/research-1/evaluation-2011

20 Covering decile 1–3 schools, which include around half of all Māori and Pasifika students, would cost around $65 million per annum.

history, which their own school cannot provide within its own roll-based staffing.

The Network for Learning could be used to connect schools facing similar challenges, such as low-decile schools working to accelerate writing for their Year 3 students. But this cannot be left to chance. Such connections will need co-ordination, planning, some additional funding and a firm anchorage. One would hope there would be a lesson learnt from the missed opportunities that came with National Standards to bring the sector and Ministry together to plan how best to use the Network for Learning to keep supporting professional school communities, and the new knowledge we need if our schools are to keep making progress.

# Chapter 9

# A new framework for secondary achievement: Gains and challenges

NCEA now dominates the learning of secondary schools. The new framework it gave freed teachers and students from the artificial constraints of the former qualifications structure. Its much more explicit framing of standards also gave secondary teaching and learning more specific goals. Student achievement of qualifications improved markedly. Retention levels improved after 2007, when the Ministry stopped granting early-leaving exemptions as a matter of course and funded schools to provide new pathways for disaffected students. Many secondary schools have also worked harder to engage their students in learning.

Treasury recently referred to a lack of improvement in student achievement over the decade to argue that increases in education funding had been ineffective (Treasury, 2012). But this is only true of New Zealand scores on the international OECD PISA assessments of 15-year-olds. And in fact our stability in PISA scores between 2000 to 2009 was a somewhat better result than other high-scoring countries that spend more on schooling than New Zealand and have less income inequality, which tends to pull country achievement levels down. PISA comparisons also show the challenge that generally high-achieving countries such as New Zealand face in reducing their proportion of low-achieving students, and how unusual it is for any country to make simultaneous gains across all three of the PISA domains of reading, mathematics and science.

Secondary qualification improvements since the introduction of NCEA show the weight that national frameworks for teaching and support for teaching play in what schools can achieve. A key question I consider in this chapter is whether we are close to the limit of what can be achieved for secondary students within the current infrastructure for school learning and support.

I start by looking at student engagement in secondary school and changes in student retention. Then I turn to what we can (and can't) learn from the international PISA assessments. How gains were made on NCEA is considered next, with a discussion of what we will need in order to see further gains, and the questions that have arisen as NCEA has become the largely taken-for-granted framework for secondary teaching and learning.

# Are schools places where students want to be?

Most New Zealand students are positive about school if they can see a purpose to what they are doing and they feel safe. Overall student engagement levels in school drop as students get older, but this is a worldwide pattern to which New Zealand is not immune. Only 4 percent of 10-year-olds in the Competent Learners study sample felt restless at school. Among the same group at age 16, 25 percent felt restless and a third were bored. A fifth wanted to leave school as soon as they could (Wylie, Hodgen, Hipkins, & Vaughan, 2008). Disengagement with school grows when students struggle to succeed (Wylie & Hodgen, 2012). This is one of the reasons for the policy concern to accelerate reading and mathematical skill development in the early school years for students who start school with little practice in these foundational domains. But there is also a question-mark over whether our current approach to education works well for all adolescents: whether our framing of secondary learning and the dominance of NCEA, which can segment learning into disparate standards, and the continued dominance of traditional 'academic subjects' gives them sufficient purpose.

Bullying also plays a part in student disengagement with school—not just for those who are victims, but also for those who bully (Wylie & Hodgen, 2012). New Zealand students report higher rates of negative interactions with other students than students in many other countries. Around two-fifths of Year 5 students reported being hit or hurt, or made fun of or called names, in the TIMSS 2006/07 study. Māori and Pasifika boys were more likely to report being at the receiving end of negative interactions with other students.[1] Nonetheless, the majority of Year 5 students also liked being at school and thought students at their school cared about each other (Caygill, Lang, & Cowls, 2010, pp. 30–31, 37–39).

At secondary level the Youth '07 survey found that most students felt safe at school in 2007 (84 percent), an increase from 78 percent in 2001. Pasifika students' sense of safety at school improved over the decade, from 72 to 84 percent (Helu, Robinson, Grant, Herd, & Denny, 2009). Six percent of secondary students overall reported being bullied at least once a week at school. Four percent had stayed away from school because of bullying at least once in the past month (Adolescent Health Research Group, 2008).[2] But that was a marked drop from the 10 percent in 2001, suggesting some improvement in their school support, or perhaps the increased role that internal assessment of NCEA standards plays, making it more costly to miss school.

The Youth '07 survey found that most secondary students thought people at their school expected them to do well. Close to 90 percent felt that adults at their school cared about them, and felt part of their school. Both these indicators of engagement had improved slightly since 2001.

One indicator of how engaged students are in secondary school is whether they stay past their 16th birthday, when school is no longer legally compulsory. Staying in school till age 17 remained relatively flat until 2007, when the Ministry of Education took a harder line on granting early-leaving exemptions to 15-year-olds. It could do so because it had retained the authority: this had not been left to individual schools. In just one year the Ministry halved the proportion of those granted an early-leaving exemption, from 6.4 percent of 15-year-olds in 2006 to 3.2 percent in 2007. By 2011 this was right down to 0.07 percent.

Interpreting the legislation more strictly was one way that central authority was used to keep students at school. But the Ministry of Education at the

---

1  Analysis prepared by Megan Chamberlain, Comparative Educational Research Unit, Ministry of Education. Source reference: Mullis, Martin and Foy (2007, p. 367). Forthcoming in the Ministry of Education's Quality Teaching for Diverse (All) Learners in Schooling (BES) online resources, as *Bullying, Racism, Identity, and Exclusion*.

2  Bullying at least once weekly over the past year was reported most in boys' schools (9.6 percent, vs. 2.6 percent in girls' schools). Boys' schools also had high rates of participation in a serious physical fight over that period (30 percent vs. 10 percent of students in girls' schools), as did low-decile schools (31 percent); this could include fights beyond school. Girls' schools have both teachers and students more likely to take action to stop bullying. In high-decile schools, teachers are more likely to do so than students, and the reverse is true in low-decile schools.

## 9 A new framework for secondary achievement: Gains and challenges

local level also talked about the value of school qualifications to parents of students who were applying for early exemption. It worked with parents and schools to find new pathways for disaffected students, including work-based learning coupled with school classes (Minister of Education, 2008, pp. 30–31). Connections were important in keeping students engaged in learning. So, too, was the ability to expand the curriculum through Ministry-funded but locally arranged work-based learning and courses with tertiary providers.

Since 2007 there has been a gradual improvement of 1 to 2 percent a year in the proportion of 17-year-olds who stay at school. By 2010, 87 percent of students were staying at school until they were 17. Māori students were least likely to stay this long, however: only 70 percent did so, and Māori students still have double the rate of early exemptions of the national figure. They are also more likely to not enrol in a new school after leaving their current one.

Then there are the students who are enrolled but lose learning time because they stay away. Some who truant become those who go on to drop out between schools, or who don't stay at school longer than age 16. Truancy rates did not change in the 2000s. In the last Ministry of Education survey of student absences in 2009, truancy rates range from around 3 percent of Year 9 students absent on any one day without a justified reason to 5 percent of Year 13 students.[3] Again, the figures are highest for Māori.

Absences from school overall, including truancy, took 12 percent of students out of the classroom on the Ministry survey days in 2009. Absence rates did not decrease over the decade. They are highest in low-decile schools: 14–15 percent, or almost double the rate in high-decile schools (Loader & Ryan, 2010).

Indeed, while students at low-decile secondary schools reported higher rates of feeling connected with school, they did not necessarily express this in their attendance or behaviour. In the Youth '07 survey over a third of students at low-decile schools said they had skipped school for a day or more without an excuse, almost twice the rate of students in high-decile schools. A fifth had been stood down from school, more than double the rate of students in high-decile schools. Teachers in low-decile secondary schools were more inclined

---

3 Much higher truancy rates were found in the Youth '07 survey, based on student self-report of having "wagged or skipped school for a full day or more without an excuse". This survey's estimated truancy rate for secondary students is 15 percent (increasing with age from 9 percent of 13-year-olds to 22 percent of 17-year-olds); 28 percent for Māori and 21 percent for Pasifika; and 22 percent for students from economically deprived backgrounds. See Denny, Galbreath, Grant and Milfont (2010).

to think that their students were disruptive and less focused on achievement (Denny, Robinson, Milfont, & Grant, 2009, p. 17).[4] These teachers also had somewhat higher rates of indications of burnout.

Interestingly, New Zealand secondary teachers in 2007 overall reported high levels of indicators of work-related burnout (28 percent, compared with 20 percent in a Danish study of stress in those working in hospitals, prisons and psychiatric wards), and indicators of student-related burnout (27 percent, compared with 17 percent client-related burnout indicators in the Danish study) (Denny et al., 2009, p. 24). This indicates that secondary schools can be demanding environments, particularly when students do not see a purpose to their school work, or a purpose that over-rides other activities or relationships in their lives. That appears to be more likely for Māori students and those in low-decile schools. Some gains were made over the decade in keeping students enrolled in school, and in feeling connected and safe. But it proved difficult to get all enrolled students to actually attend—which is a prerequisite for making the most of school.

## PISA and the questions it raises for us

New Zealand performance on the OECD PISA assessments is used by Treasury and sector groups alike as their benchmark of the performance of the system as a whole. We can certainly gain some insights through the comparisons the PISA assessments provide. But our performance on PISA should not be the sole source of judgements about our system.

The 2000s saw the rapid spread of international educational assessments, particularly the OECD's PISA assessments of 15-year-olds in 2000, 2003, 2006 and 2009. In each cycle PISA pays more attention to one of the three learning areas it has included. It was reading's turn for the spotlight in 2000 and 2009, mathematics in 2003 (and again in 2012) and science in 2006.[5] More and more countries have joined over time.

PISA addresses the question "What can you do with the science (or maths or reading skills) you have been taught?"[6] What are students near the end of their

---

4  This survey also found that around a quarter had feared being hurt by a student over the past school year; 9 percent had had a student hit or attempt to hit them.
5  In 2003 problem-solving was also assessed (Ministry of Education, 2009; OECD, 2004). New Zealand student scores were not far behind the highest-performing countries (Finland and Korea). Financial literacy is included in the PISA 2012 cycle.
6  Barry McGaw, then Director for Education of the OECD, quoted in Schagen and Hutchison (2007).

schooling carrying with them in the way of these three domains of knowledge and skill to use in work, recreation and voluntary contributions to social wellbeing? These three domains are key areas, but they do not comprise the sum of any country's curriculum or schooling goals. While PISA has added ICT skills and is undertaking work to develop measures of collaborative problem-solving, PISA can't measure, or compare, any educational system as a whole.

All too often, however, the focus of the media and politicians is on the rank of their own country, treating PISA as a competition. Yet ranks change according to who has participated, and often disguise the actual similarity of country scores. On their own, country ranks on PISA are not a sound basis on which to evaluate educational policy or make changes. The real value of PISA lies in the questions it raises about patterns of change in a country's score over time in comparison to patterns of change in other countries over the same period. PISA comparisons also allow us to look at whether we are doing as well as we think we are, or as well as we might, given socioeconomic differences and levels of country spending on education.[7]

If we start with the simple comparison of average scores, New Zealand did well in 2000 and it did well in 2009.[8] New Zealand is particularly strong in reading and science, with averages well above the OECD average. In mathematics our average score is also higher than the OECD average. In all three areas we have more high scorers, and fewer low scorers, than the OECD average.

---

7   PISA also collects information about schools and students from principals, students and (sometimes) parents. This information tends to be more useful at a country level than across countries (though economists like to use it this way), because it often has a different meaning in each country. But when I looked at the information about New Zealand from each PISA round I was disappointed to see what light it could throw on what was happening in New Zealand schools and classes over this period: the questions were too generic because they have to be pitched across so many countries, and questions change in each round. Some of the changes reflect the growing international knowledge of the importance of actual learning opportunities rather than formal structures, or counts of hours or resources. In time, PISA's greater focus on learning experiences should shed more light. Like other assessments, PISA cannot do all that a researcher might like. Another difficulty with PISA is that any analysis of student scores in relation to the things that have a bearing on them is confined to the time of the test: there is no longitudinal following of individual students, their teachers or schools. One therefore has to be very careful not to assume that linkages observed are causal.

8   New Zealand PISA results are not affected by lower retention rates for groups performing at lower levels. PISA scores in 2006 and 2009 remained much the same, despite improved retention over that period and the great reduction in early-leaving exemptions, focused on those aged 15. Second, estimated rates of coverage of the New Zealand 15-year-old population, allowing for absenteeism on the day of the PISA test, are comparable to other countries (OECD, 2010, Table A2.1, columns 13–15).

TABLE 1: NEW ZEALAND PISA 2009 HIGH AND LOW SCORERS COMPARED WITH OECD AVERAGE

|  | New Zealand high scorers % | OECD average high scorers % | New Zealand low scorers % | OECD average low scorers % |
|---|---|---|---|---|
| Reading | 16 | 8 | 14 | 18 |
| Maths | 19 | 14 | 15 | 21 |
| Science | 18 | 9 | 13 | 18 |

Source: OECD (2010, Tables V.2.2, V.3.2, V.3.5)

We scored the same as or outscored all but one of the OECD countries that had higher GDP per capita. We achieved our results with lower government spending on education than other countries with similar results. Australia had much the same average science score as New Zealand in 2006, for example, but spent US$63,675 on each student as they went through school from age 6 to age 15. New Zealand spent US$52,475 (OECD, 2007, Table 2.6, p. 45).[9]

## Challenges for high-scoring countries

How common is it for scores on PISA to increase over time? Should we be disappointed by our flat average score over the decade, good though it was? Countries whose average PISA reading scores increased over this period tend to be those with much lower initial scores than the group of high-scoring countries in which New Zealand finds itself. We fared better than other members of this high-scoring group: scores actually declined in Australia, Finland, Ireland and Sweden, after taking demographic changes into account (OECD, 2010, Table V2.7, p. 153).

The big challenge in reading for the high-scoring countries is improving the performance of their low-scoring students. None of the countries that had fewer than 15 percent of students scoring below level 2 on the PISA reading scale in 2000 reduced their proportion of these lowest scoring students by 2009. These high-scoring countries all have different education systems, with different approaches: a natural experiment of sorts. The difficulty in decreasing these proportions across different systems suggests that this may be extremely challenging, and that internationally we need new knowledge to tackle this.

---

9   Dollar amounts adjusted for differences in purchasing power.

# 9 A new framework for secondary achievement: Gains and challenges

In 2009 New Zealand had 14.3 percent of its 15-year-old students below level 2; in 2000 it was 13.7 percent, not a statistically significant difference. Looking at other English-speaking countries, we can be spurred on only by Canada, which in 2009 had 10.3 percent at this low level. Australia has much the same level as we do (14.2 percent, an increase from 12.5 percent in 2000), and the United Kingdom and the United States have more, with around 18 percent (OECD, 2010, Figures V.2.4, V.2.5; Table V.2.2, p. 147).

New Zealand had somewhat fewer high scorers in reading on PISA 2009: 15.7 percent compared with 18.7 percent in 2000. But, again, we are not alone among the countries with the highest proportion of 'top performers' to see this pattern: a decline over the decade is evident for Canada, Australia, Ireland—all English speaking—and Finland too. This may reflect wider social declines in the use of print. While New Zealand was in fact one of the few OECD countries to see a slight increase in the proportion of 15-year-olds expressing enjoyment of reading over the period, this was not true of every social group, with a decrease in the proportion of our boys in the lowest socioeconomic group who enjoyed reading.

The New Zealand average PISA score in maths also remained stable over this period. Again, countries that improved their average score in maths between 2003 to 2009 all had lower scores than New Zealand in 2003. More countries declined than improved, including Australia, whose 2003 average score was similar to New Zealand's.

Overall, it appears difficult for countries with initially high average PISA scores to make further progress on the PISA assessments. Korea is an exception, with gains in science and reading, though the reading gain was not statistically significant once demographic changes over the period were taken into account.[10] Indeed, the PISA data show that it is rare for any country's scores to improve in all three areas of reading, mathematics and science in the same period. Of the nine countries that do show progress over the 2000s, only Portugal improved its average scores for each of reading, mathematics and science. Four countries improved in two areas, and the remaining five in one area only.[11] This suggests that it is difficult for a country to make progress on PISA in a number of curriculum areas simultaneously.

---

10 The science and maths score changes were not analysed in terms of demographic changes.
11 Germany gained in reading and maths, Turkey and Italy in maths and science. Twelve countries show some score declines over the period, seven in one area only. Declines were usually not large. Finland, for example, had a lower average science score but remained among the highest-scoring countries.

## Challenges of inequality

Student performance in PISA tends to be better in countries with low levels of inequality in disposable household income. New Zealand stacks the odds against itself here with its high income inequality. Nonetheless, our average 2006 mathematics scores were comparable to countries with less income inequality (Condron, 2011). We also have a much higher proportion of students whose parents had fewer years of schooling than countries whose performance is similar. New Zealand has 23 percent of its students in the category PISA analysts call "potentially vulnerable students": those who report that their parents have not completed 12 years of schooling. Comparably performing Australia had 14 percent of such students and Canada 3 percent. The stellar Finland had only 4 percent of such students (OECD, 2011b, p. 459, Table D6.1).[12]

PISA provides a comparison of the statistical contributions that differences between schools, such as the students they enrol and where they are located, and differences within schools, such as courses students take, make to differences in individual student scores. Within-school differences in student scores are large in New Zealand, reflecting the comprehensive nature of our secondary schools. We do not allocate secondary students to separate schools on the basis of their end-of-primary school performance, as in some other systems. Between 2000 and 2009 the size of this within-school variation reduced somewhat (OECD, 2010, p. 161, Table V.4.1). This reduction suggests that some improvements occurred in terms of the educational opportunities offered to students taking different courses in the same school.

In 2000, 20 percent of the difference between student reading scores in New Zealand was attributed to differences in the schools they attended. Most of this difference between schools is due to differences in their socioeconomic intake. If school intakes were more socially even in New Zealand, differences between schools would likely contribute just 7 percent of the difference in New Zealand student scores, not 20 percent (OECD, 2001, pp. 60–61).

---

12 New Zealand also showed one of the highest rates of students with an immigrant background among OECD countries, increasing from 20 percent in the 2000 PISA round to 25 percent in the 2009 round. This proportion is similar to Australia and Canada, but much higher than Finland, Japan and Korea. The proportion of New Zealand students who spoke a different language at home than at school also rose from 10 to 15 percent over the decade (OECD, 2010, pp. 80–83).

## 9   A new framework for secondary achievement: Gains and challenges

In 2009 these differences between schools were still accounting for much the same amount of difference in individual student scores. So, over the decade, our system of self-managed schools, set up in competition with each other, could not close gaps between students in schools in different socioeconomic areas.

Nor was it able to whittle away at the gaps between individual schools (the 7 percent of variance not accounted for by socioeconomic differences) attributable to the way schools work, differences in knowledge and skill, and how those are used school-wide. One of the striking findings from the Youth '07 survey was just how wide the variation was between schools in terms of teacher and student experiences of aspects of the school climate. School self-management without a strong infrastructure makes such variation more likely.

Given that differences in school socioeconomic intakes account for the largest portion of the differences in student scores between schools, it is not surprising that New Zealand also continues to have one of the strongest links between the PISA student socioeconomic index for an individual student and that individual's reading score.

New Zealand's rate of income inequality increased markedly in the 'Rogernomics' decade, the mid-1980s to mid-1990s, with slower increases till the mid-2000s, then a decrease from 2007, with the support given to working families with children. By 2010 we were around the 10th most unequal country in the OECD (Barber, 2011). The proportion of children and young people living in hardship in New Zealand declined from 29 percent in 2000, but it was still 19 percent in 2008 (Perry, 2009).

On the one hand, our high degree of income inequality has not undermined our comparative performance as a country on PISA. On the other hand, the PISA comparisons with other countries show us how powerful those income differences can be when they result in students attending schools without more even social mixes. Our housing markets and housing supply, coupled with wide income inequality, lie behind these differences that manifest themselves in school and individual-level scores. A more even social mix in our schools would be the most powerful way to combat such differences between students, but also the most unlikely. We would need to ballot all places in ways that gave equal chances to students from poor and wealthy homes for any school, put a ceiling on and equalise all school donations, activity fees and building fees in integrated schools, and pay school transport costs to have both an even school mix and a fair school choice policy.

The profound obstacles that hinder such a change make it even more important to support teachers, particularly in low-decile schools. Improving teaching and learning is our most likely educational policy lever to improve student achievement. Even so, we do need to be realistic in our expectations. Without a more even social mix in schools, and a decrease in poverty levels, there will inevitably be a ceiling on the level of student performance that we can achieve as a country.

Hardship rates for Māori and Pasifika people in 2008 were reported as being two to three times higher than for other ethnic groups (Perry, 2009). Differences between schools related to their socioeconomic intake also affect Māori and Pasifika students, who are more likely to attend low-decile schools. Like other New Zealand students, Māori and Pasifika students show no gains in PISA scores over the decade. In 2009 substantial proportions of both groups performed at low levels on the PISA tests.

### TABLE 2: MĀORI, PASIFIKA AND PĀKEHĀ LOW SCORERS ON PISA 2009

|  | Māori: % scoring at levels 1–2 | Pasifika: % scoring at levels 1–2 | Pākehā: % scoring at levels 1–2 |
|---|---|---|---|
| Reading | 24 | 37 | 7 |
| Maths | 55 | 53 | 22 |
| Science | 45 | 65 | 23 |

Source: Telford (2010, pp. 12, 28, & 38).

To improve Māori student performance, it is important to more systematically use the knowledge that was built during this decade through seminal projects such as Te Kotahitanga [13] and the various national professional development programmes, to engage Māori and Pasifika students more, and to improve their learning, confidence and motivation to succeed in school.

Te Kotahitanga arose from the research work of Russell Bishop and Mere Berryman, beginning with finding out from Māori students what

---

13  Te Kotahitanga is based at the University of Waikato. See: http://tekotahitanga.tki.org.nz/

their class experiences were like and why they so often felt alienated. It provides secondary schools and teachers with structured feedback on their interactions with Māori students in classes, which enables teachers to test their assumptions that they are providing the 'co-constructive' environment that will best support Māori student learning. It has its own network of facilitators who work with schools, which it had to build up over time, and it also works to develop in-school leaders in this area, link schools together and keep building a knowledge base. It was greeted with some scepticism, but its worth has become clear. More schools would like to be part of this work, or to remain within the Te Kotahitanga learning community, than can be accommodated through its Ministry of Education funding.

## Limits to what we can learn from PISA

PISA shows us something about the patterns of New Zealand secondary student performance over time. But the patterns it shows us between 2000 and 2009 are limited to three curriculum areas. These areas are essential, but they do not cover all that schools do and that students learn. How they perform on PISA does not matter to individual students. How their students perform on PISA does not matter to individual teachers or schools. Qualifications that are used beyond school to access further education and employment are more motivating to students and their teachers. Qualifications also provide a good indication of how well students are prepared for the world beyond school, since to succeed requires not just content knowledge but also good levels of perseverance, communication skills, self-management, curiosity and social skills.[14] These are the sorts of skills that employers value, and that are essential in self-employment and entrepreneurship. They also matter for the whole of our lives, for the quality of our relationships and our contributions to the social fabric. Qualification levels are therefore a more meaningful measure of how well our schooling system is doing than PISA, or any other international assessment.

In contrast to the stability of our average PISA scores in the 2000s—not something to be taken for granted, since other high-scoring countries

---

14 In the Competent Learners study we found that students whose reading and mathematics performance seemed to put them on a path to achieve NCEA Level 1 at best in fact went on to achieve NCEA Level 2 if they had good levels of these competencies. See Wylie (2011a).

showed some decline—there have been marked improvements across the board in the proportion of school-leavers gaining a useful secondary qualification, including Māori and Pasifika students. This is largely thanks to the introduction of NCEA in 2002, and the shift away from the ceiling effect of norm-referenced measures to standards-based measures.

## Reframing qualifications: Secondary outcomes and NCEA

Gains in secondary student qualifications have been impressive in recent years. The birth of NCEA was messier and not as well supported by the government agencies as it should have been, leaving residues of uncertainty among parents and students as well as teachers.[15] But NCEA did give teachers and students relatively clear outlines of what they needed to do to meet given standards. Teachers use standards to construct their courses and to give feedback to students. There is therefore more alignment than previously in what happens in classrooms, in how student performance is assessed, and in student understanding of what they are aiming for. This alignment has grown over time as teachers grow more familiar with standards and how to support a range of students to gain them. Schools have also used the flexibility of the system more strategically over time, learning to check that student credit totals and kind are on track to gain the qualification a student wants, and

---

15  So messy that it led to a government-initiated review of NZQA in 2005 (State Services Commission, 2005). Judie Alison provides a historical perspective on why secondary teachers, who had wanted change in the 1990s, felt ambivalent about the reality of NCEA (Alison, 2008). She had also reported on teachers' experiences with NCEA in late 2004 (Alison, 2005).

NZCER secondary national surveys have traced the learning for teachers and schools that came with NCEA, and the growth in acceptance and understanding. The latest report is Hipkins (2010). The Learning Curves project also traced the changes for teachers and students in the initial years of NCEA, and the difficulty of bridging the vocational/academic subject divide, which was one of the original drivers of the new qualifications approach. See Hipkins and Vaughan (2005).

Research on student perceptions and experiences with standards helped pave the way for a more differentiated system, with endorsement of qualifications that reached excellence or merit levels from 2007. See Meyer, McClure, Walkey, McKenzie and Weir (2006).

The Starpath project showed how the very flexibility of NCEA could lead to Māori and Pasifika students making poor choices of subjects and courses that would limit their post-school education and career options, and the importance of adult guidance for student subject choice. See Madjar, McKinley, Jensen and Van Der Merwe (2009). The Starpath work also resulted in a book aimed at students and their parents (Madjar and McKinlay, 2011), which has also been translated into the Samoan language (Madjar and McKinlay, 2012).

if not, to provide courses or work that will cover gaps.[16] They have a more holistic picture of individual students' progress across all the courses they are taking, and they are using this knowledge more systematically. What used to be called 'pastoral' care is now better integrated with a sense of the learning career of each student.

From 2008 NZQA national subject moderators began to offer 'best practice' workshops using exemplars of student work to show different levels of student work. Initially schools had to pay to attend, but in 2012 the workshops have been funded by NZQA. There are more resources to support teachers on the NZQA website: annotated exemplars of different levels of student work, and regular reports from the national moderators on patterns they see with each standard. All secondary schools have a review by their NZQA school relationship manager at least once every 3 years. This review is described as a "partnership" between the school and NZQA, focused mainly on standards assessed internally by schools.[17] Principals and the 'principal's nominee', the senior school manager responsible for the coherence of the school's NCEA processes, often find these reviews give more than an audit; they allow the opportunity for discussion of school results and advice about strategies to improve results, such as focusing on areas where the school is strong. Good school relationship managers can also connect schools with each other where there is useful learning to be gained. There are some similarities with the former inspectorate, except that the NZQA role is limited to standards and qualifications management.

Schools have also shared strategies to improve student qualification success with each other through conferences, sector group networks and in the few secondary school clusters that continue. In a few areas these clusters have also pooled resources and gained external sponsorship to provide additional classes for students sitting scholarship exams.[18]

Over the 5 years between 2005 and 2010 the proportion of school-leavers

---

16 A compelling example of improvement is the increase in NCEA Level 1 success in Northland College, a small decile 1 school, from 11 percent of Year 11 students in 2004 to 65 percent in 2009. The principal put the change down to professional development, setting goals for each student, and offering trades academies (appealing to students who might not otherwise have made the effort to gain a qualification), conditional on achievement of NCEA Level 1. See 'Northland College tops list of NCEA big movers', *Northern Advocate*, 29 April 2010. The school also has a strong emphasis on improving literacy and numeracy in Years 9 and 10. See Curriculum Report to the Northland College Board.
17 These are called Managing National Assessment Reports, and are available on the NZQA website.
18 'Enthusiasm flows in Rotorua' and 'Taking flight in Dunedin', *New Zealand Education Gazette*, 17 September 2007, pp. 5–6.

who gained NCEA Level 1 literacy and numeracy credits increased by 13 percent to reach 86 percent. Over the same period there was a gain of 17 percent in the proportion of school-leavers who gained at least NCEA Level 2 or its equivalent. In 2010, 69 percent of New Zealand students left school with this qualification or better.[19]

Gains for the students who were particularly intended to benefit from *Tomorrow's Schools*, Māori and Pasifika students, are even more marked. Over these 5 years, 22 percent more Māori school-leavers gained NCEA Level 1 literacy and numeracy credits and 24 percent more achieved NCEA Level 2 or better. Eighteen percent more Pasifika school-leavers gained the literacy and numeracy credits, and 23 percent more achieved NCEA Level 2 or better.

In 2010 that still left 27 percent of Māori leaving school without achieving the basic Level 1 literacy and numeracy credits (whether because they lacked the knowledge and skills, or they were too disengaged from school to undertake the assessments), and 52 percent with less than NCEA Level 2. Pasifika students tend to stay at school longer than Māori, which has paid off in their gaining qualifications. Nevertheless, 20 percent left without those basic literacy and numeracy credits and 41 percent with less than NCEA Level 2.

Recently the Prime Minister announced the "very tough target" of 85 percent of 18-year-olds achieving NCEA Level 2 by 2017.[20] I would agree that this is a very tough target. It is not a target for schools alone, since 8 percent of the 74 percent of 18-year-olds in 2011 who had NCEA Level 2 or its equivalent completed or gained the qualification in tertiary education (Minister of Education, 2012, pp. 38–39). To achieve this target means adding another 1.8 percentage points on average each year. Perhaps that looks feasible given the growth in the proportion of school leavers with NCEA Level 2: an average of 3.3 percentage points more per annum. But most of this growth was achieved by 2008. The year after, growth slowed to 1.4 percentage points. Growth from

---

19 The figures are from the Ministry of Education: http://www.educationcounts.govt.nz/indicators/main/education-and-learning-outcomes. Electronic data collection allowed a full count of school-leavers for the first time in 2010 and showed slightly lower achievement rates than the previous rates using paper-based data. The full count includes students who went overseas, but it also includes students who were disengaged, such as those who left one school but did not enrol in another. The Ministry of Education provides both for 2010. I have used their 2005–10 figures based on the definition of 'school-leaver' used in the paper-based data to see the gains over time, and their 2010 figures based on all school-leaver data for the current proportions.

20 Government Sharpens Focus on Public Sector Results, 15 March 2012. http://johnkey.co.nz/archives/1413-Govt-sharpens-focus-on-public-sector-results.html. The target measures 18-year-olds; this group would include those who left school before age 18, some of whom undertake NCEA-level qualifications in tertiary institutions. However, most of those undertaking what has been called 'second chance' education do not take courses with NCEA Level 2 or equivalent qualifications, and their rate of success in gaining these school-level qualifications is also not high (Wylie & Hodgen, 2011).

## 9 A new framework for secondary achievement: Gains and challenges

2009 to 2011 rebounded, to 2.4 and 3 percentage points each year, probably reflecting the more focused NZQA work with schools and the curriculum-standards alignment work. To maintain growth at 1.8 percentage points a year will need more ongoing investment in teachers' professional learning, resources for assessment, and sharing of knowledge between schools.

Indeed, to reach 85 percent by 2017 we would need to progress as fast as one of the highest-performing and continually improving education systems, Ontario in Canada, a useful benchmark. Ontario has systematically tackled high school graduation rates and improved them from 68 percent in 2004 to 82 percent in 2011, an addition of 14 percent over 7 years, or an average of 2 percent per year. This increase came through a well-supported approach, including new funding for additional staffing in schools focused on ensuring that individual students did not fall between the cracks of subjects, or subject teachers, and that they took and passed the courses they needed in order to graduate.

Ontario did more than this to ensure that its goal of improving secondary school success could be realised. It ensured that secondary schools had access to good advice, and kept people with curriculum expertise for each subject in the Education Ministry so that there were live connections focused on curriculum running throughout the system. Indeed, the Ontario system is one of strong connections, aimed at deliberately sharing and building knowledge: between the Ministry, districts and schools, and between policy and operations (Fullan, 2010; Levin, 2008). The Ontario approach has much to offer New Zealand in terms of a coherent, long-term strategy that focuses on capability-building through joint work. It has also substantially improved literacy and mathematics achievement in primary schools. Targets that are not supported by such deliberate strategies are unlikely to be achieved.

One of the constant refrains in the school improvement research is that pressure must be combined with support to bring about change and to reach ambitious goals. The "very tough target" for secondary qualifications in New Zealand is not backed by support strategies. We lack the interconnections. We lack the advice and ongoing curriculum development. Indeed, the advisory support for secondary subjects appears to be less since 2011, and there are no dedicated curriculum positions to support secondary subjects within the Ministry of Education. NZQA has subject moderators, but they are employed on contract to focus on NCEA standards, not on broader and deeper matters of subject development and pedagogy.

We have no secure national anchors for ongoing development, no strong nodes for any networks to form around. Subject associations are voluntary, dependent on individual energy and initiative. What they produce in the way of resources and learning from each other is sometimes striking and thoughtful, but one year will differ from the next. There is no sense of reliable knowledge available to every teacher, or of continuing knowledge building, bringing research-based and practice knowledge together.

## Challenges beyond the low-hanging fruit

Our current system does not give secondary teaching strong support. But there is also another challenge to its ability to come near the "very tough target". Progress made in improving qualification success is likely to have been with students who were relatively easy to steer. "I think we've picked all the low-hanging fruit" was the summation of one low-decile school principal last year.[21] This was a principal who sought out new knowledge, an active reader of research who was very well informed about NCEA, student engagement and school improvement, someone who used the links he had established with other principals through playing active roles in sector organisations.

He was also attuned to advice from NZQA and positive about the school's connection with its NZQA school relationship manager. He was already using the results of the Starpath project. These had shown how important it is for schools to offer coherent pathways for students to secure a *meaningful* qualification that will allow them to access further learning or work that interests them, rather than just an assortment of credits amounting to a qualification. Schools need to track their students' accumulation of credits and work with them to ensure they complete a qualification.

I suspect there is more progress to be made with the "low-hanging fruit", because not all principals are as well connected and knowledge-seeking as this one. Nor do all secondary principals lead schools with strong internal cultures and collective ways of working that enable the kind of changes this school has made to improve its students' qualification levels. Working more collectively means forging better connections inside the school as well as outside, across different subject departments. It means being open to learning from colleagues who have found effective ways to engage the same students one is struggling to support, as the Te Kotahitanga project has shown. Sharing knowledge systematically is still a challenge in many secondary schools, which

---

21 Interview, July 2011, with highly experienced principal of a multicultural Auckland school.

because of their size and the division into different subjects, are much less likely than primary schools to have professional learning or inquiry cultures (Wylie, 2011b). However, there is insufficient Ministry of Education funding to reach all secondary schools with projects that help develop such collective capability. Unless we provide better support and challenge to schools that are currently not well connected, both externally and internally, they will continue to lack the knowledge and initiative they need to improve student qualification levels.

This very tough target of 85 percent of 18-year-olds achieving NCEA Level 2 by 2017 is also unlikely to be reached without the Ministry, NZQA and the sector working together, making the target a common purpose. Schools and the government agencies need to support this purpose by having and sharing better information and understanding of where and how things work well and are changing for the better, so that a cohesive national strategy with the right kind of interconnections and support can be developed and regularly revisited to use what has been learnt in the meantime. We will also need to link joint work at the national level with careful inquiry into practice that engages students and deepens their learning at the local level. Without interconnections of this kind, which use what knowledge we have and also build the new knowledge we need, we are unlikely to come near the worthy ambition of having every student leave secondary school with a useful and meaningful qualification.

There are two challenges that can only be successfully met by the system as a whole pulling together. First, we need to pick the low-hanging fruit, and we have the knowledge to make more progress here. These are the students who are readily engaged with school, not waiting out their time to leave. The low-hanging fruit are also the school processes and structures that can be tweaked or accommodated, with hard work and with the infrastructure described above.

The deeper challenge is posed by those students who are harder to engage. Recall that probably around a third of secondary students coming up to NCEA express boredom and restlessness: these are the students who will need new approaches to teaching and learning. Ministry of Education strategy has succeeded in finding a more attractive option for many of those who would have left school early, working with both the student and their family, and the school. But truants and those who fade out from one school without reappearing in another, and those who skip school, have proved harder to reorient. They include students who have not built up sufficient knowledge and skills over their schooling to successfully tackle NCEA. Many of these students who struggle with course demands keep coming to school: present, but not really engaged in learning.

To reach disengaged students who have not enjoyed much school success will also mean more changes to how secondary schools work. A more collective approach will be needed, along with changes in the courses schools can offer and in how standards are used to construct courses. It will also mean more sharing of resources with other schools. It will mean overcoming the competitive incentives inherent in our self-managed school system, to hold onto anything that may give one school an edge over other schools or allow it to retain operational funding and staffing associated with students. It will mean more joint work with tertiary providers and workplaces, which current policy under the 'Youth Guarantee' has begun to support much more than before.

High-decile schools have already reached the Prime Minister's target for 18-year-olds: 85 percent of all their school-leavers gain NCEA Level 2 or more. But without substantial systemic work, interconnections and more support, it is hard to see how it will be possible for decile 1–2 schools to leap from 57 percent in 2011 to close to 85 percent by 2017. It is also hard to see how we can ensure this level of success for an additional 34 percent of Māori school-leavers and an additional 22 percent of Pasifika school-leavers across the country.

We do need some shared ambition to keep improving, to see our system as one that is in continuous development: a learning system as well as a schooling system. This very tough target should be used as a responsibility shared between the government agencies, the sector and schools to spur continuous improvement, not as a stick to beat any one part of the system. We also need to guard against the measure of the goal becoming the goal itself, as numeric targets so often do. It would probably be better to set a goal of continual improvement, as was done with the stellar reduction in the use of early exemptions, and use rates of progress as the yardstick, rather than an arbitrary figure. Arbitrary figures encourage gaming behaviour: a shallow focus on what is easiest, what is most achievable, rather than what is good learning.

## Building on NCEA

NCEA is not without its problems. It has retained the peculiar New Zealand structure of a three-level series of school-leaving qualifications, one for each senior school year, allowing qualifications to continue their dominant role in teaching and learning and making it harder to introduce innovations. If we were inventing a secondary qualification system for the first time I

## 9  A new framework for secondary achievement: Gains and challenges

doubt we would use this structure. The three-tier structure of our secondary qualifications is like a human appendix: something that has outlived any use it once had.

The three-tier structure in itself creates an unnecessarily large workload for teachers and schools, and more work for NZQA. The qualification workload is substantial anyway,[22] because NCEA is much more explicit than the previous qualifications. It is much more individualised and involves more internal assessment, which also means external moderation of in-school moderation processes. These changes in the nature of the workload amount to a real shift for secondary teachers and schools. It is a shift that is still occurring, and that has some way to go.

For example, secondary courses were originally designed to offer 24 credits, to fit with course structures from the previous qualifications system. That meant a larger than necessary workload for both teachers and students, focusing learning on credit-earning. Schools and teachers—and students—have found it hard not to measure value in terms of numbers of credits. Numbers can be tallied; they look authoritative. Decisions on the number of credits per course have been left to each school to make, where some central guidance or limits on credits per course would have been much more effective. The opportunity to do so was there with the revision of the New Zealand Curriculum, but could not be taken because of the separation of curriculum and qualifications within government, each dealt with by a different government agency.

Standards are a double-edged sword. Too rigidly adhered to they can make a course and student learning too superficial, particularly when teachers—and often students—use NZQA material (including marking schedules) readily available on the Internet (Moed & Hall, 2011).[23] The quality of NCEA standards is mixed. The recent review of standards to align them to the New Zealand Curriculum did not provide a single clear overarching rationale for the review work, nor did it systematically bring together people with different expertise—curriculum specialists, professional developers and teachers, people who understood the new key competencies and the challenge of weaving them through 'subjects'. That kind of co-construction would have been able to yield a set of standards that would take secondary teaching and learning further.

Instead, the work was contracted out to the subject associations. As

---

22  A flavour of what is involved in this work at school level is available in PPTA (2010).
23  Moed and Hall also illustrate how the framework of a standard can edge out the intention behind it.

noted earlier, these are voluntary organisations and are not all the vibrant organisations they were becoming in the late 1980s, when they were deliberately fostered through ongoing Department of Education support and linkage with subject specialists employed in its Curriculum Division. Realignment of standards meant that teachers were asked to produce standards in the absence of the sharing of knowledge, challenge, discussion with advisers and researchers with curriculum expertise, and trialling that should be essential for these frameworks, which shape so much of secondary teaching and learning. This realignment was a missed opportunity to make much more of the framework that secondary teachers rely on.

For those who see the New Zealand Curriculum as a bridge to a new kind of teaching and learning, with more likelihood of engaging a wider range of students and equipping them with the understanding and intellectual, creative, problem-solving and social skills they need to navigate through an increasingly complex and demanding world, NCEA has also proved a disappointment.

A cogent critique of the way NCEA has not changed the essential 'sorting' role of secondary school qualifications, and did not provide the flexibility to bridge the academic/vocational subject divide and link schools more with their communities, is given by Bolstad and Gilbert (2008). Jane Gilbert (2005) provides a strong case for the importance of fundamentally rethinking this divide, and for how we therefore should approach teaching and learning and judge student capability and performance.

Last year another principal I spoke with was grappling with the powerful way the structure of the qualifications frames teachers' thinking and willingness to innovate:

> We still have the tail wagging the dog: the assessments. The teachers start with the standards. But I want to throw the standards in a cupboard—give them back to NZQA—because we can't start with them if we're truly designing a curriculum that is focused on what students need in [this part of the country], if we were to have a completely integrated theme-based curriculum.
>
> Teachers are apprehensive of such change. Their first instinct is to go to the suite of assessments. So we have the standard, it defines the unit of work, it gives exemplars. It's destroying creativity, the opportunity for project work. Students can't think up their own project—only in technology—and the scope can be banal—find a client, design a business card.
>
> If we had more project work, we would have more creative, thinking, risk taking

## 9 A new framework for secondary achievement: Gains and challenges

students. I think instead that students play it very safe, pedestrian—they have their eye on the outline, following a sequence, not daring to deviate—'Is this ok?'

Teachers know the theory—the value of project work, themes across the curriculum that reinforce learning in each area. But they're not prepared to take the risk. They default back to how we look in the league tables. I can't shift it.

This isn't the original promise of NCEA. It isn't what was so exciting when it began. I don't think NCEA has dumbed things down. But it has restricted and constricted, made things very narrow.[24]

It seems unlikely to me that secondary teachers, parents and employers—and probably students—are ready to float free of qualification measures. That makes it doubly important to ensure the qualification measures we use really will enable deep and useful learning. The next generation of qualification measures needs the kind of careful strategic development, co-construction and trialling that was so successful with the 2007 New Zealand Curriculum. It needs to occur within ongoing and knowledgeable networks, anchored at nodal points such as the Ministry of Education, NZQA, researchers at universities and NZCER, and advisers/professional development providers.

Ten years after the introduction of NCEA, there appears to be much more coherent support offered by NZQA. But it is confined to technical aspects of assessment: it does not cover curriculum content and purpose, and pedagogy. Recent studies of the schools' initial interpretation and use of the New Zealand Curriculum are pointing clearly to the need for "ongoing and innovative alignment work" between the New Zealand Curriculum and NCEA (and the National Standards) (Cowie, Hipkins, Keown, & Boyd, 2011). We need much more coherent joint work to really progress secondary students' learning.

---

24 Interview, June 2011, with highly experienced principal of a rural secondary school.

# Chapter 10

# What self-managing schools need to succeed

New Zealanders need our schools to give our children and young people attractive learning opportunities that build in them the knowledge, skills, understanding and values that will enable them to lead meaningful and contributing lives, that build our society and economy as well as themselves. We need students to experience learning and effort as worthwhile so that they leave school with all the habits of good learners.

As framed in the New Zealand Curriculum, they should be confident and curious, able to take the initiative, able to think for themselves and reflect on what they have learnt and how they have learnt it. They should be able to connect information and ideas in new ways, undaunted by change, difficulties or issues that have no obvious solution, and be able to grapple with these challenges in thoughtful ways. We need them to respect and understand what lies behind the differences between people while being secure in their own identity. We seek this for all our children and young people, whatever their background, whatever the needs they bring to school. In an increasingly complex and ever-changing world with its daunting economic, ecological and social challenges, schools matter more than ever.

The current New Zealand schooling system cannot meet these expectations. We have not been able to make the most of what is best about self-managing schools: the greater coherence within an individual school's activities that comes from a deeper sense of the school as a community in itself, whose wellbeing, worth and effectiveness are dependent on its own actions.

*Tomorrow's Schools* has certainly enhanced school initiative. But initiative and the deeper sense of a school as a community need to be informed and enriched. On their own they are not sufficient to improve educational opportunities and outcomes across the board. "If I knew then what I know now", as the low-decile primary principal in Chapter 8 lamented to me, looking back to a decade of lost time for his students and teachers. What he knows now came from his school's good fortune to take part in well-grounded national professional development, which linked him with others facing similar challenges and provided the opportunity to undertake joint work with researchers and professional developers. What he knows now built on the long-standing strengths of New Zealand education: the endeavour to treat each student as an individual, and the flexibility of our curriculum.

This new knowledge has enabled the inclusion of a new sharpness, an analytical inquiry cycle that enables teachers and school leaders to check the efficacy of learning, and to share and in some schools co-construct goals for learning with students in ways that increase student engagement and effort. Many New Zealand schools are taking this approach, supported by the similarly inquiry-using mandatory frameworks of the revised *New Zealand Curriculum*, and by the school planning and reporting cycles.

However, the progress we have been able to make with this new knowledge and the greater coherence between the frameworks that schools and teachers work in has been too uneven. It has yet to reach all students. Our system lacks the national and local infrastructure of connections to share and keep building effective teaching practices so that all our schools can do what we ask of them.

In this conclusion I discuss three fundamental flaws in our system. These impede our ability to make the best use of self-managing schools. I draw some contrasts with other schooling systems that have given more attention to the connections that enable schools to keep developing so they can improve learning opportunities and outcomes. I end with recommendations for the real change that I believe is needed in our system.

The fundamental flaws we need to address are:

1. equating school self-management with schools standing alone
2. fragmentation of the government agencies
3. hidden costs.

# 1. The cost of equating school self-management with stand-alone schools

Between 16 and 20 percent of the schools that ERO reviews each year are clearly struggling with the responsibilities they have as self-managing schools. It has proven harder to run schools this way in low-income or rural communities, and in small schools. But if these categories of schools were removed from the current school-self-management framework and run a different way, we would still find struggling schools among the remainder.

The proportion of schools that can't reach the ERO bar may change in make-up, but has not reduced over time. This points to the chronic inability of our system to improve the overall capacity and capability of schools to self-manage. What the system has offered schools in the way of support and challenge has been more piecemeal than sustained. Too often schools have run into large problems they cannot solve on their own, and which grow more intractable, particularly when schools cannot find or do not seek the help they need. Too often there are personality clashes between board members, or between board members and principals. Too often schools have not been able to find and employ a good principal who will stay. Too often they have had to grapple with a high turnover of teachers without the critical mass of experience that schools need to sustain strong professional cultures. As one person with wide experience in different roles across the system concluded:

> It's much less about the individual prerogatives of boards and principals, and much more about the entitlements and rights of student citizens, regardless of the socio-economic setting, to get an effective education ... But I don't think it's fair to say to the school in Raupunga or the school at Mitimiti: that's your job on your own. Or the school in Mangere: that's your job on your own. I don't think that's fair.[1]

It is not only unfair to ask this of every school; it has also proved impractical. Far too much of the relationship between New Zealand schools and government has been conducted at a distance since *Tomorrow's Schools*. The frequent experience of both schools and the government officials they deal with has been one of feeling that officials' hands are tied when it comes to supporting schools and building their capability.

ERO's contact with schools is only sporadic. Its new offer, of something more akin to the kind of support and challenge relationship that schools need, is restricted to those 20 percent of schools that are now failing to meet the criteria for the regular 3-yearly review. However, what it can offer may not actually meet a school's needs, as described in Chapter 7, and is limited in duration.

Even in the early days of *Tomorrow's Schools*, schools were hoping for something more from ERO. They wanted advice and connections, as well as a judgement of whether they were meeting legal requirements. Over the last decade ERO reviews have often given schools a more useful outside perspective

---

[1] Personal interview, July 2011, with former principal, ERO reviewer, and Ministry of Education official.

on how they operate than they did in those early days. Nonetheless, few primary principals in the NZCER 2010 national survey wanted to stick to the current ERO framework. Principals want more ongoing feedback than ERO can provide. They want the opportunity to regularly discuss their school's progress on its goals with someone who can bring insight and knowledge to the discussion to help the school keep developing.

The Ministry has largely played a hands-off role with schools since 1989. Regional and local Ministry offices have had a chequered and unclear role. Although educationalists could see the need for closer relations, the Lough review hobbled the development of the Ministry regional and local offices and their ability to work with schools to harness and deepen local knowledge and energy.

Ironically, although more attention has finally been given to the Ministry–school relationship at the local level, the framing of the relationship is still largely one of separate roles, with separate responsibilities. The Ministry–school relationship at the local level appears to schools more bureaucratic than capability-building.

Unfortunately, repeated restructuring and the downsizing of the Ministry have at the same time resulted in instability, and some loss of important institutional knowledge and expertise. The Ministry has difficulty attracting and keeping experienced educators. Without sufficient expertise in its ranks it struggles to have the credibility it needs for its work with schools to succeed. At the local level, Ministry officials' work with schools is not with the schools of an area as a collective, sharing responsibility for improving learning, but is limited to contact with individual schools. Yet this contact seems not so much individual, with the school as a (distinct) community, as 'one size fits all'. Schools merely see more checking that what they are doing complies with regulations. They see professional development allocation decisions based on standardised templates.

Although there is more emphasis today on Ministry–school contact at the local level, the local level appears limited to behaving as a branch office of the policy-oriented Ministry in Wellington, with little ability to take the initiative itself. There is wide talk of 'recentralisation' as a result. And yet these changes at the local level, irksome as they are experienced by schools, do not actually alter the casting of schools as stand-alone entities, They seem wasteful to me given the system's real need for a stronger infrastructure. Back in 1994 Sir John Anderson was struck by the New Zealand system's unique absence of any decision-making "junction point" between the centre (Ministry of Education) and the school (Anderson, 1994, p. 244). He suggested regional support units that could tackle some of the issues that could not be left to schools that were now competing with each other. This included property management, dispute resolution and the "sharing of best practice". He did not flesh out this suggestion, but implicit in it is the idea of a body that has authority in relation to schools in an area, a body that is taking an area-wide perspective.

Currently the 11 Ministry offices around the country lack the authority to take such an area-wide perspective. They also do not serve as the conduits through which best practice could be shared among schools. They do not bring the Ministry and schools either individually or collectively together in joint ongoing work to keep developing the quality of learning. They do not encourage the openness that is needed for such work.

On the contrary. Their powers are limited, particularly since they are not treated as key parts of the infrastructure that a strong schooling system needs. They have few of the "marvellous weapons" of resources the inspectorate had to connect people, so that best practice could be developed, trialled and shared. Funding for each school does not come through the local Ministry offices but directly from the centre. That makes it harder to pool resources to provide support or learning opportunities that would otherwise be unaffordable for some schools, or unavailable in an area.

## Obstacles to schools working together

The Picot taskforce did not envisage self-managing schools working in isolation. However, it underestimated the pressure that school self-management would come under without some inbuilt connections to other schools: first, to make sense of large new responsibilities, and second, to meet growing expectations within constrained budgets. Per-student funding and per-student staffing both position schools more as competitors than as colleagues. Schools did not gravitate to work together long term to share knowledge or resources: the incentives of the *Tomorrow's Schools* system led them in the opposite direction.

It has been striking throughout the NZCER national surveys since 1989 to see how many teachers want the opportunity to learn from their peers in other schools, and how rare is this opportunity. There is an unmet need for the cross-fertilisation role that inspectors and advisers once played, such as arranging inter-school visits so that teachers and principals can see more effective practices for themselves in action and have the opportunity to discuss how these practices work, how to bring about change. Fortunately, the principal and senior school leadership professional associations (which received some Ministry of Education funding) and teacher unions have been keen to provide some opportunities where school leaders can learn from one another. But these opportunities have been too uneven in reach and quality.

It is not as if the need for schools to work together has gone unrecognised by the Ministry all these years. But because of the absence of any local presence which had the authority and resources to bring schools together, the means used have usually been short term, largely clusters dependent on competitive funding, with voluntary membership and voluntary levels of commitment. Often the main rationale for cluster membership was to secure additional funding or professional development for a school rather than to share a project with other schools.

All of this means that clusters have not been sufficiently effective. If gains have been made in student learning they have occurred unevenly and may not be sustained, and they often don't travel very far. Exceptions to this do exist, mainly in some schooling improvement and ICT clusters that were funded for more than 3 years, and which saw benefits from their involvement in national initiatives and networks that could provide the infrastructure of knowledge, support and challenge. Some EHSAS clusters using inquiry cycles to deepen their understanding of the New Zealand Curriculum have also produced new knowledge that was useful to other schools.

The clusters that have been the most productive and enlivening for their members have been those that could draw on external expertise and work with it to develop their own capability, focused on well-identified goals to improve particular aspects of learning and performance. Some originally Ministry-funded and some self-organised clusters have developed sufficient trust to open the doors to each other, to act as critical friends. But the voluntary cluster approach has not proved a reliable way to lift the overall quality of teaching practice.

Mandatory clusters have also been tried. Resource teachers of learning and behaviour (RTLBs) were allocated to clusters of schools to share among themselves. ERO evaluated these clusters twice in 5 years (ERO, 2004, 2009). Both times it found too much variation in cluster governance, management and quality. Little had changed over the 5 years. This suggests that ERO's national reports are limited in their impact on the practice of individual schools or clusters. The Ministry has now reorganised RTLBs in larger regional groupings.

## The challenge of suspicion

If our system is to provide self-managing schools with the stronger infrastructure they need, it has to recast school–government relations and tackle unwarranted assumptions. It also needs to rethink what is asked of boards of trustees.

Currently, although principals would like more ongoing dialogue about their school's progress, they are suspicious of closer relations with the government agencies: the Ministry and ERO. This is partly because of the recent swing-back to a greater weight placed on regulations than experienced since the 1990s, and partly because of the loss of the joint-work approach that enabled them to feel like respected partners with the Ministry. Suspicion of closer relations is also fed by encounters with Ministry staff who are inexperienced and lack knowledge, or by officials' rigidity.

I think a brake on the system's ability to strengthen itself also stems from the over-characterisation in the Picot report of the more connected 1980s schooling system in New Zealand as "bureaucratic" and "centralised". I hope Chapters 2 and 3 show how this is a skewed portrayal. *Tomorrow's Schools* unnecessarily limited the development of our schooling system by casting all school–government relations as bureaucratic and antithetical to good local decision making. Our system in the 1980s was strained, but not because it was rigidly and pervasively bureaucratic. It was faced with rapidly growing expectations of what it should achieve, but without the curriculum and qualifications frameworks it needed to change practice, and with the need to have a more coherent and concerted approach to school and teacher development.

Schools already enjoyed considerable latitude in what was taught and how it was taught, and secondary schools were already making many of their own allocation decisions. The Picot report did not distinguish the (generic) government processes that were irksome in terms of this existing latitude, such as approval processes for spending and staffing, from the sources of challenge and support that every school needs, which were also part of the government role in relation to schools. The role of government in ensuring the system benefited from cross-fertilisation of ideas and understanding through joint work between people with different roles also got knocked out when school self-management was seen as something that could occur only if schools were cut loose from "apron-strings". Connections were wrongly characterised as dependency that would inhibit the capacity of individual schools to make their own decisions. But self-management of schools is enabling only when it is well supported, when government actively works to develop the capability of every school to become a strong professional community.

It is not enough for government to try to steer from a distance via regulations, guidelines, accountability frameworks, and publication of research and advice. That leaves too much scope for schools to see regulations and accountability frameworks negatively, in terms of compliance, a restriction on their scope as self-managing schools that are also accountable to their community. It also means there is no-one ultimately responsible for ensuring that no school falls through the cracks—as history shows us too many New Zealand self-managing schools can, and do.

## A fresh approach

We need a fresh approach. We need to construct a network of education authorities that support and challenge the schools that comprise them, in ways that make more of the schools than the schools can make of themselves individually—ways that nurture the capacity of schools to self-manage, while at the same time ensuring they contribute to the capacity of their fellow schools and to the authority as a whole. I use the term 'authority' because there does need to be some locus of decision making coupled with ultimate responsibility. Also, 'authority' conveys something that is worthy of note because what it offers is based on expertise, on wise knowledge. I certainly don't mean an enforcement entity that seeks conformity or takes over: that would achieve nothing, at great cost. 'Federation' might be another way to convey the concept of an entity that is greater than the sum of its parts and is constructed to maximise the development of those parts in harmonious, efficient connections.

The recent McKinsey analysis of how 20 schooling systems around the world have improved student performance notes the critical role of what it calls "mediating layers" between individual schools and the policy centre. This was not something the authors expected to find. They had expected to find changes in teaching practice. They had expected to find "changes in the support and stewardship provided by the center" (Mourshed, Chijioke, & Barber, 2010, p. 81). But without this intermediate role providing support and challenge, and encouraging collaboration and sharing between schools, they concluded, it would have been hard to have the integration needed to sustain system-wide improvement.

I started this book with a conversation with the principal of a secondary school in the city of Edmonton, Alberta. What I learnt about how the Edmonton Public Schools district worked (Wylie, 2007b) showed me that the choice was not between self-managed schools or 'centralisation' and 'bureaucracy'. The choice was between struggling on as we were or creating a better infrastructure. The Edmonton district of close to 200 schools, serving over 80,000 students, impresses me because it works well, and it works well because of a lattice of connections between schools, and between schools and the district's hub, its 'central office'. Central office has the ultimate responsibility for the quality of the schools and student learning. It has the authority that comes from employing the principals and holding them accountable. It actively develops those who lead schools, and it supports them.

Central office staff also have the authority that comes from successful performance as a principal or school leader themselves. They know what they are asking, and school leaders generally respect them. Anyone who goes into the central office has served on district committees that work with the central office on matters such as staffing or property. They already have a district overview. Anyone who goes into the central office to work with principals has also mentored new principals in a systematic process.

Authority in the Edmonton district also comes from the connections principals have beyond their own school. It would be difficult to stay isolated in this district. Every principal is part of a support group of principals, meeting monthly to share news and issues, and to initiate collaborations, such as sharing resources. One principal from each of the support groups takes part in a monthly meeting with the district superintendent (the district head), allowing regular discussion of issues, two-way flows of information, sharing of perceptions, and joint problem-solving.

Like New Zealand schools, Edmonton schools are responsible for their own school plans, teacher appointments and budget allocation. Unlike New Zealand principals, the accountability is face to face and ongoing, through discussions several times a year about the school's progress on its goals. I was particularly struck by the sense of shared responsibility that came through one principal's description of her discussions with her central office supervisor:

> She asks me very hard questions, challenges that push us forward. I don't feel threatened by them. They [central office] want me to be a success—that looks good for them, reflects on them.

Here is authority used well. It adds value to the schools and educators it is responsible for. Here, principals and schools are not left struggling. New principals are on probation for 2 years, and not all are confirmed in the role. Existing principals whose schools show no progress on their goals despite additional central office support are likely to be shifted out. Recruitment of principals is not left to chance. The district runs its own principal preparation course. To be considered, teachers need to provide evidence that they have taken leadership roles within their schools, and have contributed to their school's professional collective learning.

Edmonton schools are also connected with each other through shared inquiry projects, focused on student learning and addressing both school and district priorities. Schools work in small groups of two or three, sharing professional development related to their common inquiry focus. They present the results of their projects—what they did to change their practice, what effects are evident in students' actual learning opportunities and outcomes, what new needs they now identify—to other inquiry groups, so that one group's learning is available to other schools, in small enough forums that real discussion and connections can occur.

This inquiry approach stems from the larger Alberta Initiative for Schooling Improvement (AISI), summarised in a recent evaluation as an "impressive change strategy that is perhaps without parallel in the world today" (Hargreaves et al., 2009, p. 17). The evaluators note a culture that is "dynamic, intellectually rigorous and sustainable" (p. 16), one which often made teacher learning and change simply part of ongoing life in schools rather than something separate or imposed. The AISI culture has had most effect in districts that emphasised connections and working together, allowing "strong personal relationships, high trust and intense professional learning" (p. 4).

Other districts that have made gains in student learning have also harnessed the power of schools working collectively—with support. Michael Fullan describes York Region district in Ontario, with 192 schools, forming "local learning networks" of six to 10 schools each. These networks include principals, teacher leaders, the district supervisor who is responsible for these schools, and district curriculum consultants. They work to improve a specific challenge in learning, which they identify from student performance data, and to develop the schools in the network. Fullan (2010, p. 72) was struck by the lack of hierarchy in the network meetings, their focus on solving problems, and by district and school staff working together as "colearners with great focus".

A recent description of several US districts with good school and student performance also notes the priority these district authorities give to building school capacity through real joint work (Anderson, Mascall, Stiegelbauer, & Park, 2012). Not only is there district office support for individual schools, differentiated according to school need, but also structured processes that harness knowledge in individual schools so that it can be shared. One district has regular meetings for teachers of specific subjects or year levels at different schools to share what they are doing, so that they can learn from each other's responses to similar challenges and build a greater collective knowledge of effective practices. These meetings are part of a wider network of teacher leaders in each school for each subject and each year level, anchored by district curriculum and programme specialists. The district staff spearhead continual improvement through supporting and focusing schools' own initiatives, and encouraging experimentation where the common approaches used in the district seem to be stalling or not working well with all students. Principals and teachers are treated as partners in a shared endeavour. As in the York Region district, this engenders enthusiasm and well-focused energy. And it pays off in teaching and learning.

These four North American districts are small enough to allow meaningful interaction. The two US districts were smaller than the two Canadian ones, at 60 and 70 schools each. What is striking to a New Zealander is that these education authorities include curriculum and assessment experts. *Tomorrow's Schools* did not leave this expertise in the local Ministry of Education offices. Individuals might bring it with them, but that was not what they were employed to provide. Instead, access to such expertise was contracted, held separately in the support services provided by the colleges of education. That fragmentation resulted in thinner connections and less knowledge of individual schools as a whole, less continuity in that knowledge, and more time having to be spent to establish relations and knowledge that could help a school. The support services in New Zealand have tended to work with individual schools, without the ability and resources to develop and sustain networks of subject or year-level teachers that could share and build useful knowledge to improve teaching.

These North American education authorities are providing schools with a more co-ordinated infrastructure. They are not separating educational 'content' (the curriculum and pedagogy) from 'structure' (the employment and development of principals, and the accountability of schools). Their staff are also putting the development of school and professional capacity first and foremost, through ways that strengthen and use collective energy and responsibility. That is the kind of approach we need here in New Zealand.

We cannot achieve this greater co-ordination without rethinking the role of boards of trustees. New Zealand and England are the only two countries that have a mandated governance layer at the individual school level. England has increasingly emphasised school partnerships and federations as a means to improve school and system performance. Had we moved to school self-management in a different era, I doubt there would have been such a weight placed on parent representatives employing principals. That isn't essential for open communication and respect between school professionals and parents, or with the wider community around a school. In fact, few trustees see employing school staff or overseeing the principal as key elements in their role. What they emphasise in the NZCER national surveys is setting the strategic direction for the school, followed by scrutinising the school's performance, the partnership with the school staff, and representing parents. Boards need to be part of the appointment process of a principal, but they do not need to undertake it on their own. Nor is their work in setting the school's strategic direction, scrutinising the school's performance, and representing parents dependent on their being the principal's employer.

In Edmonton, school councils are mandatory, but the form they take is left to each school and its community to decide. Parents and others who become involved do not have the legal and time obligations of New Zealand trustees. They do not wrestle with 'paperwork'. But they certainly play a regular and valued role in informing their school about the needs of its students and community, and in discussing the school's programme, reports of its achievements, and progress on its goals with school staff.

# 2. Costs of fragmentation

To provide a more co-ordinated infrastructure at the local level, we also need to tackle the fragmentation of roles at the national level of the government agencies and the recent return to the contractual 'purchase' model of the 1990s, which precludes the kind of joint work and ongoing relationships that can build and embed the knowledge schools need to be effective.

In 1994 Sir John Anderson was warning the Government that there needs to be "overall effective co-ordination of the various policy strands" if schools were to successfully translate government policy into teaching and learning (Anderson, 1994, p. 244). He was thinking particularly of the curriculum and qualifications work, which he could see had to be developed alongside staffing, funding and teacher training policy. A whole decade later a similar point has to be made again, in the reviews of the mucky introduction of NCEA (State Services Commission, 2005). These reviews led to the Ministry of Education being given a clearer co-ordinating role, but the government agencies remained separated. Even though there is more communication between the agencies now, such contact does not give the strength that comes from joint work on shared projects.

This continued separation has weakened the coherence of the New Zealand Curriculum (Ministry of Education, 2007) and secondary qualifications. That is one challenge. Fast approaching is another: to develop the next generation of student performance measures that can match and foster the changing approaches to learning that I described at the end of Chapter 9. Our current fragmented system is ill-suited to these challenges.

In addition to the weak links between curriculum and qualifications work at the national level, we have no permanent networks of teachers, researchers, academics and professional developers with secure processes of real two-way communication at the national level to work on these challenges together. Without such ongoing joint work, based on existing relationships, trust, and shared knowledge, new resources or standards are unlikely to be as well-grounded as they need to be to really make a difference in teaching and learning.

We haven't the time or money to reinvent the wheel. But to build on knowledge of effective change, teachers need to be connected with that knowledge in ways that support them to use it well.

It is hard to envisage how this can happen. Ministry-funded school support has become extremely targeted in terms of school eligibility and focus. It is also more piecemeal than focused on knowledge sharing and building. Contracts with providers are framed as the purchase of specified services, not the developmental partnerships that were so productive in work such as the Literacy Professional Development Project, Assessment for Learning, or the Numeracy Development Projects. We do not have all the answers we need, and the knowledge that has grown over the past decade is far from evenly shared or used. Without national investment in such joint work we will find it hard to make continued progress.

Spending on education at the national level on this support for schools and teachers is currently more cost-conscious than cost-effective. It is unlikely to produce value for money because it is too piecemeal. It will not be able to lift the system as a whole over time. Nor can this approach sufficiently connect providers of professional development or schools in new ways, creating vibrant networks of inquiry.

I think the separation of school inspection from school support has also served a narrow purpose, at the cost of the development of the system as a whole. The Edmonton example shows that they do not have to be kept separate, and that the combination is more powerful than either element on its own. It is worth recalling that the original vision for the Audit and Review Agency did not hold school accountability and school support in entirely separate compartments. That vision did not blur or soften school accountability: a board was to be dismissed if a school could not make progress on its goals. This spelling out of the consequences for schools if they did not keep developing is, ironically, far more hard-edged than what did actually occur when ERO was distanced from schools and the Ministry. This distancing stemmed from the Lough report's rigid enforcement of the generic state services model of how the much larger Crown-owned enterprises and government departments should be held accountable: an approach based on the ideology of provider capture. With the loss of connection of accountability and support at the local level, allowing real shared responsibility, we also lost an everyday means for the essential cross-fertilisation a good education system needs, enabling schools to learn from each other and principals to gain a wider perspective through serving on review teams.

Fragmentation of the government agencies has also led to an underuse and underdevelopment of principals and curriculum leaders. Separating policy and operations in the Ministry, and chopping its curriculum functions right back, has hindered the circulation of knowledge through the system. While the opportunity to see a wide range of schools has drawn some principals and teachers into working for ERO, limits on their ability to use this increased knowledge to work with schools to improve them have also led to their exit.

# 3. Hidden costs

> New Zealand expectations are so high! For a country with a population the size of Melbourne, we think we should be Olympians, climb mountains, rule the world: on a shoestring budget![2]

In an international context, New Zealand spending for the compulsory school years has been and continues to be lower than in other countries whose scores

---

2   Interview, August 2011, with experienced principal.

on the international assessments it has matched or bettered.[3] In crude terms, one could say that ours has not been an unproductive education system. While I think that progress on our own measures—the ones that motivate learners and teachers, such as leaving school with a meaningful qualification—is more relevant than the international assessments, these international comparisons do put our ambitions in relation to the size of our purse in a sobering context.

Most education systems that have made real gains for their students and schools have been able to provide more funding to enable changes to occur. A real increase in the investment we make in New Zealand children and young people's education is currently unlikely. Therefore we need to make better use of the funding available. Simply continuing what we do now will not allow that to happen. It will not allow us to make all the headway we could make on improving the learning opportunities and outcomes for Māori and Pasifika students, for students from low-income homes, for those with special needs. It will not allow us to keep developing teaching and learning as they need to be developed for the demands of this era.

School self-management and the separation of roles have had hidden costs. There has been a growth in administrative work and the need for every school to undertake some things that could probably be undertaken more efficiently if resources were pooled to hire expertise. Principals have long pointed to their frustration that they cannot focus sufficiently on educational leadership. A large part of their attention in the 1990s went into administration, property and financial management.

It is hard to make the most of any government investment in new knowledge and resources for schools if these are not systematically built on and spread. "A history of little lurchy things" was what one e-learning expert recalled of much of the last 20 years when we spoke in 2011. I think we did see some real gains made in the 2000s in literacy, maths, the incorporation of assessment for learning, and the synergy of the emphasis on inquiry and evaluation cycles in the New Zealand Curriculum, the planning and reporting framework, and the iterative best evidence syntheses. We saw real gains through NCEA and Te Kotahitanga in secondary teaching. We saw gains coming from ongoing joint work, and partnerships working towards a common purpose.[4]

---

3   In the latest OECD comparisons of country spending, for 2009, converted into US dollars, New Zealand spending per primary student is given as $6,812; Australia as $8,328; Canada as $8,262; the United States as $11,109. Finland spent $7,368 and Japan, $7,729. Secondary education spending shows a similar pattern (OECD, 2012, Table B1.1a).

4   See, for example, Alton-Lee (2012); Annan et al. (2002); Timperley and Parr (2009); Wylie (2011c).

But these gains of knowledge and relationships of challenge and trust have been uneven and not sufficiently capitalised on. Overall, there has been too much reinvention of the wheel, too many separate things with their separate start-up costs. And too much time has been lost establishing relations, bringing new officials and providers up to speed so they can operate knowledgeably and efficiently.

There has been insufficient joint work during crucial periods, such as the development of NCEA and the National Standards, with long-term costs seen in the weakness in what is developed and its implementation. The international literature is clear about how important it is, as the OECD (2011a) puts it, to include the teaching profession as "part of the solution", co-constructing solutions with policy makers, rather than as "part of the problem" (see also Fullan, 2010; Levin, 2008, 2012; Sahlberg, 2011). It is telling that both Sir John Anderson's report to the Government in 1994 and Gary Hawke's final report to the Minister, in his role chairing the National Standards Sector Advisory Group, emphasise that including the teaching profession in such joint work is vital for the success of major policy intended to change teaching practice to improve learning.

Separate government departments are also likely to have needed more operating funding than if they had been working more closely together. The contractual emphasis, resurgent again, also takes its toll in the time spent for all involved, leaving less time to be spent on the heart of education, on student learning opportunities.

# Making the most of self-managing schools

In the light of these three fundamental flaws, what could we do differently now to make the most of self-managing schools? The past 23 years in New Zealand have certainly shown the limitations of positioning each school as a separate island. It will be connections that increase the effectiveness of our schools and the ability of our education system to better meet our expectations, not any further extension of New Zealand schools' longstanding latitude. What I suggest in conclusion as the changes we need is designed to integrate the key strengths of what was lost with *Tomorrow's Schools* with the knowledge we have about the frameworks and relationships that would allow us to make the most of self-managing schools.

Self-managed schools work best, and most efficiently, when they:

- use inquiry cycles to pursue clear goals for student learning and engagement
- operate as collective learning organisations
- work within and contribute to a supporting and challenging education authority
- work within a national system that is also focused on continuous learning and capacity development, using ongoing joint work
- work within national policy frameworks that are well grounded in strong evidence.

To achieve this means more than tweaking our current structures and ways of doing things. It means changes in the government agencies, and some changes for schools and boards. These are changes that I think can be made without increasing government education funding.

I suggest more challenging support at the local level, more connections to share and build knowledge, and more coherence between the different layers of the schooling system. We need more dialogue and joint work between policy and operations if we are to keep developing teacher and school capability, and to overcome the suspicion that mars our system. Here are my recommendations:

1. *A national network of education authorities*

    (a) There should be a national network of around 20 education authorities, responsible to a national director who is part of the senior leadership team in the Ministry of Education.

    (b) Each education authority would work with and for around 120 schools: a size large enough to provide schools with the infrastructure they need, while small enough to allow good interaction and relationships.

    (c) The education authorities would be staffed with experienced, proven and credible educators, and with human resource, finance and property expertise. They would provide schools with the specialist support needed for students with special educational needs.

    *Role of the education authorities*

    (d) Each education authority would have ultimate responsibility for the quality of schools in their area. They would work with principals to allocate the authority's funding and resources to ensure as equitable as possible learning opportunities for the area's students and the ongoing development of the physical capacity and capability needed for the area's schools. They would set school enrolment zones. They would work with principals to decide the authority's own goals for school capability and student performance, setting ambitious but achievable goals that are aligned with national goals.

(e) The education authorities would employ principals, but include school boards in the selection process. They would have regular discussions with principals on the school's performance and progress on its goals, based on the school's charter. This would provide formative accountability and challenging support, and would thereby minimise the chances of schools struggling and getting into difficulty. They would provide advice and connect school leaders with the sources of knowledge they need. They would work more closely with principals who are not making headway on the school's goals, and could remove them if there were no improvement.

(f) Education authority leaders would be 'champions' for education and schools in the area. They would maintain good connections with business, iwi, community groups and the non-profit sector. They would use the media to encourage public understanding and discussion of education.

*Vital connections within each education authority*

(g) The education authority would ensure that its principals meet regularly with each other in purposeful groups, based on location, and also on common contexts or challenges (e.g., secondary, Māori medium, iwi groupings, low-decile). They would ensure there is two-way communication between these groups and the authority's leadership.

(h) The education authorities would also ensure that schools and teachers are connected in order to learn from each other, and would provide anchorage for networks of teachers in this work (e..g,. primary writing, Māori medium, e-learning).

(i) Education authority staff would be connected with researchers and professional developers in enduring joint work, using them to support authority and school priorities for ongoing inquiry and capability development, and student performance, and to keep building on what is learnt.

*Vital connections across education authorities*

(j) Education authority staff would also be nodes in national networks with a particular focus (e.g, science, accelerating maths learning in low-decile schools, threading key competencies through secondary subjects). These networks would also include teachers, professional developers, subject experts and researchers. They would have an inquiry focus. They would undertake periodic national reviews of teaching, learning and student performance, to check progress and gain insight into what needs development, so that network plans could focus on the next set of needs.

(k) Education authority leaders would also form a national network to share progress and challenges. They would meet (physically or electronically) as a group once a quarter with the Secretary of Education to evaluate progress and what needs development, and discuss any barriers to development.

*Vital connections across the system*

(l) Representatives from this education authority leaders' national group and the Secretary would meet with the Minister of Education to discuss progress and the capability development needs after these national meetings. This should ensure there is shared knowledge. It should also mean there can be substantive discussion on goals and common purpose, which will also increase shared 'ownership', and strategic thinking that is most likely to be successful in achieving long-term educational goals.

(m) The education authorities should have their own director, with a small team focused on supporting the education authority network and acting as a clearing house for relevant new knowledge.

(n) Because of the need for closer links and real dialogue between operations and policy, this director should be part of the Ministry of Education's senior leadership team. The director should have no responsibilities other than to work with the 20 leaders of the education authorities, and to provide input from this work into the Ministry's senior leadership team and its strategic thinking, while drawing that strategic thinking and direction back into the work with the education authority leaders. The education authority network needs to have sufficient standing to ensure that it remains focused on capability development.

2. *A single government educational agency*
   (a) There should be a single Ministry of Education at the national level (Wellington) that has the responsibility for the strategic direction of education as a whole, aimed at continual development and capacity building, so that student learning and outcomes keep pace with our expectations.
   (b) Curriculum and qualifications work should be undertaken in tandem, to ensure that there is coherence between them, and in the guidance and resources that support them.
   (c) Reshaping the Ministry of Education around strengthening the capability of self-managing schools, and around achieving greater coherence between policy and operations through closer relations and action at the level of education authorities, along with the work of the education authorities would have implications for the current work and roles of the Ministry of Education, NZQA, ERO and the NZSTA. Some of their current work would now be better provided through the educational authorities, and some through more coherence at the national level.
   (d) The national Ministry of Education needs to operate in such a way that it can attract and keep sufficient educational expertise and credibility, organised in ways that allow continual capitalisation on what is achieved. That means there should be a less piecemeal, short-term approach than at present.
   (e) I recommend the use of Ben Levin's (2012) invaluable outline of the essentials that enable a Ministry of Education to provide strong, positive and successful leadership, together with his checklist of characteristics of effective ministries of education, to reshape the Ministry and the way it operates, and set goals for its performance.
   (f) Joint work and ongoing programmes from them should be a cornerstone of our strengthened system. We need national anchoring of the networks of inquiry outlined in relation to the role of education authorities, which would be responsible for periodic review of capacity and performance in given curriculum or student areas. This anchoring does not necessarily have to be within the Ministry staff, but if it is not, it should be with centres or organisations that can be contracted on a long-term basis (with the usual regular reviews of performance), and who contribute to the development of relevant frameworks and policy so that we can maintain coherence of policy and practice.

(g) Similarly, there should be ongoing joint work with the teaching profession's representatives in key policy areas, with cycles of periodic review of progress. This would also ensure greater coherence across different aspects of policy, as well as underline the sense of common purpose.

(h) Six-monthly reviews of national progress involving the sector's representatives, Ministry senior leadership team and the Minister of Education that also took an inquiry approach are essential. These would do much to forge the essential sense of common purpose and respect needed for a system to progress, and to provide the understanding and energy needed to keep developing together.

3. *Connected and contributing self-managing schools*

Schools should remain self-managing. Boards of trustees should continue to provide schools with parent–community links, work with school leaders to set school goals, and review performance against those goals. They should be involved with the education authority on the appointment of the school's principal. Principals and teachers should also be active members of networks beyond their own schools so that their work is better supported and they can contribute to others as well.

This book has been about the policy and structures that lie behind teaching and learning, the infrastructure that can get forgotten or taken for granted. I hope I have shown what a critical difference infrastructure actually makes. It deserves far more attention to ensure its strength, vitality and coherence. We have the experience and knowledge now to create the more dynamic schooling system that our students need. It is time to think afresh. It is time to give all our self-managing schools the vital connections, support and challenge they need to succeed.

# Glossary

AIMHI Achievement in Multicultural High Schools. Cluster started in 1995 to improve nine secondary schools serving low income multicultural urban areas; one of the most successful and enduring school clusters.

Assessment for Learning Using assessment tasks not just as a gauge of performance, but to analyse student needs and 'next steps'. Assessment thus becomes an integral part of teaching and learning; the term was also used for a national professional development programme in the 2000s.

Audit and Review Agency The original name given to the government agency that would periodically review and evaluate the progress of self-managing schools; ERO's precursor.

BES Iterative Best Evidence Synthesis. Syntheses of research relating teaching and school leadership to student outcomes, using an iterative process that engaged school sector representatives alongside researchers and government officials to discuss emergent findings and their implications as the synthesis was building.

Board of Studies Government body with wide stakeholder input, set up to bring greater coherence in secondary curriculum, assessment, qualifications and pedagogy; 1988–1990.

Board of Trustees Governance body for each school, usually with around seven members: five parent representatives elected triennially by current parents of children at the school, with the board having power to co-opt also; the principal; and a staff representative, elected by the school staff. Secondary schools also have a student representative, elected by students.

BSM Beginning School Mathematics. A national mathematics framework and resource for primary schools that was rolling out as *Tomorrow's Schools* began.

Competent Learners A longitudinal study following a cohort of Wellington region children from their last months of early childhood education in 1994–95 through their schooling, with the most recent follow-up in 2009, as they turned 20.

Decile All New Zealand state and state-integrated schools are assigned to a category reflecting the socio-economic nature of their intake, for funding purposes. High decile schools have the lowest proportion of students from low socioeconomic homes; low decile schools, the highest proportion of these students.

Department of Education The government agency responsible for education policy and provision until 1989.

DSI District Senior Inspector, leader of the team of inspectors based in one of the 10 education boards in the era before *Tomorrow's Schools*. Inspectors worked with education board staff, but were employed by the Department of Education.

Education board Until 1989, 10 education boards around the country were responsible for primary school provision in their area; they were governed by people from primary school committees and local government.

Education Development Conference In fact, several national conferences, which spurred discussions around the country about the purpose and issues of education, in which some 60,000 people took part, between 1971 and1974, and whose results fed into subsequent reviews of education.

ERIC Early Reading In-service Course, the first national programme to provide primary teachers with professional development in teaching reading for the first years of school, running in the 1970s.

ERO Education Review Office. The government agency responsible for regular evaluations of schools.

hapū sub-tribe.

hui meeting, gathering.

Inquiry into the Quality of Teaching (Scott report) 1986 Education and Science parliamentary select committee report, with cross-party participation, named after its chair, Noel Scott.

Inspectorate Department of Education officers with school leadership experience, working at education board or regional office level, charged with both reviewing and supporting schools, a role which ended with the *Tomorrow's Schools* reforms.

iwi tribe.

kura kaupapa Māori Māori medium school.

LARIC Later Reading In-service Course; followed on from ERIC to provide the first national programme for primary school teachers working with Standard 2 (now Year 4) to Form 2 (now Year 8) students.

Literacy taskforce A government taskforce reporting in 1999.

Lough report (*Today's Schools*) 1990 government review of progress with the implementation of *Tomorrow's Schools* which further reinforced the separation of schools from the government education agencies.

LPDP Literacy Professional Development Programme, which ran in the mid-2000s with a national network of facilitators working with individual schools to improve school capability in teaching reading and writing, analytical capacity, and more collective ways of working.

Mathematics and Science Taskforce 1997 A government taskforce set up in the wake of New Zealand's disappointing performance on the TIMSS international assessments.

NAGs National Administration Guidelines. Mandatory regulations framing self-managing schools' operations.

National Curriculum Framework The first national curriculum in New Zealand, introduced from 1991.

National Qualifications Framework Developed in the 1990s to bring all school and vocational qualifications into a single framework, to encourage more flexibility of provision.

NCEA National Certificates of Educational Achievement, the secondary qualification since 2002, with three levels.

NEMP National Education Monitoring Project. Started in the early 1990s to provide a national picture of student achievement over time, across the curriculum.

NEGs National Education Guidelines. These provide the mandatory framework for schools' work. They now have five components: National Education Goals, Foundation Curriculum Policy statements, National Curriculum statements, National Standards, and the National Administrative Guidelines.

Network for Learning. Government initiative to support schools to make more use of the Internet, including sharing across schools and between schools and homes to support learning.

New Zealand Curriculum The current national curriculum, mandatory since 2010.

Numeracy Development Projects National framework and resources to support primary and secondary mathematics, with a national network of facilitators providing professional development to schools during the 2000s.

NZCER New Zealand Council for Educational Research.

NZEI New Zealand Educational Institute, the early childhood education and primary teachers' and principals' and school support staff professional association and union.

NZPF New Zealand Principals' Federation. National body set up to represent and support principals after *Tomorrow's Schools* enlarged the principal's role.

NZQA New Zealand Qualifications Authority. Responsible in the 1990s for secondary qualification reform, now responsible for operation of qualifications.

NZSTA New Zealand School Trustees Association. National body representing and supporting boards of trustees.

Picot taskforce The group charged with reviewing education administration for the Government in 1987–88, and responsible for the Picot report. Named after its chair, Brian Picot.

PISA Programme for International Student Assessment, run by the OECD, to provide yardsticks of 15-year-olds' performance, and analysis of how performance relates to student and country factors.

PPTA Post-Primary Teachers' Association. National body representing secondary teachers and principals.

Reading Recovery National programme providing one-to-one teaching for students with low reading levels at age 6, access dependent on individual school choice and resources.

Rogernomics Short-hand for the radical neo-liberal economic and public sector reforms begun in 1984, named after Roger Douglas, the Government Minister who led them.

Royal Commission on Social Policy Intended to assuage public concern about the impact of Rogernomics, with wide consultation and analysis of social policy provision and issues, including education. It ran from 1987 to 1988.

RTLB Resource Teacher: Learning and Behaviour. Specialist support for teachers to help them with strategies for students with learning or behaviour difficulties, located in school and now regional clusters.

School Certificate Originally intended as the school-leaving qualification for those not heading to university; became the universal qualification sat in Form 5, now Year 11.

Schools Without Failure Resource developed in the mid-1980s to support schools to better engage Māori and other students not being well served by schools, and to improve their educational performance.

SEMO Strengthening Education in Mangere and Otara, the seminal schooling improvement cluster set up in the wake of a damning ERO area-wide review in 1996.

Starpath University of Auckland applied research programme to improve the pathways to tertiary education for students in schools in low-income areas.

SIMS Second International Maths Study. Carried out in 1981 across 20 countries.

Taskforce to Review Education Administration The Picot taskforce (see above).

TIMSS Third International Maths and Science Study.

Tomorrow May Be Too Late The first study to analyse the shortcomings of educational provision for students in Mangere-Otara, in 1981.

Tomorrow's Schools The radical reform that separated schools from government in 1989, making all schools self-managing.

University Entrance: the qualification required to gain entrance into university.

whānau family.

# References

Adolescent Health Research Group. (2008). *Youth '07: The health and wellbeing of secondary school students in New Zealand: Initial findings.* Auckland: University of Auckland.

Aikin, S. (1994). Primary problems and the New Zealand curriculum framework. *New Zealand Annual Review of Education, 4,* 57–76.

Aitken, G., & Sinnema, C. (2008). *Effective pedagogy in the social sciences / tikanga-a-iwi: Best evidence synthesis iteration.* Wellington: Ministry of Education.

Alcorn, N. (1999). *To the fullest extent of his powers: C. E. Beeby's life in education.* Wellington: Victoria University Press.

Alison, J. (2005). *Teachers talk about NCEA.* Wellington: New Zealand Post Primary Teachers Association.

Alison, J. (2008). The NCEA and how we got there: The role of PPTA in school qualifications reform 1980–2002. *New Zealand Journal of Teachers' Work, 5*(2), 119–138.

Alison, J., Cross, B., & Willets, R. (2003, December). *Bloodied but unbowed: The effect on New Zealand secondary school teachers' work and lives of the neoliberal reform of the 90's: A union perspective.* Paper presented at the New Zealand Association for Research in Education & Australian Association for Research in Education joint conference, Auckland.

Alton-Lee, A. (2012, April). *The use of evidence to improve education and serve the public good.* Paper given at the AERA 2012 Annual Meeting, Vancouver. Retrieved from http://www.educationcounts.govt.nz/__data/assets/pdf_file/0004/109039/The-Use-of-Evidence-to-Improve-Education-and-Serve-the-Public-Good.pdf

Anderson, J. (1994). Education priorities in the schools sector, & teaching staffing resource delivery mechanisms options: Final report to the Minister of Education. Appendix III. In Pearce, D. F. (1996). *Two years of peace?: The schools consultative group and the state in New Zealand.* Unpublished doctoral thesis, University of Canterbury.

Anderson, S. E., Mascall, B., Stiegelbauer, S., & Park, J. (2012). No one way: Differentiating school district leadership and support for school improvement. *Journal of Educational Change.* DOI: 10.1007/s10833-012-9189-y

Annan, B. (2007). *A theory for schooling improvement: Consistency and connectivity to improve instructional practice.* Unpublished doctoral thesis, University of Auckland.

Annan, B., Fa'amoe-Timoteo, E., Carpenter, V., Hucker, J., & Warren, S. (2002). *A three-way partnership to raise student achievement: Strengthening Education in Mangere and Otara outcomes report July 1999–June 2002.* Auckland: Ministry of Education.

Anthony, G., & Walshaw, M. (2007). *Effective pedagogy in mathematics: Best evidence synthesis iteration.* Wellington: Ministry of Education.

Anthony, G., & Walshaw, M. (2009). *Effective pedagogy in mathematics: Educational practices series, 19.* International Academy of Education & International Bureau of Education, UNESCO. Retrieved from http://www.ibe.unesco.org/en/services/publications/educational-practices.html

Barber, P. (2011). How to get closer together: Impacts of income inequality and policy responses. *Policy Quarterly, 7*(4), 62–68.

Barrington, J. (1981). The politics of school government. In M. Clark (Ed.), *The politics of education*. Wellington: New Zealand Council for Educational Research.

Barrington, J. (1990). Historical factors for change in education. In P. McKinley (Ed.), *Redistribution of power?: Devolution in New Zealand*. Wellington: Victoria University Press.

Barrington, J. (1991). *Report to the Ministry of Education: OECD: Educational evaluation and reform strategies*. Wellington: Education Department, Victoria University of Wellington.

Beeby, C. E. (1986a). Introduction. In Renwick, W. L. (1986). *Moving targets: Six essays on educational policy*. Wellington: New Zealand Council for Educational Research.

Beeby, C. E. (1986b, 8 November). The place of myth in educational change. *New Zealand Listener*. Retrieved from http://www.educationaotearoa.org.nz/all-stories/2010/7/18/the-place-of-myth-in-educational-change.html

Bell, B. (1991). Science curriculum development: A recent New Zealand example. In A. Begg, B. Bell, F. Biddulph, M. Carr, J. McChesney, & J. Young-Loveridge (Eds.), *SAMEpapers 1990* (pp. 1–31). Auckland: Longman Paul.

Bell, B., & Baker, R. (1997). Curriculum development in science: Policy-to-practice and practice-to-policy. In B. Bell & R. Baker (Eds.), *Developing the science curriculum in Aotearoa New Zealand* (pp. 1–17). Auckland: Addison Wesley Longman New Zealand.

Bennie, N., Henry, E., & Ratcliff, B. (1990). *Beginning school mathematics: A study of the implementation*. Wellington: Ministry of Education.

Benton, R. (1988). Fairness in Māori education: A review of research and information. In *Report of the Royal Commission on Social Policy, Volume III (2): Future directions* (pp. 285–404). Wellington: Royal Commission on Social Policy.

Biddulph, F. (1999). The legacy of schooling: Student teachers' initial mathematical feelings and competence. *Mathematics Teacher Education and Development, 1*, 64–71.

Boag, P. (1977). Foreword. In N. Scott, *A survey of some aspects of New Zealand secondary schools*. Wellington: Department of Education.

Bolstad, R., & Gilbert, J. (2008). *Disciplining and drafting, or 21st century learning?* Wellington: NZCER Press.

Bolstad, R., & Gilbert, J., with McDowall, S., Bull, A., Boyd, S., & Hipkins, R. (2012). *Supporting future-oriented learning and teaching—a New Zealand perspective*. Wellington: Ministry of Education.

Boston, J., Martin, J., Pallot, J., & Walsh, P. (Eds.) (1991). *Reshaping the state: New Zealand's bureaucratic revolution*. Auckland: Oxford University Press.

Boven, R., Harland, C., & Grace, L. (2011). *More ladders, fewer snakes: Two proposals to reduce youth disadvantage*. Auckland: The New Zealand Institute.

Boyd, R. (1998). A case study of change in national education administration post-Picot. In *NZEAS biennial conference: Ten years on: Reforming New Zealand education: Proceedings: Vol 1* (pp. 143–175). Wellington: New Zealand Educational Administration Society.

Breakwell, J. (1999). The pendulum swings: Back to reasonably convenient schools. *Australia and New Zealand Journal of Law & Education, 4*(2), 3–17.

Bull, A. (2011). *Primary science education for the 21st century: How, what, why?* Wellington: New Zealand Council for Educational Research.

Bull, A., Gilbert, J., Barwick, H., Hipkins, R., & Baker, R. (2010). *Inspired by science: A paper commissioned by the Royal Society and the Prime Minister's Chief Science Advisor.* Wellington: New Zealand Council for Educational Research.

Burgon, J., Ferral, H., Hodgen, E., & Wylie, C. (2012). *Educational leadership practices survey: Report on the national norms and benchmarking.* Wellington: Ministry of Education.

Burstein, L. (1993). Prologue: Studying learning, growth, and instruction cross-nationally: Lessons learned about why and why not engage in cross-national studies. In L. Burstein (Ed.), *The IEA Study of Mathematics III: Student growth and classroom processes.* Oxford: Pergamon Press.

Butterworth, G., & Butterworth, S. (1998). *Reforming education: The New Zealand experience 1984–1996.* Palmerston North: Dunmore Press.

Cain, M. (2009). *The school charter: Planning and reporting: Principal sabbatical report 2009.* Retrieved from http://www.educationleaders.govt.nz

Calhoun, E., & Joyce, B. (1998). Inside-out and outside-in: Learning from past and present school improvement paradigms. In A. Hargeaves, A. Lieberman, M. Fullan, & D. Hopkins (Eds.), *International handbook of educational change* (pp. 1286–1298). Dordrecht, The Netherlands: Kluwer Academic.

Cameron, M., & Baker, R. (2004). *Research on initial teacher education in New Zealand, 1993–2004: Literature review and annotated bibliography.* Wellington: New Zealand Council for Educational Research.

Campbell, E. (1978). *Realities of curricula.* Wellington: Department of Education.

Capper, P. (1992). Curriculum 1991. *New Zealand Annual Review of Education, 1,* 15–27.

Capper, P. (1994). *Participation and partnership: Exploring shared decision-making in twelve New Zealand secondary schools: Part One.* Wellington: Post Primary Teachers' Association.

Caygill, R., & Kirkham, S. (2008). *Mathematics: Trends in year 5 mathematics achievement 1994 to 2006.* Wellington: Ministry of Education.

Caygill, R., Lang, K., & Cowls, S. (2010). *The school context for year 5 students' mathematics and science achievement in 2006.* Wellington: Ministry of Education.

Clark, E. T. (1988). *Primary teacher accountability: The role of the inspector of schools.* Unpublished Master of Public Policy research paper, Victoria University of Wellington.

Clay, M. (1990). The Reading Recovery programme, 1984–88: Coverage, outcomes and Education Board district figures. *New Zealand Journal of Educational Studies, 25*(1), 61–70.

Codd, J., & Hermansson, G. L. (1976). *Directions in New Zealand secondary education.* Auckland: Hodder and Stoughton.

Coleman, B. R. (1976). *The changing role of the principal of the New Zealand urban primary school, of moderate size, with special reference to the following: Professional leadership, personal attributes, and role as interpreter of the school to the local and wider community.* Unpublished MA thesis, Victoria University of Wellington.

Committee on Secondary Education. (1976). *Towards partnership: Report of the Committee on Secondary Education.* Wellington: Government Printer.

Condron, D. J. (2011). Egalitarianism and educational excellence: Compatible goals for affluent societies? *Educational Researcher, 40*(2), 47–55.

Controller and Auditor-General. (2001). *Providing and caring for school property*. Wellington: Author.

Coopers and Lybrand. (1988). *Local management of schools*. London: Author.

Cowie, B., Hikpins, R., Keown, P., & Boyd, S. (2011). *The shape of curriculum change: A short discussion of key findings from the Curriculum Implementation Studies project*. Wellington: New Zealand Council for Educational Research.

Davies, D. (2001). *School entry assessment: June 1997–Dec 2000*. Wellington: Research Division, Ministry of Education.

Day, D. W. A. (1984). *The role of the board of governors in the New Zealand state secondary school*. Unpublished Master of Public Policy research paper, Victoria University of Wellington.

Deloitte Touche Tohmatsu. (1997). *School accommodation management resource capability*. Author.

Denny, S., Galbreath, R. A., Grant, S., & Milfont, T. L. (2010). *Youth '07: The health and wellbeing of secondary school students in New Zealand: Students who truant: What makes a difference?* Auckland: University of Auckland.

Denny, S., Robinson, E., Milfont, T., & Grant, S. (2009). *Youth '07: The social climate of secondary schools in New Zealand*. Auckland: University of Auckland.

Department of Education. (1978). *Educational standards in state schools*. Wellington: Author.

Department of Education. (1981). *State Secondary Schools in New Zealand: a baseline survey*. Wellington: Author.

Department of Education. (1983). *Advisory services available to New Zealand teachers: A research report*. Wellington: Department of Education.

Department of Education. (1986). *State secondary schools in New Zealand: A 1985 follow-up of the 1975 baseline survey*. Wellington: Author.

Department of Education. (1987a). *Briefing papers provided to Hon David Lange, Minister of Education*. Wellington: Author.

Department of Education. (1987b). *Report for the year ended 31 March 1987*. (E.1). Wellington: Author.

Department of Education. (1987c). *The Curriculum Review: Report of the Committee to Review the Curriculum for Schools*. Wellington: Author.

Department of Education. (1988a). *Secondary education in New Zealand: Reorientation and Reform: An appraisal for UNESCO*. Wellington: Author.

Department of Education (1988b). *Twenty thousand: A summary of responses to the Report of the Taskforce to Review Education Administration*. (1988). Wellington: Author.

Department of Education (1990). *Today's Schools: A review of the education reform implementation process* [the Lough report]. (1990). Wellington: Author.

Doake, D. B. (1972). Teacher education in the field of reading. In C. S. Brockett (Ed.), *Reading, books and children: Selected proceedings: Third New Zealand conference, 1972* (pp. 24–34). Auckland: International Reading Association, Auckland Council.

Dumont, H., & Istance, D. (2010). Analysing and designing learning environments for the 21st century. In H. Dumont, D. Istance, & F. Benavides (Eds.), *The nature of learning: Using research to inspire practice* (pp. 19–34). Paris: OECD.

Dweck, C. (2000). *Self-theories: Their role in motivation, personality and development*. Philadelphia, PA: Psychology Press.

Education and Science Select Committee. (1986). *Report on the inquiry into the quality of teaching (Scott report)*. Wellington: Government Printer.

Elley, W. (1994). Curriculum reform: Forwards or backwards? *New Zealand Annual Review of Education, 3*, 38–49.

Elley, W. (2004). New Zealand literacy standards in a global context: The uses and abuses of international literacy surveys. *English Teaching: Practice and Critique, 3*(1), 32–45.

Elley, W. B. (1985). *Lessons learned about LARIC*. Christchurch: University of Canterbury.

Elley, W. B. (2010, 20 February). Meeting standards. *The Listener*, p. 6.

Ellis, S. (1996, December). *Public policy, public scrutiny, and secondary schools in trouble*. Paper presented at the New Zealand Association of Researchers in Education Conference, Nelson.

Eng, G. (1992). *The use of grade related criteria in Sixth Form Certificate English: A comparative study*. Christchurch: Education Department, University of Canterbury.

Eppel, E. (2009). Curriculum, teaching and learning: A celebratory review of a very complex and evolving landscape. In J. Langley (Ed.), *Tomorrow's Schools 20 years on…* (pp. 51–62). Auckland: Cognition Institute.

Ernst & Whinney. (1987). *Report on the future costs of school administration, prepared for the Taskforce to Review Education Administration*. Auckland: Author.

ERO. (1994). *Report of the Education Review Office for the year ended 30 June 1994*. Wellington: Author.

ERO. (1996). *Improving schooling in Mangere and Otara*. Wellington: Author.

ERO. (2000). *Annual report of the Education Review Office for the year ended 30 June 2000*. Wellington: Author.

ERO. (2004). *Evaluation of the Resource Teacher: Learning and Behaviour service*. Wellington: Author.

ERO. (2007). *School governance: An overview*. Wellington: Author.

ERO. (2009). *Resource Teachers: Learning and Behaviour: An evaluation of cluster management*. Wellington: Author.

ERO. (2010). *Criteria for timing decisions*. Wellington: Author.

ERO. (2011). *Directions for learning: The New Zealand curriculum principles, and teaching as inquiry*. Wellington: Author.

ERO. (n.d.). *Information for learning institutions*. Wellington: Author.

Ewing, J. L. (1963). *The appointment and promotion of primary school teachers in New Zealand: Some explanatory notes for teachers*. Wellington: Department of Education.

Fancy, H. (2000). Commentary. In G. Sullivan (Ed.), *The Tomorrow's Schools reforms: An American perspective* (pp. 16–20). Wellington: Institute of Policy Studies, Victoria University of Wellington.

Fiske, E., & Ladd, H. (2000). *When schools compete: A cautionary tale*. Washington, DC: Brookings Institute Press.

Flockton, L. (2003, November–December). *The first two cycles of New Zealand's National Education Monitoring Project: 1995–1998 and 1999–2002*. Paper presented at the New Zealand Association for Research in Education & Australian Association for Research in Education joint conference, Auckland.

Fountain, G. (2008). Caught in between: How the scientific management of education in New Zealand made history history. *Curriculum Matters, 4*, 134–146.

Fountain, G. (2012). *Caught in-between: The impact of different forms of mandated national assessment for qualifications on teacher decision-making in Year 12 history in New Zealand, 1986–2005*. Master of Education thesis, Victoria University of Wellington.

Fullan, M. (2010). *All systems go: The change imperative for whole system reform*. Thousand Oaks, CA: Corwin.

Garden, R. (1997). The Third International Mathematics and Science Study: Some implications for New Zealand. *New Zealand Annual Review of Education, 7*, 181–196.

Gardiner & Parata Ltd. (2008). *Te hiringa i te mahara: The power of the mind*: Māori secondary teachers and professional development. 1998–2008: 10 years on. Wellington: Author.

Gilbert, J. (2005). *Catching the knowledge wave? The knowledge society and the future of education*. Wellington: NZCER Press.

Gilmore, A. (1999). *The NEMP experience: Professional development of teachers through the National Education Monitoring Project*. Christchurch: Unit for Studies in Educational Evaluation, Education Department, University of Canterbury.

Gilmore, A., & Hattie, J. (2000). *Evaluation of the assessment resource banks in schools*. Wellington: Ministry of Education.

Gluckman, P. (2011). *Looking ahead: Science education for the twenty-first century*. Auckland: Office of the Prime Minister's Science Advisory Committee.

Glynn, T., Crooks, T., Bethune, N., Ballard, K., & Smith, J. (1989). *Reading Recovery in context*. Report to the Department of Education.

Grant, D. (2003). *Those who can, teach: A history of secondary education in New Zealand from the union perspective*. Wellington: Steele Roberts.

Gray, J., Hopkins, D., Reynolds, D., Wilcox, B., Farrell, S., & Jesson, D. (1999). *Improving schools: Performance and potential*. Buckingham, UK: Open University Press.

Hall, C. (1997). The National Qualifications Framework in 1996 and beyond: A call for reflection on the nature of outcomes-based education. *New Zealand Annual Review of Education, 6*, 71–87.

Hamilton, B. (1998). There must be a pony: Education reform: A colonising experience for Māori. In *NZEAS biennial conference: Ten years on: Reforming New Zealand education: Proceedings, Vol 1* (pp. 235–240). Wellington: New Zealand Educational Administration Society.

Hargreaves, A., Crocker, R., David, B., McEwan, L., Sahlberg, P., Sumara, D., et al. (2009). *The learning mosaic: A multiple perspectives review of the Alberta Initiative for School Improvement (AISI): Summary report*. Calgary, AB: Alberta Education. Retrieved from http://education.alberta.ca/aisi

Harker, R. (2000). Roll change and the removal of zoning, 1991–1998. *set: Research Information for Teachers, 2*, 4–6.

Hartevelt, J. (2008, 1 September). Boys sell mascara to help cash-strapped school. *The Press.* Retrieved from http://www.stuff.co.nz/national/606164/Boys-sell-mascara-to-help-cash-strapped-school

Hattie, J. (2009). *Horizons and whirlpools: The well travelled pathway of national standards.* Retrieved from http://www.cognitioninstitute.org/files/docs/horizons-whirlpools-the-well-travelled-pathway-of-national-standards.pdf

Helu, S. L., Robinson, E., Grant, S., Herd, R., & Denny, S. (2009). *Youth '07: The health and wellbeing of secondary school students in New Zealand: Results for Pacific young people.* Auckland: University of Auckland.

Heylen Research Centre. (1987a). *Opinion poll: Public attitudes towards the New Zealand education system.* Prepared for the Department of Education. Wellington: Author.

Heylen Research Centre. (1987b). *Public attitudes towards the New Zealand education system: Opinion poll.* Wellington: Author.

Heylen Research Centre. (1989a). *Education administration reform: Parents: Public opinion poll.* Wellington: Author.

Heylen Research Centre. (1989b). *Education administration reform: Principals/teachers opinion poll.* Wellington: Author.

Higgins, J., & Hendry, D. (1992). *Teacher development contract: Beginning school mathematics.* Wellington: Wellington College of Education.

Higgins, J., & Parsons, R. (2009). A successful professional development model in mathematics: A system-wide New Zealand case. *Journal of Teacher Education, 60*(3), 231–242.

Hill, J., & Hawk, K. (2003, December). *Achieving is cool: What we learned from the AIMHI project to help schools more effectively meet the needs of their students.* Paper presented at the New Zealand Association for Research in Education conference, Auckland.

Hill, M. (1999). Assessment in self-managing schools: Primary teachers balancing learning and accountability demands in the 1990s. *New Zealand Journal of Educational Studies, 34*(1), 176–185.

Hill, R. (1992). *Managing today's schools: The case for shared decision-making.* Wellington: New Zealand Institute for Social Research and Development.

Hinchco, B. (2011, 16 June). *So why are principals opposed to National Standards?* Paper for NSSAG meeting. Retrieved from http://nssag.minedu.govt.nz

Hipkins, R. (2010). *The evolving NCEA.* Wellington: New Zealand Council for Educational Research.

Hipkins, R., Joyce, C., & Wylie, C. (2007). *School planning and reporting in action: The early years of the new framework.* Wellington: New Zealand Council for Educational Research.

Hipkins, R., & Robertson, S. (2011). *Moderation and teacher learning: What can research tell us about their interrelationships?* Wellington: New Zealand Council for Educational Research.

Hipkins, R., & Vaughan, K., with Beals, F., Ferral, H., & Gardiner, B. (2005). *Shaping our futures: Meeting secondary students' needs in a time of evolving qualifications.* Wellington: New Zealand Council for Educational Research.

Hodgen, E., & Wylie, C. (2005). *Stress and wellbeing among New Zealand principals.* Wellington: New Zealand Council for Educational Research.

Hood, D. (1998). *Our secondary schools don't work anymore: Why and how New Zealand schooling must change for the 21st century.* Auckland: Profile Books.

James, C. (1992). *New territory: The transformation of New Zealand, 1984–92.* Wellington: Bridget Williams.

Kifer, E., & Burstein, L. (1993). Concluding thoughts: What we know, what it means. In L. Burstein (Ed.), *The IEA Study of Mathematics III: Student growth and classroom processes.* Oxford: Pergamon Press.

Laking, R. (1996). *Ministry of Education management audit.* Wellington: Ministry of Education.

Lauder, H., & Hughes, D. (1999). *Trading in futures: Why markets in education don't work.* Buckingham, UK: Open University Press.

Lennox, B. (1995, December). *Advocacy, evolution and learning: School assessment for the National Qualifications Framework.* Paper presented at New Zealand Association for Research in Education conference, Palmerston North.

Levin, B. (2008). *How to change 5,000 schools: A practical and positive approach for leading change at every level.* Cambridge, MA: Harvard Education Press.

Levin, B. (2012). *System-wide change in education.* Education Policy Series 13. International Academy of Education. Retrieved from http://www.iiep.unesco.org/fileadmin/user_upload/Info_Services_Publications/pdf/2012/EdPol_13.pdf

Literacy Taskforce. (1999). *Report of the Literacy Taskforce.* Wellington: Ministry of Education.

Loader, M., & Ryan, T. (2010). *Attendance in New Zealand schools in 2009.* Wellington: Ministry of Education.

Lubienski, C. (2009). *Do quasi-markets foster innovation in education?: A comparative perspective.* OECD Education Working Papers 25. Paris: OECD Publishing.

Madjar, I., & McKinlay, E. (2011). *Understanding NCEA: A relatively short and very useful guide for secondary school students and their parents.* Wellington: NZCER Press.

Madjar, I., & McKinlay, E. (2012). *Malamalama i le NCEA.* Wellington: NZCER Press.

Madjar, I., McKinley, E., Jensen, E., & Van Der Merwe, A. (2009). *Towards university: Navigating NCEA course choices in low-mid decile schools.* Auckland: University of Auckland, Starpath Project.

Mansell, H. (1999, November–December). *Curriculum reform in New Zealand: What is really being done and is it worth the trouble?* Paper presented at Australian Association for Research in Education & New Zealand Association for Research in Education joint conference, Sydney.

Mansell, R. (1985). The Schools Without Failure project. *Delta, 36,* 3–14.

Mansell, R. L. (1993). *Community forum on education in Wellington's eastern suburbs: A case study on choice and democratic community participation in New Zealand education policy.* Unpublished master's thesis, Victoria University of Wellington.

McCauley, L., & Roddick, S. (2002). *An evaluation of Schools Support.* Wellington: Research Division, Ministry of Education.

McDonald, G. (1989). Pupil progress, Reading Recovery, and the 1:20 teacher–pupil ratio policy in the junior school. In G. McDonald (Ed.), *More teachers, fewer pupils: A study of the 1:20 teacher–pupil ratio policy in the junior school* (pp. 69–86). Wellington: New Zealand Council for Educational Research.

McDowall, S., Cameron, M., & Dingle, R., with Gilmore, A., & MacGibbon, L. (2007). *Evaluation of the Literacy Professional Development Project.* Wellington: Ministry of Education.

McGee, C., Jones, A., Bishop, R., Cowie, B., Hill, M., Miller, T., et al. (2002). *Curriculum stocktake: National school sampling study: Teachers' experience in curriculum implementation: General curriculum, mathematics and technology.* Wellington: Ministry of Education.

McGee, C., Jones, A., Cowie, B., Hill, M., Miller, T., Harlow, A., et al. (2003). *Curriculum stocktake: National school sampling study: Teachers' experience in curriculum implementation: English, languages, science and social studies.* Wellington: Ministry of Education.

McNaughton, S. (2011). *Designing better schools for culturally and linguistically diverse children: A science of performance model for research.* New York, NY: Routledge.

McQueen, H. (1986). *Education: Pointers to a crisis.* Wellington: National Business Review reprints.

McQueen, H. (1991). *The ninth floor: Inside the Prime Minister's Office: A political experience.* Auckland: Penguin Books.

Meyer, L., McClure, J., Walkey, F., McKenzie, L., & Weir, K. (2006). *The impact of NCEA on student motivation.* Report prepared for the Ministry of Education. Wellington: Victoria University of Wellington.

Minister of Education. (1988). *Tomorrow's Schools: The reform of education administration in New Zealand.* Wellington: Government Printer.

Minister of Education. (1999). *New Zealand schools 98.* Wellington: Ministry of Education.

Minister of Education. (2008). *New Zealand schools 2007: Nga kura o Aotearoa.* A report on the compulsory schools sector in New Zealand. Wellington: Ministry of Education.

Minister of Education. (2012). *New Zealand schools 2011: Ngā kura o Aotearoa.* A report on the compulsory schools sector in New Zealand. Wellington: Ministry of Education.

Ministerial Task Group Reviewing Science and Technology Education. (1992). *Charting the course: Report of the Ministerial Task Group Reviewing Science and Technology Education.* Wellington: Ministry of Research, Science and Technology & Ministry of Education.

Ministry of Education. (1990). *Quality education for all according to their needs: Brief for the incoming government.* Wellington: Author.

Ministry of Education. (1991). *The national curriculum of New Zealand: A discussion document.* Wellington: Learning Media.

Ministry of Education. (1996). *Meeting the challenge: Teacher supply.* Wellington: Author.

Ministry of Education. (2002a). *Briefing for the incoming Minister of Education.* Wellington: Author.

Ministry of Education. (2002b). *Curriculum stocktake report to Minister of Education: Executive summary.* Wellington: Author.

Ministry of Education. (2002c). *Planning for better student outcomes.* Wellington: Author.

Ministry of Education. (2003). *Reading literacy in New Zealand: Final results from the PIRLS and the repeat of the 1990–1991 Reading Literacy Study (10-Year Trends Study) for Year 5.* Wellington: Author.

Ministry of Education. (2006). *Review of schools' operational funding.* Wellington: Author.

Ministry of Education. (2007). *The New Zealand curriculum.* Wellington: Learning Media. Ministry of Education. (2009). *Problem solving for tomorrow's world: Results of New Zealand 15-year-olds in the 2003 PISA survey.* Wellington: Author.

Ministry of Education. (2010). *Homeschooling as at 1 July 2010.* Retrieved from http://www.educationcounts.govt.nz/statistics/schooling/homeschooling

Ministry of Education. (2011a). *Briefing to the incoming Minister.* Wellington: Author.

Ministry of Education. (2011b). *Developing communities of mathematical enquiry.* Retrieved from http://www.educationcounts.govt.nz/__data/assets/pdf_file/0010/88075/Case1-Developing-Mathematical-Communities.pdf

Ministry of Education. (2011c). *New Zealand schools 2010: Nga kura o Aotearoa: Report of the Minister of Education on the compulsory schools sector in New Zealand.* Wellington: Author.

Mitchell, D., with McGee, C., Moltzen, R., & Oliver, D. (1993). *Hear our voices: Final report of Monitoring Today's Schools research project.* Hamilton: University of Waikato.

Moed, A., & Hall, C. (2011). Teaching, learning, and assessment of science investigation in year 11: Teachers' response to NCEA. *New Zealand Science Review, 68*(3), 95–101.

Mourshed, M., Chijioke, C., & Barber, M. (2010). *How the world's most improved school systems keep getting better.* McKinsey & Company. Retrieved from http://www.mckinsey.com/client_service/social_sector/latest_thinking/worlds_most_improved_schools

Mullis, I., Martin, M. O., & Foy, P. (2007). Findings from IEA's trends in mathematics and science study at the fourth and eighths grades. In J. F. Olson, C. Preschoff, E. Erberber, A. Arora, & J. Galia (Eds.), *Index of students' perception of being safe in school (SPBSS) and trends.* Chestnut Hill, MA: TIMSS & PIRLS International Study Center, Boston College.

Munro, R. (1976). Investigative science in contemporary classrooms. In J. Codd & G. L. Hermansson (Eds.), *Directions in New Zealand secondary education* (pp. 129–139). Auckland: Hodder and Stoughton.

Murfitt, D. (1995). *The implementation of New Right reform in education: Teachers and the intensification of work.* Unpublished Master of Education thesis, University of Canterbury.

Musset, P. (2012). *School choice and equity: Current policies in OECD countries and a literature review.* OECD Education Working Papers 66. Paris: OECD Publishing.

Neill, A., Fisher, J., & Dingle, R. (2010). *Exploring mathematics interventions: Exploratory evaluation of the Accelerating Learning in Mathematics pilot study.* Wellington: New Zealand Council for Educational Research.

Nelson, B. G. (1986). *A review of support and advisory services.* Wellington: Department of Education.

New Zealand School Trustees Association. (2008). *School governance: Board of trustees stocktake.* Wellington: Author.

Nightingale, D. (1993). *Principal development and curriculum leadership projects: 1992 evaluation report.* Blenheim: Author.

O'Connell, P. (2010, July). *Coherence and inquiry as key dimensions for sustainability of professional learning.* Paper presented at the 23rd World Congress of Reading, Auckland. Retrieved from http://www.learningmedia.co.nz/sites/all/modules/filemanager/files/Research_files/ProLearning5.pdf

OECD. (1983). *Reviews of national policies for education: New Zealand.* Paris: Author.

OECD. (2001). *Knowledge and skills for life.* Paris: Author.

OECD. (2004). *Problem-solving for tomorrow's world.* Paris: Author.

OECD. (2007). *PISA 2006: Vol 2 data.* Paris: Author.

OECD. (2010). *PISA 2009 results: Learning trends: Changes in student performance since 2000.* Paris: Author.

OECD. (2011a). *Building a high-quality teaching profession: Lessons from around the world.* Paris, France: Author.

OECD. (2011b). *Education at a glance 2011.* Paris: Author.

OECD. (2012). *Education at a glance 2012.* Paris: Author.

Office of the Auditor-General. (2008). *Ministry of Education: Monitoring and supporting school boards of trustees.* Wellington: Author.

Ofsted reveals how its star exemptions fell from grace. (2011, 25 November). *Times Educational Supplement*, pp. 12–13.

Openshaw, R. (2009). *Reforming New Zealand secondary education: The Picot reform and the road to radical reform.* New York, NY: Palgrave Macmillan.

Openshaw, R. (2012). Researching New Zealand's education reforms: Problems and prospects 1988–2011. In R. Openshaw & J. O'Neill (Eds.), *Critic and conscience: Essays on education in memory of John Codd and Roy Nash* (pp. 63–86). Wellington: NZCER Press.

Openshaw, R., & Walshaw, M. (2010). *Are our standards slipping?: Debates over literacy and numeracy standards in New Zealand since 1945.* Wellington: NZCER Press.

Patterson, L. (2011). *Tracks to adulthood: Post-school experiences of 21-year-olds.* Wellington: Ministry of Education.

Pearce, D. F. (1996). *Two years of peace?: The schools consultative group and the state in New Zealand.* Unpublished doctoral thesis, University of Canterbury.

Pearce, D., & Gordon, L. (2005). In the zone: New Zealand's legislation for a system of school choice and its effects. *London Review of Education, 3*(2), 145–157.

Peddie, R., & Tuck, B. (Eds.). (1995). *Setting the standards: The assessment of competence in national qualifications.* Palmerston North: Dunmore Press.

Penetito, W. (2010). *What's Māori about Māori education?* Wellington: Victoria University Press.

Perris, L. (1998). Implementing education reforms in New Zealand: 1987–97: A case study. *World Bank, Education Reform and Management Series, 1*(1).

Perry, B. (2009). *Non-income measures of material wellbeing and hardship: First results from the 2008 New Zealand Living Standards Survey, with international comparisons.* Wellington: Ministry of Social Development.

Pountney, C. (2000). *Learning our living: A teaching autobiography.* Auckland: Cape Catley.

PPTA. (2010). *The cost of change: PPTA survey on NCEA workload.* Wellington: Author.

Purves, A. (1979). *Achievement in reading and literature in the secondary schools: New Zealand in an international perspective.* Wellington: New Zealand Council for Educational Research.

Ramsay, P. (1991). *Local school management: Possibility or impossibility?* Speech delivered to the Annual Conference of the New Zealand School Trustees Association, Nelson.

Ramsay, P. (1992, May). Picot—four years on: The reform of education administration in New Zealand: An insider's commentary of events. *New Zealand Principal, 7*(2), 8–17.

Ramsay, P. D. K., with Oliver, D. (1993). *Teacher quality: A case study prepared for the Ministry of Education as part of the OECD study on teacher quality.* Hamilton: School of Education, University of Waikato.

Ramsay, P. D. K., & Sneddon, D. (1983). Teacher turnover in an economically depressed area. *New Zealand Journal of Educational Studies, 18*(1), 79–84.

Ramsay, P. D. K., Sneddon, D. G., Grenfell, J., & Ford, I. (1981). *Tomorrow may be too late: Schools with special needs in Mangere and Otara: Final report.* Hamilton: Education Department, University of Waikato.

Renner, J. M. (1976). Diffusion and implementation: The case of social studies. In J. Codd & G. L. Hermansson (Eds.), *Directions in New Zealand secondary education* (pp. 108–128). Auckland: Hodder and Stoughton.

Renwick, M., & Gray, A. (1995). *Implementing the New Zealand curriculum in primary schools.* Wellington: New Zealand Council for Educational Research.

Renwick, M., Vize, J., & Smith, L. (1989). An evaluation of the implementation of the 1:20 teacher-pupil ratio policy in the junior school. In G. McDonald, V. N. Podmore, M. Renwick, L. Smith, J. Vize, & C. Wylie (Eds.), *More teachers, fewer pupils: A study of the 1:20 teacher-pupil ratio policy in the junior school* (pp. 21–68). Wellington: New Zealand Council for Educational Research.

Renwick, W. L. (1976). Social change and objectives of secondary education. In J. Codd & G. L. Hermansson (Eds.), *Directions in New Zealand secondary education.* (pp. 15-28). Auckland: Hodder and Stoughton.

Renwick, W. L. (1979, 11 May). *Lay and community participation in education.* Address to the New Zealand School Committees' Federation Annual Conference, Christchurch.

Renwick, W. L. (1981, 18 January). *The midwife and the crow: The Department of Education and educational effectiveness.* Opening address to the 2nd International conference of the New Zealand Educational Administration Society (NZEAS), Upper Hutt.

Renwick, W. L. (1983, January). *Accountability: A tangled skein.* Opening address to the 3rd NZEAS conference, Accountability in a Changing Community, Auckland.

Renwick, W. L. (1986). *Moving targets. Six essays on educational policy.* Wellington: New Zealand Council for Educational Research.

Robertson, S. (2011). *Principal vacancies and appointments 2009–2010.* Wellington: New Zealand Council for Educational Research.

Robinson, V., Hohepa, M., & Lloyd, C. (2009). *School leadership and student outcomes: Identifying what works and why: Best evidence synthesis iteration (BES).* Wellington: Ministry of Education.

Robitaille, D. (1989). Students' achievements: Population A. In D. Robitaille & R. A. Garden (Eds.), *The IEA Study of Mathematics II: Contexts and outcomes of school mathematics.* Oxford: Pergamon Press.

Ross, J. A. (1976). Development of the secondary school curriculum: An overview. In J. Codd & G. L. Hermansson (Eds.), *Directions in New Zealand secondary education* (pp. 83–94). Auckland: Hodder and Stoughton.

Sahlberg, P. (2011). *Finnish lessons: What can the world learn from educational change in Finland?* New York, NY: Teachers' College Press.

Schagen, I., & Hutchison, D. (2007). Comparisons between PISA and TIMSS: We could be the man with two watches. *Education Journal, 101,* 34–35.

Schagen, S., & Wylie, C. (2009). *School resources, culture and connections.* Wellington: New Zealand Council for Educational Research.

Scott, D. (1997). The primary science curriculum. In B. Bell & R. Baker (Eds.), *Developing the science curriculum in Aotearoa New Zealand.* Auckland: Addison Wesley Longman New Zealand.

Scott, N. (1977). *A survey of some aspects of New Zealand secondary schools.* Wellington: Department of Education.

Scott, R. A. (1980). The inspectorate and educational standards: A New Zealand experience. In *The inspector and the quality of education,* Conference papers, Australasian Association of Institutes of Inspectors of Schools biennial conference, Hamilton.

Shallcrass, J. (1973). *Secondary schools in change: Papers collected by Jack Shallcrass.* Wellington: Price Milburn/PPTA.

Shallcrass, J. (1978). *Forward to basics.* Wellington: New Zealand Educational Institute (NZEI).

Sheehan, M. (2010). The place of 'New Zealand' in the New Zealand history curriculum. *Journal of Curriculum Studies, 42*(5), 671–691.

State Services Commission. (2005). *Report on the performance of the New Zealand Qualifications Authority in the delivery of secondary school qualifications, by the review team led by Doug Martin.* Wellington: Author.

State Services Commission, Treasury, & Department of the Prime Minister and Cabinet. (2011). *Formal review of the Ministry of Education (MOE): Performance improvement framework.* Wellington: Authors. Retrieved from http://www.ssc.govt.nz/pif

Statistics New Zealand. (n.d.). *School leavers with no qualifications, 1991–2000.* Wellington: Author.

Strachan, J. (1996, December). *Moderation—swan or ugly duckling?* Paper presented at the New Zealand Association for Research in Education conference, Nelson.

Taskforce to Review Education Administration. (1988). *Administering for excellence: Effective administration in education.* Wellington: Government Printer.

Telford, M., with May, S. (2010). *PISA 2009: Our 21st century learners at age 15.* Wellington: Ministry of Education.

Thrupp, M., Harold, B., Mansell, H., & Hawksworth, L. (2000). *Mapping the cumulative impact of educational reform: A study of seven New Zealand schools.* Hamilton: School of Education, University of Waikato.

Thrupp, M., Hattie, J., Crooks, T., & Flockton, L. (2009, 23 November). Open letter to the Minister of Education, Hon. Anne Tolley: Warning about the new National Standards system. *New Zealand Education Review 7(1)*, 8-14.

Timperley, H., Wilson, A., Barrar, H., & Fung, I. (2007). *Teacher professional learning and development: Best evidence synthesis.* Wellington: Ministry of Education.

Timperley, H. S., & Parr, J. M. (2009). Chain of influence from policy to practice in the New Zealand literacy strategy. *Research Papers in Education, 24*(2), 135–154.

Treasury. (2012). *Treasury's advice on lifting student achievement in new Zealand: Evidence brief.* Wellington: Author. Retrieved from http://www.treasury.govt.nz/publications/ media-speeches/speeches/economicleadership/ sanz-evidence-mar12.pdf

Wagemaker, H. (1993). Review of research. In H. Wagemaker (Ed.), *Achievement in reading literacy: New Zealand's performance in a national and international context* (pp. 5–22). Wellington: Department of Education.

Waslander, S., Pater, C., & van der Weide, M. (2010). *Markets in education: An analytical review of empirical research on market mechanisms in education.* OECD Education Working Papers 52. Paris: OECD Publishing.

Whitcombe, J. (2008). Contributions and challenges of 'New Public Management': New Zealand since 1984. *Policy Quarterly, 4*(3), 7–13.

Wylie, C. (1980). *Reflective surfaces: The individual as the key social relationship in New Zealand society.* Unpublished doctoral thesis, Victoria University of Wellington.

Wylie, C. (1988a). Education. In *Report of the Royal Commission on Social Policy*, Vol IV (pp. 117–148). Wellington: Royal Commission on Social Policy.

Wylie, C. (1988b). Fair enough? (How fair is New Zealand education?) *set: Research Information for Teachers, 1*, 1–4.

Wylie, C. (1989). Fleshing out the bones: The origins and development of the 1:20 teacher–pupil ratio policy in the junior school. In G. McDonald (Ed.), *More teachers, fewer pupils: A study of the 1:20 teacher–pupil ratio policy in the junior school.* Wellington: New Zealand Council for Educational Research.

Wylie, C. (1995a). Contrary currents: The application of the public sector reform framework in education. *New Zealand Journal of Educational Studies, 30*(2), 149–164.

Wylie, C. (1995b). The shift to school-based management in New Zealand: The school view. In D. Carter & M. O'Neill (Eds.), *Case studies in educational change: An international perspective.* London: Falmer Press.

Wylie, C. (1997a). *At the centre of the web: The role of the New Zealand primary school principal within a decentralized education system* Wellington: New Zealand Council for Educational Research.

Wylie, C. (1997b). *Primary principals' experiences of ERO reviews.* Wellington: New Zealand Principals' Federation.

Wylie, C. (1997c). *Self-managing schools seven years on: What have we learnt?* Wellington: New Zealand Council for Educational Research.

Wylie, C. (1999). *Ten years on: How schools view educational reform.* Wellington: New Zealand Council for Educational Research.

Wylie, C. (2006). *What is the reality of school competition?* Retrieved from http://www/ncspe.org/publications_files/OP126.pdf

Wylie, C. (2007a). *School governance in New Zealand: How is it working?* Wellington: New Zealand Council for Educational Research.

Wylie, C. (2007b). *What can New Zealand learn from Edmonton?* NZCER occasional paper. Retrieved from http://www.nzcer.org.nz/system/files/15845.pdf

Wylie, C. (2011a). *Competent Learners @ 20: Summary of key findings.* Wellington: Ministry of Education.

Wylie, C. (2011b, April). *Opportunities for teacher collaborative practices in a self-managed school system: The New Zealand experience.* Paper presented at the American Educational Research Association 2011 Annual Meeting, New Orleans. Retrieved from http://www.nzcer.org.nz

Wylie, C. (2011c). The development of leadership capability in a self-managing schools system: The New Zealand experience and challenges. In T. Townsend & J. MacBeath (Eds.), *International handbook of leadership for learning.* Dordrecht, Heidelberg, London, New York: Springer.

Wylie, C. (forthcoming). *New Zealand: Challenges around capability improvements in a system of self-managed schools.* San Francisco, CA: WestEd.

Wylie, C., & Hodgen, E. (2010). *NZCER primary and intermediate schools national survey: A snapshot of overall patterns and findings related to the National Standards.* Wellington: New Zealand Council for Educational Research.

Wylie, C., & Hodgen, E. (2011). *Forming adulthood: Past, present and future in the experiences and views of the Competent Learners @ 20.* Wellington: Ministry of Education.

Wylie, C., & Hodgen, E. (2012). Trajectories and patterns of student engagement: Evidence from a longitudinal study. In S. L. Christenson, A. L. Reschly, & C. Wylie (Eds.), *Handbook of research on student engagement* (pp. 585–600). New York, NY: Springer.

Wylie, C., Hodgen, E., & Darr, C. (2009). *National Standards consultation analysis: Report for the Ministry of Education.* Wellington: Ministry of Education.

Wylie, C., Hodgen, E., Hipkins, R., & Vaughan, K. (2008). *Competent learners on the edge of adulthood: A summary of key findings from the Competent Learners @ 16 project.* Wellington: Ministry of Education.

Wylie, C., & King, J. (2004). *How do effective schools manage their finances?* Wellington: New Zealand Council for Educational Research.

Wylie, C., & King, J. (2005). *An increasing tightness: Pressure points for schools' financial management.* Wellington: New Zealand Council for Educational Research.

Wylie, C., & Smith, L. (1995). *Learning to learn: Children's progress through the first 3 years of school.* Wellington: New Zealand Council for Educational Research.

Young-Loveridge, J. M. (2010). A decade of reform in mathematics education: Results for 2009 and earlier years. In *Findings from the New Zealand Numeracy Development Projects 2009* (pp. 15–35). Wellington: Ministry of Education.

# INDEX

3Rs 57

accountability 7, 46, 65, 78, 80, 81, 85, 91, 162, 172, 174, 185, 243, 244–5, 247, 249, 253
*Administering for Excellence, see* Picot taskforce
advisers 8, 19, 22, 24, 25, 35, 37, 39–40, 42, 72, 75, 81, 82, 83, 97, 241
colleges of education advisory (support) services 40, 85, 95–6, 101, 129, 134, 137, 141, 146, 165, 179, 199, 229, 246
AIMHI (Achievement in Multicultural High Schools) 120, 122, 152, 257
Aitken, Judith 122
Alberta Initiative for Schooling Improvement (AISI) 245
Alcorn, Noeline 50
ALiM pilot study 194
Alison, Judie 226
Allen, Peter 158
Alton-Lee, Adrienne 176
Anderson, Sir John 109, 126, 156, 187, 240, 247, 251
ARBs (Assessment Resource Banks) 137
art 205
assessment *see also* examinations; NCEA; PISA assessments; qualifications
Committee of Inquiry into Curriculum, Assessment and Qualifications 71–2
consistency 205
curriculum, and 61, 66, 70, 71–2, 135, 136, 166
international student assessments 67, 68
low-decile schools 208
primary schools 21, 189, 202, 205
purpose 136–8
reading 37–8, 59
Schools Without Failure project 28

standards-based 153–6
use of data for decisions on resource allocation 164
use of historical data 152
Assessment for Learning 195, 198, 199, 248, 251, 257
AsTTle (Assessment Tools for Teaching and Learning) 196
Auckland 104, 107, 181, 212; *see also* Mangere; Otara
Audit Office 171–2, 257
Australia
PISA scores 220, 221, 222
spending per primary student 250

Ballard, Russ 88, 89
Barrington, John 73–4
Beeby, Clarence 50, 70, 88
*Beginning School Mathematics* (BSM) 143–5, 257
Berryman, Mere 224–5
BES *see* Iterative Best Evidence Synthesis
Bishop, Russell 224–5
Board of Studies 71–2, 257
boards of trustees 1, 2, 80, 82, 83, 89–90, 98, 108–12, 147, 163, 247, 256, 257
accountability 91, 162, 172, 185, 249
charters, and 91–2, 95, 172, 184–5
ERO, and 87, 108, 171
financial management 111, 171, 187
'individual competence' 86–7
Māori members 149
national network of education authorities (proposed), and 253
National Standards, and 172
personality clashes 112, 238
planning and reporting framework, and 164, 171, 173
principals, and 92, 99, 100, 101, 102, 103, 110, 111–12, 173, 180, 185, 238, 247, 256

professional development 111, 171, 172, 173
property management 90–1, 103–4, 171
relations with staff 111–12
replacement with commissioners 112, 124, 172, 184
roles 108–9, 129, 173–4, 247
Schooling Improvement clusters, and 120
statutory interventions 170, 171–2, 172, 173, 181, 184, 185
Boyd, Ross 96, 113
bullying 215–16
bureaucracy see also Department of Education; education boards; Ministry of Education
after *Tomorrow's Schools* 47, 127, 156
before *Tomorrow's Schools* 20, 42, 43–6, 51, 67, 242
Bursary 153

Cabinet Committee on Employment and Training 78
Caldwell, Brian 100
Campbell, Elizabeth 61–2
Canada 1, 178, 221, 222, 229, 244–7, 250
capacity development 95, 96, 166, 178, 184, 229, 238, 239, 240, 243, 246, 247, 252, 254, 255, 256
Carpinter, Paul 94
Chamberlain, Mary 165
Chamberlain, Megan 216
charters 80, 81, 85, 87, 91–2, 93, 94, 95, 128, 152, 162, 163–4, 166, 172, 184–5, 190, 253
Christchurch Teachers' College 36
Claxton, Guy 202
Clay, Marie 36
Clover Park middle school 125
clusters 92–3, 102, 117, 119–22, 127–8, 152, 181, 198, 199, 200, 201, 202, 209, 212, 241–2
coherence in education 12, 14, 16, 31, 56, 65, 71–2, 76, 81, 108, 130, 136, 140, 143, 151–2, 177–8, 188, 193, 210, 235, 236, 237, 252, 255

collective approaches 3, 20, 25, 26, 76, 86, 87–8, 93, 96–7, 125, 126, 130–1, 251 see also clusters; fragmentation; interconnections in public education; Ministry of Education—disconnection and reconnection of schools
Assessment for Learning 195, 198, 199, 248, 251
'collaborative competition' 106
Leadership BES 177
limits on sharing of new practice 41–3, 87
Literacy Professional Development Project (LPDP) 195, 196–7, 198–9, 248
Literacy Taskforce 140
local 41–2, 87, 102, 114, 118, 181–3, 186, 187–8, 202, 239–40, 245–6, 252
low-decile schools 210
NCEA 158–9, 229, 230–1, 235, 251
Network for Learning 212–13
North America 1, 244–7
Numeracy Development Projects (Numeracy Programme) 148, 190–4, 248
PB4L (Positive Behaviour for Learning) strategy 180–1
policy work 88–9, 93, 248, 256
property management 90–1, 93
proposed single government educational authority, and 256
reading 34–9
revised curriculum framework 165–6, 251
school clusters 92–3, 102, 117, 119–22, 127–8, 152, 181, 198, 199, 200, 201, 202, 209, 212, 241–2
school culture 62, 189, 196, 198, 205, 230–1
Schools Without Failure project 27, 28–32, 131
secondary schools 151–2, 251
colleges of education 100, 101, 105, 129, 134, 143

advisory (support) services 40, 85, 95–6, 101, 134, 137, 141, 146, 165, 179, 199, 229, 246
Committee of Inquiry into Curriculum, Assessment and Qualifications 71–2
Committee on Secondary Education 44
community–school interconnections 48, 72–6, 111, 181, 247 *see also* boards of trustees; parents
   accountability to community 172, 185, 243
   charters, and 91–2, 93
   community education forums 81–2, 93
   community expectations 63, 67
   consultation 72, 89, 172
   curriculum developments 31, 61
   Māori education 149
   Picot taskforce report 80
   resources to supplement government provision 50, 58
   Schools Without Failure project 29
   teacher turnover, and 60
Competent Learners project 204, 215, 225, 257
Coopers and Lybrand 94–5
corporal punishment 52
Correspondence School, The (Te Aho o Te Kura Pounamu) 142
Cowie, Donald 94
Crooks, Terry 158
curriculum *see also* syllabuses
   1970s 61
   1980s 19, 20–1, 26, 30–1, 39, 40, 44, 50, 53, 71
   academic nature of 52, 67, 71, 157, 215, 234
   advisers, and 39, 40, 229–30
   assessment, and 61, 66, 70, 71–2, 135, 136, 166
   barriers to change 44
   Committee of Inquiry into Curriculum, Assessment and Qualifications 71–2
   'essential skills' 131–2, 157
   flexibility 237
   inspectorate 1978 report 57–8
   key competencies 204
   local decision making 71–2
   national framework 85, 130, 131–7, 142–3, 156, 157, 164, 189, 198, 201, 202, 204, 235, 237, 241, 251
   national framework, revised 165–6, 177, 179, 184, 233–4
   OECD report 50, 53
   Picot taskforce, and 83
   professional development 134, 140, 143, 145, 146, 147, 148, 149
   qualifications, and 67, 76, 153, 156–9, 160–1, 205, 248, 255
   resources for 44
   review, 1987 72, 75
   secondary schools 61, 66, 67, 229–30
   subject associations 41, 128, 155, 229–30, 234
   *Tomorrow's Schools*, and 2, 85, 130
Curriculum Stocktake report 2002 134

decile ratings 107, 137, 257; *see also* low-decile schools
Deloitte 104
Department of Education 257; *see also* advisers; inspectors; Ministry of Education
   Committee of Inquiry into Curriculum, Assessment and Qualifications, and 71–2
   Curriculum Division 31, 85, 86, 234
   curriculum review, 1987 31, 72
   evaluation of school quality 75
   funding 20, 42, 45–6, 90
   interconnections with schools 19, 20, 22, 28, 32, 41, 42, 45, 50
   Māori and Island Education Division 31
   Māori education, and 70–1, 154
   Maths, and 143–4
   Picot taskforce, and 79, 83
   Reading, and 34–9
   school committees, and 74

School Publications 85
Schools Without Failure project, and 30
secondary schools, and 61–5
sharing of new initiatives, and 42
*Tomorrow May be Too Late* study, and 59, 60
*Tomorrow's Schools*, and 2, 80, 88, 93, 97, 100
transition to Ministry of Education 2, 80, 136
Department of the Prime Minister and Cabinet 180
*Directions in New Zealand Secondary Education* 65–6
Douglas, Roger 79, 223
Dunedin 96, 128

East Coast 98, 120, 121, 123
Edmonton Public Schools district 1, 244–5, 247
Education Act 1989 89–90
education authorities, proposed national network 252–5
education boards 2, 19, 23, 25, 32, 39, 43, 44, 45, 74, 80, 88, 89, 97, 257
 secondary 21, 45, 74, 88
Education Development Conference 46, 62, 63, 73, 74. 258
education policy 6, 13–15, 16–18, 49, 50, 56–7, 117, 248; *see also* guidelines, national; Picot taskforce; self-managing schools; *Tomorrow's Schools*
 collective work on 88–9, 93, 248, 256
 evidence-based 5, 7, 14, 18, 160, 252
 primary schools' dissatisfaction with level of involvement 129
 separation from operations 77, 79, 88, 96, 98–9, 100–1, 112–14, 119, 127, 162, 210, 249, 252, 255
 teacher involvement 251, 256
Education Policy Council 82, 85
Education Review Office (ERO), 258 *see also* Review and Audit Agency
 advice and assistance to schools 87, 95, 99, 100, 111, 129, 169, 181, 183, 238–9, 249
 assessments of *Tomorrow's Schools* 122–6
 beginning of 2
 boards of trustees, and 108, 111, 120, 171
 criticism of teachers for low expectations 144
 curriculum, and 134, 135, 136
 'effectiveness' reviews 120
 Inquiry, and 200
 longitudinal review category 169, 182, 183
 Lough report, and 94, 95, 97
 Mangere–Otara report 98, 123–6
 Māori education 150
 National Standards, and 206, 207
 principals, and 103, 168–9, 175, 182–3
 proposed single government educational authority, and 255
 rural education, and 139
 school charters, and 162
 school clusters, and 119, 120, 241–2
 schools in difficulty, and 98, 99, 116, 118–19, 169–71, 182, 237–8
 schools' self-management capability, and 167–9, 237–9
 teacher education, and 143
Education Standards Act 2001 163
*Educational Leadership Practices Survey* 179
*Effective Governance: Working in Partnership* 172
Eide, Ingrid 49
electronic learning 211–13
Elley, Warwick 58–9, 133
Employers' Federation 44
employment, and education 2, 3, 12, 13, 68, 78
England: exemption of 'outstanding' schools from regular inspection 168
 mandated governance at school level 247;
 self-managed school framework 160

279

English curriculum 132, 133, 137, 149
environmental initiatives 205
Eppel, Elizabeth 132
equality of access to education 6, 44, 70–1, 81, 82–3, 84, 91, 106–7, 120, 210, 214, 220–5
ERIC (Early Reading In-service Course) 37, 141, 258
Ernst & Whinney 95
ERO *see* Education Review Office
Extending High Standards Across Schools (EHSAS) clusters 198, 199, 200, 241
External Policy Group 178

failure 12, 58, 71, 140, 203, 204; *see also* Schools Without Failure project
Fancy, Howard 115, 142, 162
financial literacy 218
Finland: PISA scores 218, 220, 221, 222
    spending per primary student 250
First-Time Principals programme 174, 176
fragmentation 4, 14–15, 96–7, 99, 246
    costs of 156–9, 247–9
frameworks, national, *see* guidelines and frameworks, national
freedom 6, 86–7
    'ordered freedom' in teaching 25
Fullan, Michael 106, 178, 245, 246
funding 6, 14, 84, 95
    bulk funding 7, 109–10
    competition for 98, 99, 104, 105–8, 119, 125, 240
    Department of Education 20, 42, 45–6, 90
    e-learning 212–13
    full funding 110
    locally raised funds 104–5, 187
    low-decile schools 211
    Ministry of Education 1, 90, 92–4, 96, 104, 115, 130, 142, 146, 163, 186–8, 214, 225, 231, 240, 241, 250–1, 252
    operational funding 46, 104, 105, 107, 123, 124, 129, 130, 141, 163, 186–7, 209
    roll numbers, and 104, 106, 107, 109
    school clusters 92–3, 102, 117, 119–22, 127–8, 200, 209
    Schools Support project 114–15
    student needs, and 141–2
    tagged 45, 146
    targeting 46
    weighted 81

Gammie, Darren 176
Garden, Robert 142–3
Gianotti, Maurice 80
governance 1, 2, 73–4, 80, 108–12, 162, 163, 171–4, 247; *see also* boards of trustees
government agency–school links 2, 77, 80, 92, 95, 97, 113–14, 161, 162–88, 242–7, 251; *see also* Ministry of Education—disconnection and reconnection of schools
    mediating layers 243–4
    proposed single government agency 255–6
Greig, David 94
guidelines and frameworks, national 14, 15, 16, 17–18, 20, 50, 61, 63, 65, 72, 80, 91, 100, 107, 128–9, 214–15, 237, 243, 256; *see also* New Zealand Curriculum
    local autonomy, and 82, 91
    National Administration Guidelines (NAGs) 103, 128–9, 149, 165
    National Education Guidelines (NEGs) 128–9, 149, 150
    National Qualifications Framework 155, 157, 158
    National Standards 172, 179, 184–5, 189, 192, 194, 201–7, 208, 210, 235, 251
    planning and reporting framework 94–5, 163–7, 168, 171, 177, 182, 183, 193, 237, 251
    self-review guidelines 169

Hales, Doug 170
Hattie, John 196
Hawke, Gary 206, 251

healthy schools initiatives 205
Hearn, Shona 158
Hillary College 60
history syllabus 136
Hohepa, Margie 176
home-schooling 11
Hood, David 157

ICT professional development cluster programme 199, 200, 241
IEA (International Association for the Evaluation of Educational Achievements) reading assessments 59
immigrants 222
income inequality 214, 222–5; *see also* equality of access to education
infrastructure 2, 7, 76, 188, 211, 231, 242–7, 257
  absence of / deficiencies in 3, 8, 65–6, 76, 85, 102, 110, 129, 130, 140, 141, 142, 155, 157–8, 159, 160, 161, 163, 223, 237, 239–40
  hallmarks of effective infrastructure 15–18; local 118, 124, 125, 142, 237
  maths 142–5
  proposed national network of education authorities 252–5
  inquiry in schools 197–9, 200–1, 205, 210, 211, 230, 237, 241, 245, 251, 252, 254, 256
Inquiry into the Quality of Teaching (Scott report) 62–5, 74–5, 87. 258
in-service training, *see* professional development
inspectors
  advisers, and 39, 40, 43, 56
  innovations in schools, and 41, 42, 64
  Inquiry into the Quality of Teaching, and 75
  interconnecting role 19, 22–5, 34, 41–2, 43, 47, 56, 64, 75, 86, 128
    lack of subsequent Department work 87
  liaison 23, 24, 25, 32, 67
  loss of inspectorate 86, 90, 97
  Māori 83

  Principals, and 23, 24, 25, 26, 27, 32, 241
  professional development, and 25, 26, 27–8, 32, 34, 55, 57, 58, 64, 241
  reading, and 34, 35, 37; report, 1978 57–8
  rural education, and 43
  Schools Without Failure project, and 28
  sources of authority 25–7
  staffing, and 45
interconnections in public education 3, 16, 17–18, 65, 256–7; *see also* advisers; collective approaches; community–school interconnections; fragmentation; government agency–school links; inspectors; Schools Support Project
  1980s 19–20, 22–5, 30–1, 34, 39, 242
  after *Tomorrow's Schools* 30, 47, 93–7, 99, 102, 110, 126, 130, 242–3
  costs of fragmentation to qualifications reform 156–9
  national network of education authorities (proposed) 252–5
  NEMP project 137–8
  roads not taken 72–4
intermediate schools 51, 84, 125
  new practice 41
Intermediate Schools Association 114
International Mathematics and Science Study
  Second 143
  Third (TIMSS) 139, 142–3, 148, 190, 192, 215
Ireland, PISA scores 220, 221
Irwin, Kathy 158
Iterative Best Evidence Synthesis (BES) programme 176, 194, 251, 257

Japan 222, 250
joint approaches, *see* collective approaches

Karmel, Peter 49
*Kiwi Leadership for Principals* 176, 178

knowledge development and use  3, 4, 15, 16, 17–18, 19, 39, 41, 42, 43, 47, 72, 75, 76, 126, 141, 160, 184, 201, 206, 230, 248–9, 252, 254, 255
    advisers and support services  40, 96, 114, 246
    boards of trustees  110–11
    ERO  97, 124, 125, 168, 169
    funding for  187
    inspectors  22, 24, 27, 32, 34, 40
    Ministry of Education  115, 116, 117, 118, 124, 166, 183–4, 185–6, 189, 190, 239, 249
    Network for Learning, and  213
    Picot report  81
    school clusters  93, 119, 121, 127, 200, 209, 241
    school leadership, and  175–8
    Schools Support  114
    *Tomorrow May Be Too Late*  59, 60
    *Tomorrow's Schools*  85, 88, 129, 145, 186, 240
Korea, PISA assessments  218, 221, 222
kura kaupapa Māori  8, 120, 150, 258

Labour and Labour-led Governments  110, 163
    restructuring, 1980s  62, 77–8, 79, 88, 123, 223
Lange, David  45, 61, 70, 79, 80, 88, 92, 95, 124
LARIC reading in-service course  37–8, 258
Leadership Best Evidence Synthesis (BES)  176–7, 178–9, 211
leadership development  163, 174–80, 241
Learning Curves project  226
learning difficulties  55
Learning Media  196
'learning muscles'  202
learning organisations  161, 177
Levin, Ben  178, 255
literacy  165, 185, 204, 205, 227, 228, 229, 251; *see also* reading; writing
    National Standards  179, 204

professional development  140, 141, 148, 181, 196–7
Literacy Leadership project  196
Literacy Learning Progressions  208
Literacy Professional Development Project (LPDP)  195, 196–7, 198–9, 248, 258
Literacy Taskforce 1999  140–2, 258
Lough report *(Today's Schools)*  93–6, 97, 239, 249, 258
low-decile schools
    absence rates  217–18
    change in  210–11
    e-learning  212, 213
    inquiry in  197, 210, 211
    NCEA  227, 228, 230–2
    Reading Together programme  211
    roll decline  107
    self-management difficulties  120–1, 151, 181–3, 209
    student achievement and performance  108, 137, 139, 141, 181–3, 192, 207–9
    teacher burnout  218
low-income areas  6, 7, 17, 26, 59–61, 99, 107, 109, 123; *see also* equality of access to education; income inequality
    difficulty of schools' self management  120, 238
    ERO concerns about school capability  169
    inequities in families' living standards  210, 211
    Ministry of Education, and  183
    science teaching  146
    student achievement and performance  71, 124, 137, 250
    student engagement, and  201
    student reading levels  59, 141
    truancy rates  217

mainstreaming  39
Manaiakalani cluster  212
Mangere  27, 41–2, 59–61, 98, 120, 122, 123–6
Māori education *see also* kura kaupapa Māori

# Index

1970s and 1980s 27, 30, 40, 49, 59–61, 69–71
advisers 40
Board of Studies, and 72
curriculum, and 131
ERO concerns about 123, 169
funding 46
low-decile schools 107, 194, 207, 210, 224
Māori concerns about 72–3, 83
Ministry of Education, and 120, 148–51, 165, 180, 183
OECD report 52, 53
Picot taskforce, and 83
readers 34, 35
school principals 99
Schooling Improvement clusters 120
socioeconomic factors 107, 210, 224
te reo Māori 49, 52, 53, 72, 83, 91, 123
*Tomorrow's Schools*, and 2, 7, 8, 14, 17, 87, 148–51
Māori students
achievement and performance 2, 52, 69–71, 87, 125, 139, 149, 150, 167, 170, 190, 210, 224–5, 250
assessment scores 137
bullied 215–16
engagement 2, 125, 149–51, 201, 218, 228
holding back 55
length of time at school 217, 228
maths 192, 194, 224
PISA assessments 224
qualifications 13, 70, 78, 150, 226, 228, 231
reading 59, 139, 141, 207, 224
truancy rates 217
mathematics; *see also* numeracy
advisers 27, 40
assessment 137
*Beginning School Mathematics* (BSM) 143–4
curriculum 133, 139
in early school years 215
insufficient infrastructure 142–5
Literacy Taskforce 1999 140–2
National Standards 179, 204

PISA assessment 214, 218, 219, 220, 221, 222, 224
primary schools 54, 139, 140, 190–5, 204, 229
professional development 139, 140, 143, 145, 148, 191–2, 193
student performance 57, 68–9, 185, 225, 251
Wellington maths units 27–8
Mathematics and Science Taskforce 1997 148, 190, 258
Maths New Zealand website 194
McCombs report (review of secondary education) 62–3, 73
McMahon, Tim 164
McNaughton, Stuart 207, 208, 210
McQueen, Harvey 33, 63
middle schools 125
Mills, Mary-Anne 165
Ministerial Task Group Reviewing Science and Technology Education 145–6
Ministry of Education *see also* Department of Education
Assessments, and 137
boards of trustees, and 108, 171–3
curriculum, and 85, 130, 131, 136, 143, 146, 147, 148, 156, 165–6, 229
disconnection and reconnection of schools 97, 98–9, 100–1, 107, 112, 126–9, 162, 174, 178–86, 190, 201–2, 239–40, 251, 252, 255–6
early-leaving exemptions, and 151, 214, 216–17, 219
Education Policy Council, , and 82, 85
ERO, and 123–4
funding 1, 90, 92–4, 96, 104, 115, 130, 142, 163, 186–8, 214, 225, 231, 240, 241, 250–1, 252
Literacy Taskforce, and 140
Māori education, and 120, 148–51, 165, 180, 183, 225
national network of education authorities (proposed), and 252, 254, 255

National Standards, and 172, 179, 184–5, 198, 201, 202–3, 206–7
NCEA, and 13, 159, 228, 229, 231, 235
Pasifika education, and 183
Performance Improvement Framework Review 180
policy advice 82; and principals 174–80, 242
professional development, and 93, 101, 128, 135, 146, 147, 148, 149, 151, 160, 170, 172, 173, 183, 184, 185, 187, 195, 198, 201, 202, 212, 237, 239, 240, 241
property management, and 90–1, 94, 96, 104, 108
Reading Together programme, and 211
regional and district offices, and 96, 113, 115, 116, 128–9, 164, 166, 167, 171, 181, 186, 239–40
salaries, and 185–6
school charters and annual reports, and 80, 91, 92, 93, 94, 128, 162, 164, 166, 170, 184–5
school clusters, and 92–3, 119–22, 129, 200, 202, 241, 242
Schools Consultative Group, and 109
Schools Planning and Reporting project, and 94–5, 163–7
Schools Support project, and 112–22, 126
single government educational agency, as 255–6
Special Education section 180–1
suggested cuts, to redirect money to schools 94
Te Aho o Te Kura Pounamu (The Correspondence School), and 142
*Tomorrow's Schools*, and 2, 80, 82, 85, 88, 93–5, 96, 108, 239–40
turnover of staff and contractors 185–6, 239
music 205

National Administration Guidelines (NAGs) 103, 149, 165, 184, 258

National and National-led Governments 74, 79, 96, 109, 123, 130, 141, 156, 163, 187, 202, 223
National Education Guidelines (NEGs) 128–9, 149, 150, 184, 259
National Education Monitoring Project (NEMP) 137–8, 139, 190, 259
national network of education authorities (proposed) 252–5
National Qualifications Framework 155, 157, 158, 258
National Standards 172, 179, 184–5, 190, 192, 194, 201–7, 208, 210, 235, 251
National Standards Sector Advisory Group (NSSAG) 206–7, 251
NCEA (National Certificates of Educational Achievement) 15, 38, 154–5, 179, 184, 214–15, 226–30, 251, 250, 259
  building on 232–5
  disengaged students, and 230–2
  internal assessment 216
  introduction of 158–9, 206, 226, 248
  Level 1 225, 227, 228
  Level 2 13, 150, 151, 204, 210, 225, 228–9
  low-decile schools 227, 228, 230–2
  regional achievement data 167
  target of 85 percent of 18-year-olds achieving Level 2 228–32
Network for Learning 212–13, 259
'new public management' 79
New Zealand Committee on Secondary Education 63
New Zealand Council for Educational Research (NZCER) 6, 7, 103, 105, 111, 134, 137, 149, 159, 171, 172, 198, 235, 240–1, 247, 259
*New Zealand Curriculum* (curriculum national framework) 85, 130, 131–7, 142–3, 156, 157, 164, 189, 198, 201, 202, 204, 235, 237, 241, 251, 259; revised 165–6, 177, 179, 184, 233–4
New Zealand Educational Institute (NZEI) 41, 43, 74, 170, 259
Māori Advisory Council 31

New Zealand Qualifications Authority (NZQA) 2, 130, 153–4, 155–7, 158, 227, 229, 233, 235, 255, 259
New Zealand School Trustees Association (NZSTA) 109–11, 112, 128, 165, 172, 186–7, 255, 259
  'black book' 110–111
  field officers 110, 111
Nga Tapuwae College 45, 124
Nightingale, David 101–2
Northland 120, 121, 123
Northland College 227
numeracy 165, 190–5, 196, 205, 227, 228; see also maths
Numeracy Development Projects (Numeracy Programme) 148, 190–4, 199, 248, 259

O'Connell, Pam 196
OECD
  PISA assessments 214, 218–26
  report, 1983 33, 49–53, 57, 72, 74
OFSTED 168
Ontario school system 178, 229
O'Rourke, Maris 94
Otara 27, 41–2, 59–61, 98, 120, 122, 123–6
Otara Language Group 60
Otara Principals' Association 125–6

Parent Advocacy Council 82
parents 7, 31, 42, 46, 50, 61, 66, 73–4, 103; see also boards of trustees; community–school interconnections
  choice of school 2, 24, 86, 104, 107
  early exemption, and 217
  level of education 17, 67, 68, 69, 222
  National Standards, and 203, 206
  partnership role 74–5, 80, 108, 211
  responses to Picot report 82, 84
  satisfaction with children's education 159
  special needs students, of 8
parent–teacher associations 73, 74, 88, 89

Parr, Judy 196
Pasifika education
  1980s 27, 30, 40, 59–61
  advisers 40
  curriculum, and 131
  funding 46
  low-decile schools 107, 194, 207, 210, 224
  Ministry of Education, and 120, 148–51, 165, 180, 183
  Schooling Improvement clusters 120
  socioeconomic factors 107, 210, 224
  *Tomorrow's Schools*, and 17
Pasifika students
  achievement and performance 139, 190, 210, 224–5, 250
  assessment scores 137
  bullied 215–16
  engagement 201
  length of time at school 228
  maths 192, 194, 224
  PISA assessments 224
  qualifications 226, 228, 231
  reading 59, 139, 141, 207, 224
  sense of safety at school 216
  truancy rates 217
PB4L (Positive Behaviour for Learning) strategy 180–1
pedagogy 31, 58, 76, 100
  equipment linked to 44
  pedagogical leadership 175
Penetito, Wally 49
Perris, Lyall 46, 89, 97, 138
Picot taskforce 6, 14, 19, 20, 43, 79–82, 95, 96–7, 109, 116, 240, 242–3, 259
  responses to report 82–4
PISA assessments 214, 218–20, 259
  challenges for high-scoring countries 220–1
  challenges of inequality 222–5
  limits to what can be learnt from 225–6
  'potentially vulnerable students' category 222

285

planning and reporting framework 94–5, 163–7, 168, 171, 177, 182, 183, 193, 237, 251
Point England school 212
policy, *see* education policy
Porirua area 26, 28, 41–2, 120, 122
Portugal, PISA scores 221
Post Primary Teachers' Association (PPTA) 41, 128, 158, 159, 259
Pountney, Charmaine 44, 84, 125–6
poverty 41, 123–4, 223, 224
primary schools 53–4
    advisers 39
    appointment of teachers 43
    assessment 189, 202
    charters 184–5, 189
    constraints 199–201
    drawbacks in teachers' knowledge and support 54–7
    frameworks for teaching, 2000s 189–213
    funding 104
    graduate teachers 51, 53
    holding back students 55
    inquiry 197–9, 200–1, 205
    inspectors 22, 23, 24, 25, 27, 55
    internal connections and coherence 193
    latitude before *Tomorrow's Schools* 21, 56, 128
    learning related to students' experiences 35, 53
    maths 139, 140, 190–5
    new practice 41, 87
    NZCER surveys 7, 103, 105, 111, 159, 171, 198–9, 239
    OECD comparisons of spending 250
    OECD report 51, 53
    parent satisfaction with 84
    principals 21, 27, 43, 44, 98, 99, 104, 105, 128, 166–7, 168–9, 174–5, 202, 205, 239
    professional development 143, 145, 189, 191–2, 193, 196–7, 198–200, 201
    property, resources and equipment 43, 44
    recapitation 125

rolls 121
student achievement and performance 53–4, 138–40, 189, 198–9, 203–4, 205
student:teacher ratio 56–7
principals
    accountability 174, 185, 253
    administrative support 63, 99, 105
    advisers, and 39, 40
    appointment of 103, 173, 245, 253
    appointment/dismissal of teachers, and 43
    boards of trustees, and 92, 99, 100, 101, 102, 103, 110, 111–12, 173, 180, 185, 238, 247, 256
    clusters, and 119
    curriculum, and 135, 136–7, 177
    demands on 174–5
    ERO, and 103, 168–9, 175, 182–3, 242
    financial management 98, 103, 104–5, 119, 175, 187, 250
    First-Time Principals programme 174, 176
    'individual competence' 86–7
    inspectors, and 23, 24, 25, 26, 27, 32, 241
    Iterative Best Evidence Synthesis (BES) programme 176
    Leadership Best Evidence Synthesis (BES) 176–7
    low-decile schools 181–3, 208–9, 210, 230, 236–7
    management role 21, 32, 63, 98, 100, 104
    Māori 181
    Māori education, and 149
    Ministry of Education, and 174–80, 242
    national network of education authorities (proposed), and 253–4
    Picot taskforce, and 83–4
    planning and reporting framework, and 164, 166–7
    primary schools 21, 27, 43, 44, 98, 99, 104, 105, 128, 166–7, 168–9, 174–5, 202, 205, 239
    professional development 32–3, 42, 63, 75, 101–2, 103, 173, 174, 178–9, 241

# Index

professional supervision and performance appraisal 102–3
property management 98, 103–4, 119, 175, 250
rural schools 26, 42, 99, 101, 103, 170–1
salaries 185
Schools Support project, and 116
secondary schools 21, 23, 45, 63, 67, 69, 100, 128, 152, 166–7, 219, 227, 230, 234
stress levels 175
teaching 21, 99, 175
*Tomorrow's Schools*, and 33, 43–4, 86–7, 89–90, 92, 94, 95, 97, 99–103, 128, 129, 163, 177, 238
*Tomorrow's Schools*, before 21, 23, 24, 25, 26, 27, 32–3, 43, 45, 63, 66–7
workload 63, 65, 99, 100, 152–3
Principals' Federation 114, 128, 170, 175
problem-solving, PISA assessment 218
professional development *see also* teacher education
advisers 40
curriculum, and 134, 140, 143, 145, 146, 147, 148, 149
cuts of 1980s, and 33–4, 55; ICT 199
inspectors, and 25, 26, 27–8, 32, 34, 55, 58, 64, 241
literacy, and 140, 141, 148, 181, 196–7
low-decile school teachers 209, 210
Māori education, and 149, 151
maths 139, 140, 143, 145, 148, 191–2, 193
Ministry-funded 93, 101, 128, 135, 146, 147, 148, 149, 151, 160, 170, 172, 173, 183, 184, 185, 187, 195, 198, 201, 202, 212, 237, 239, 240, 241
NCEA 155, 159, 227
new practice 41
NZQA 155–6, 227
OECD report 50, 51–2, 57
primary teachers 143, 145, 189, 191–2, 193, 196–7, 198–200, 201
principals 32–3, 42, 63, 75, 101–2, 103, 173, 174, 178–9, 241
reading in-service courses 37–9

rural areas 42
science 139, 140, 145–8
secondary teachers 64, 155, 224, 227, 235
standards-based assessment, and 155–6, 159
syllabus change, and 51
teacher release days 27–8, 30, 33
*Tomorrow's Schools*, and 86–7, 127–8, 145, 159, 160, 163
trustees 171, 172, 173
Professional Leadership Forum 178–9
'provider capture' 77, 88, 249
psychologists 81
public opinion polls 84
Purves, Alan 67–8

qualifications 12, 13, 14, 15, 44, 48, 53, 55, 71, 76, 87, 130, 151 *see also* assessment; NCEA; New Zealand Qualifications Authority (NZQA); School Certificate; Sixth Form Certificate; University Entrance
changes 153–6
Committee of Inquiry into Curriculum, Assessment and Qualifications 71–2
costs of fragmented system 156–9
curriculum, and 67, 76, 153, 156–9, 160–1, 205, 248, 255
low-decile schools 108
Māori students 13, 70, 78, 150
as a measure of school system success 225–6, 250

Ramsay, Peter 60, 79, 92, 99–100, 123–4
reading 54–5, 57, 58–9
advisers 34, 37, 40
assessment 137
in early school years 215
joint work to advance 34–9
Literacy Taskforce 1999 140–2
PISA assessment 214, 218, 219, 220–1, 223, 224
student performance 67–8, 139, 204, 214, 225

Reading Recovery  36–7, 55–6, 82, 141, 259
Reading Together programme  211
Ready to Read series  34–5, 54, 86
Renwick, Bill  35, 45–6, 70, 72, 73
resource production and development  24, 27, 28–31, 39, 55–6, 60, 85, 86, 136, 143–4, 145, 147, 148, 191, 194, 227
resource teachers: learning and behaviour (RTLBs)  241–2, 259
responsibility, shared  17, 56, 95, 114, 127, 163, 170, 180, 184, 186, 201–2, 231, 239, 240, 245
Review and Audit Agency  87–8, 90; *see also* Education Review Office (ERO)
Richardson, Ruth  84
Robinson, Marijke  80
Robinson, Viviane  176, 179
'Rogernomics'  79, 223, 259
Rosemergy, Margaret  79
Royal Commission on Social Policy  6, 80, 81, 260
rural areas  6, 50, 64–5, 83, 107, 139
    administrative support school clusters  127
    advisers  40, 43, 101;
    difficulty of schools' self management  120, 238
    ERO concerns about school capability  139, 169, 170
    quality of education  42–3, 123, 139
    school principals  26, 42, 99, 101, 103, 170–1
    science teaching  146
    teacher supply and turnover  26, 42, 43, 121, 170
    Virtual Learning Network, and  212

School Certificate  2, 44, 64, 70, 71, 153, 260
School Certificate Examinations Board  44, 53
school cultures and values  20, 28, 30, 31, 32, 121, 128, 146, 151, 169, 189
    collective  62, 189, 196, 198, 205, 230–1
    inquiry  198–9, 200–1, 205, 230
School Trustees Association  114

Schools *see also* intermediate schools; primary schools; secondary schools; self-managing schools
    capacity  17, 24, 30, 32–4
    communities, as  74–6, 80
    latitude before *Tomorrow's Schools*  20–2, 44, 75–6, 242–3
    new practice  41–3, 87
    working on their own  72, 77
Schools Consultative Group 1992–1994  109
Schools Planning and Reporting project  94–5, 163–7
Schools Support project  112–18, 119, 124, 126, 134, 137
Schooling Improvement clusters  119–22, 241
Schools Without Failure project  27, 28–32, 131, 260
science  66, 131, 132, 137, 139, 142, 145–8, 192, 205
    Mathematics and Science Taskforce 1997  148, 190
    PISA assessment  214, 218, 219, 220, 221, 224
    professional development  139, 140, 145–8
Scott, Noel (Scott report)  62–5, 74–5, 87
Second International Maths Study (SIMS)  68–9, 260
secondary schools *see also* NCEA; PISA assessments
    advisers  39
    challenges  65–7, 151–3
    comprehensive  51, 69, 222
    curriculum  136
    Department of Education-funded studies  61–5
    examinations  21
    fee-paying international students  104
    funding  104–5
    inquiry in  230
    inspectors  22, 23–4, 25, 64
    lack of coherence  151–2

## Index

latitude before *Tomorrow's Schools* 15, 21, 67, 242
new practice 41, 64, 87
NZCER surveys of 7, 171
objectives 67
OECD report 50, 51, 52–3
parent satisfaction with 84
principals 21, 23, 45, 63, 67, 69, 100, 128, 152, 166–7, 219, 227, 230, 234
professional development 64, 155, 224, 227, 235
programme shortcomings 48
property, resources and equipment 44
qualifications regime 15, 44, 48, 52–3, 64, 67, 76, 87, 205, 214, 232–3, 234–5
reading 38–9
reputation 23–4
self-review 63, 152
staffing cuts 158
student achievement and performance 15, 131, 151–3, 214, 225–6, 230–2
subject associations 128
truancy rates 217
Virtual Learning Network, and 212
zoning 50
self-interest 77
self-managing schools *see also* boards of trustees; collective approaches; community–school interconnections; Education Review Office (ERO); guidelines and frameworks, national; infrastructure; intermediate schools; Ministry of Education; primary schools; principals; secondary schools; teachers; *Tomorrow's Schools*
1990s, in 98–129
absence rates 217–18
annual reports 128, 162, 163, 164, 166, 167, 183
capacity development 95, 96, 166, 178, 184, 229, 238, 239, 240, 243, 246, 247, 252, 254, 255, 256
charters 80, 81, 85, 87, 91–2, 93, 94, 95, 128, 152, 162, 163–4, 166, 172, 184–5, 190, 253
clusters 92–3, 102, 117, 119–22, 127–8, 152, 181, 198, 199, 200, 201, 202, 209, 212, 241–2
communities, as 91, 236, 239, 243
competition between 98, 99, 104, 105–8, 116, 119, 125, 126–7, 147, 151, 170, 201, 223, 231, 240
conditions and changes needed for success 160, 252–7
connected and contributing 256
'continuous improvement culture' 164
costs of administration 14, 94–5
in difficulty 98, 99, 116, 118–19, 162–3, 169–71, 182, 237–8
England 160, 247
enrolment criteria 106–7
fees 104–5
fundamental flaws 236–51
government agency links 2, 77, 80, 92, 95, 97, 113–14, 161, 162–88, 242–7
hidden costs 108, 250–1
local decision making and latitude 83, 85–6
planning and reporting framework 94–5, 163–7, 168, 171, 177, 182, 183, 193, 237, 251
property management 90–1, 93, 94, 98, 103–4
recommendations for making the most of 252–7
reviews of 81, 87–8
Schools Support project, and 112–22, 124, 126
self-management as a barrier 2
self-review 117–18, 152, 164, 169
shift to 1–3, 6–9, 14–15, 20, 77, 78–93
social stratification 138
socioeconomic differences, and 222–5
statutory interventions 170, 171, 172, 173, 181, 184, 185
United States 160
self-managing schools as stand-alone schools 97, 125, 126–7, 128, 152, 160, 164, 174; *see also* fragmentation; Ministry of Education—disconnection and reconnection of schools

289

approaches to more co-ordinated infrastructure 243–7
costs of equating self-management with stand-alone schools 237–40
obstacles to schools working together 130–1, 240–2
suspicion of government agencies 242–3
Shallcrass, Jack 41
shared responsibility 17, 56, 95, 114, 127, 163, 170, 180, 184, 186, 201–2, 231, 239, 240, 245
Sinclair, Mary 114
Sixth Form Certificate 154
skills 11, 12, 20, 67, 133, 138, 145, 156, 157, 195, 196, 197, 204, 211, 219, 223, 225, 231, 234, 236
  'essential skills' 131–2, 157
  levels 3, 78
Smelt, Simon 80
Smith, Lockwood 131
social studies curriculum 66, 132, 205
Special Education Service 102
special needs students
  advisers, and 39
  PB4L (Positive Behaviour for Learning) strategy 180–1
  Picot taskforce report 81, 82
  primary schools 201
  proposed changes to education system, and 253
  secondary schools 45
  shared responsibility for 17
  student achievement practitioners, and 183
  *Tomorrow's Schools*, and 8, 85, 250
Spinks, Jim 100
Starpath project 226, 230, 260
State Services Commission 79, 80, 90, 94, 113, 116, 180, 226
streaming 51, 69
Strengthening Education in Mangere and Otara (SEMO) 120, 122, 126, 260
student achievement and performance 2, 48–9, 76, 159; *see also* assessment; ERO; National Standards; NCEA; PISA assessments; qualifications
  achievement objectives 133–4, 135, 136, 137, 139, 145, 193
  early years of school 203–4
  Extending High Standards Across Schools (EHSAS) clusters, and 198
  individual progression 203–4
  international comparisons 67–9
  low-decile schools 108, 137, 139, 141, 181–3, 192, 207–9
  Māori students 2, 52, 69–71, 87, 125, 139, 149, 150, 167, 170, 190, 210, 224–5, 250
  McKinsey analysis of world schooling systems 243–4
  National Education Monitoring Project (NEMP) 137–8, 139, 190
  OECD report 57–9
  Pasifika students 139, 190, 210, 224–5, 250
  policy emphasis on improving 156, 185, 224, 251
  primary schools 53–4, 138–40, 189, 198–9, 203–4, 205
  proposed national network of education authorities, and 253, 254
  proposed single government educational agency, and 255
  school practices and principles to improve 163–4, 165, 176, 189, 198–9, 202, 205, 232–5, 236–7, 246–7, 251
  Schools Without Failure project 27, 28–32, 131
  secondary schools 15, 131, 151–3, 214, 225–6, 230–2
  student achievement practitioner 183
  Treasury reference to 214
Students *see also* learning; Māori students; Pasifika students; special needs students
  early-leaving exemptions 151, 214, 216–17, 219
  engagement 6, 12, 76, 122, 131, 151, 152, 153, 158, 204, 214, 215–18, 230–2
  failure 12, 58, 71, 140, 203, 204

ideal results of school experience 236
immigrants 222
international comparisons of
motivation 203, 204
performance 67–9
personal value systems 67
secondary, surveys 61–2, 67, 215–16
subject associations 41, 128, 155, 229–30, 234
suspensions and expulsions 23–4, 151
Sweden, PISA scores 220
syllabuses, *see also* curriculum
history 136
*Tomorrow's Schools*, before 20–1, 24, 26, 39, 50–1, 53, 64, 66

Taskforce to Review Education
Administration, *see* Picot taskforce
Tate, Ormond 63
Taumata Whanonga 2009 181
Taylor, William 49
Te Aho o Te Kura Pounamu (The Correspondence School) 142
Te Kotahitanga 224–5, 230, 251, 250
Te Puni Kōkiri 150
te reo Māori 49, 52, 53, 72, 83, 91, 123
teacher education, *see also* professional development
maths 143, 195
reading 35–6, 38
teacher release days 27–8, 30, 33
teachers, *see also* collective approaches; inspectors; learning; principals; professional development
administrators, and 49–50
appointments 43, 64–5
assessment, and 135, 136, 137–8, 157–8
bulk funding, and 110
burnout 218
capacity 17, 24, 247
curriculum, and 133, 134, 135, 136, 143–4, 157–8, 229–30
dismissals 43
feed forward 195, 211

feedback 26, 31, 195, 211
grading 22–3, 25, 64
improvement 23, 30
'individual competence' 86–7
initiative 17
knowledge building and use 13–14, 17, 19, 27, 34, 39, 51–2, 62, 75, 121, 125, 130–1, 134, 138, 140, 142, 143, 147–8, 155, 157, 164, 188, 205, 230
latitude before *Tomorrow's Schools* 20–2, 56
learning from peers 61, 116, 119, 123, 128, 192, 201, 229–30, 240–1, 245, 254
low-decile schools 120–1, 181–2, 194, 208–9, 211, 217–18, 224
Māori 52, 123, 149, 150, 194
maths 69, 142–5, 190–5
national network of education authorities (proposed), and 254
NCEA, and 226–7
OECD report 51, 52
Picot taskforce, and 83–4
policy and regulatory frameworks 14–15, 19, 20–1, 24, 55, 76
policy work 251, 256
primary 54–7, 142–3, 145, 189–213
quality of teaching 19, 40, 42, 43, 57, 58, 62, 67, 69, 71, 84, 169, 181, 185
salaries 64, 81, 83, 110, 121, 185
science 142, 145–8
secondary 61–3, 64–5, 66, 67, 142, 149, 155, 158, 179, 217–18, 224, 227, 229–30, 233–5
shortages 120, 121, 143, 158
standards-based assessment, and 154–5, 157–8
students' experiences of 12, 13
student:teacher ratios 50, 51, 56–7, 121, 211
*Tomorrow's Schools*, and 88
turnover 51, 60, 146, 170, 193, 238
working on their own 66, 67, 75, 148
workload 61, 62, 135, 151, 152–3, 179, 199, 233

thinking skills 12
Timperley, Helen 196
TIMSS, *see* International Mathematics and Science Study - Third
*Today's Schools* (Lough report) 93–6, 97, 239, 249
*Tomorrow May Be Too Late* study 59–62, 79, 124, 260
*Tomorrow's Schools* 2, 3, 6–8, 14, 20, 60, 75, 85–8, 236–7, 260; *see also* self-managing schools
   Advisers, and 40
   ERO assessments of 122–6
   fleshing out the bones 88–9
   implementation 85, 89–93, 100
   lessons for the 1990s 159–61
   Lough review of 93–6, 97, 239, 249
   NZCER surveys of effectiveness 7, 15–16, 105, 134, 149, 159, 171, 172, 239, 240–1, 247
   principals, and 33, 43–4
Treasury 20, 77, 79, 80, 90, 94, 115, 178, 180, 186, 214, 218
Treaty of Waitangi 91, 149
truancy 217, 231

unemployment 78
UNESCO 70
uniforms 52, 62
unions 32, 41, 72, 82, 88, 112, 113, 114, 128, 132, 178, 241; *see also* New Zealand Educational Institute (NZEI); New Zealand School Trustees Association (NZSTA); Post Primary Teachers' Association (PPTA); Principals' Federation
United Kingdom: PISA scores 221; *see also* England
United States
   PISA scores 221
   self-managing schools 160, 246–7
   spending per primary student 250
Universities Examination Board 53
University Entrance 52–3, 70, 71, 260

Virtual Learning Network 212–13
vocational education 12, 68, 69, 151, 153, 157, 217, 227, 234

Waikato 96, 125
Wanganui 43
Wellington 27, 30, 32–3, 74, 80; *see also* Porirua area
   maths units 27–8
Wereta, Whetu 79
West Auckland Principals' Association 127–8
West Coast 120, 123
whānau concept 60
Wise, Colin 79–80
Woolf Fisher Research Centre, University of Auckland 207
work-based learning 12, 68, 69, 151, 153, 157, 217, 227, 234
World Bank 89
writing 195–7, 208–9

Youth '07 survey 216, 223
Youth Guarantee policy 180, 231

www.ingramcontent.com/pod-product-compliance
Lightning Source LLC
Chambersburg PA
CBHW081328230426
43667CB00018B/2864